PROJECT
MOON DUST

Other Avon Books by
Kevin D. Randle

CONSPIRACY OF SILENCE
A HISTORY OF UFO CRASHES

With Donald R. Schmitt
THE TRUTH ABOUT THE UFO CRASH AT ROSWELL
UFO CRASH AT ROSWELL

PROJECT MOON DUST

BEYOND ROSWELL—
EXPOSING THE GOVERNMENT'S CONTINUING COVERT
UFO INVESTIGATIONS AND COVER-UPS

KEVIN D. RANDLE, Captain, U.S.A.F.R.

AVON BOOKS NEW YORK

AVON BOOKS, INC.
1350 Avenue of the Americas
New York, New York 10019

Copyright © 1998 by Kevin D. Randle
Published by arrangement with the author
Visit our website at http://www.AvonBooks.com
ISBN: 0-380-72692-0

Library of Congress Cataloging in Publication Data:

Randle, Kevin D., 1949–
   Project Moon Dust : beyond Roswell—exposing the government's continuing
covert UFO investigations and cover-ups / Kevin D. Randle.
      p.   cm.
   Includes bibliographical references.
    1. Unidentified flying objects—Research—United States.
2. Conspiracies—United States.   I. Title.
TL789.4.R36   1998   98-10452
001.942'0973—dc21   CIP

First Avon Books Trade Printing: July 1998

AVON TRADEMARK REG. U.S. PAT. OFF. AND IN OTHER COUNTRIES, MARCA REGISTRADA,
HECHO EN U.S.A.

Printed in the U.S.A.

OPM   10 9 8 7 6 5 4 3 2 1

Contents

Introduction

As a specialized aspect of its over-all material exploitation program, Headquarters USAF has established Project Moon Dust to locate, recover
and deliver descended foreign space vehicles.
ICGL #4, 25 April 1961, delineates collection responsibilities—

> —*Official Air Force document
> recovered throught the Freedom of
> Information Act.*

T he history of the UFO phenomenon is filled with
dozens of government and military studies that
have concluded, time and again, that flying sau-

cers are real and interplanetary. The history is filled with government statements that are in direct conflict with established facts and documentation. The history is a confusing blend of fact and fiction. This is an attempt to sort some of it out, providing us with a few clues about the situation.

With the Freedom of Information Act and a new candor on the part of some officials, we have been able to piece together part of that history. But even with that, we find ourselves caught in word games and arguments over semantics. It doesn't lead us to the truth. It keeps us in the dark, which, in some cases, is exactly what *they* want.

If that wasn't true, then why in a letter, does Lt. Colonel John E. Madison, an Air Force officer, insist there were no missions named Moon Dust (See *Conspiracy of Silence*, pp. 167–179). Why does he tell Jeff Bingaman, United States senator, that no such mission ever existed when that is clearly in error. Yes, I used the term "error" on purpose here, though a good case can be made for using the word "lies." In fact, in a follow up letter written by Colonel George M. Mattingley (see *The Truth about the UFO Crash at Roswell* for a copy of the letter), the errors are admitted. Clearly the situation about Project Moon Dust and Operation Blue Fly, as outlined in that original letter, was wrong. The question is whether the misinformation was a deliberate or a simple mistake.

Other letters, from other military officers to the Senate, provide more clues. The second letter, by Mattingley, has as much wrong in it as the first, claiming, for example, that the UFO mission didn't begin until 1957 when the documentation proves it began in 1953. If it wasn't a deliberate attempt to mislead, then why continue after being caught the first time? Why tell that same senator more lies about UFOs, Project Moon Dust and Operation Blue Fly?

We have been told that the Air Force investigated UFOs for more than twenty years and never found any information to suggest they were real, that they posed a threat to the United States, or that they were from other solar systems. That is what we've been told, but as we'll see, such is not the case. Arguments at the highest levels suggest that the information that flying saucers are real has been found, that they might pose a threat, and that they *are* from other worlds.

What I have tried to do here is provide the information that I have found during my investigations of UFOs for the last decade. I have, over the last several years, scoured the Project Blue Book files at the National Archives, at the Air Force Archives at Maxwell Air Force Base, and the photo files held at various Air Force facilities. I have searched through documents at presidential libraries, and piles of documents held at the Center for UFO Studies. I have ordered dozens of microfilmed records from everywhere from the National Archives to the National Climatic Center in Asheville, North Carolina. I have reviewed hundreds of hours of video and audio taped interviews held in various repositories and in private hands. And I have interviewed, literally, hundreds of witnesses to various aspects of the UFOs.

To fully understand the UFO phenomenon, it is often necessary to understand what precipitated the activities. Does the creation of the 4602d Air Intelligence Service Squadron seem nefarious? In and of itself, no. But plug in the history of what was happening at the time the

4602d was given its mission of UFO investigation and suddenly the situation seems more geared to a coverup than it does to investigation.

Does the creation of Project Moon Dust reflect the advancement of terrestrial science as we step into space, or is it a response to the growing number of UFO reports? Moon Dust did, in fact, retrieve returning space debris launched from other countries. But the mission also included investigation of UFOs. Why set up a special team to recover "returning space debris" prior to the launch of the first Soviet satellite?

It is clear, from the documentation, that Moon Dust preceded the launch of Sputnik in 1957. The mission began, at least on paper, in 1953. That is what the Air Force told one U.S. senator at that time. However, there would be no returning space debris until 1957.

The problem goes beyond government deceit. There are those in the UFO community, those who are supposedly trying to find the truth, who have been no more candid than the government and the Air Force. They are the ones out there who have been contradicting everything that has been said and published, often without evidence to back up their claims.

Some of the best known UFO cases have become confused over the years. To understand the UFO phenomenon, it is necessary to understand how these situations are created. Nothing takes place in a vacuum, though the government would often like us to believe exactly that.

What I have tried to do here is sort through some of that confusion. I have tried to accurately report on the situations that existed as decisions were made at the highest levels. To do so properly, it is necessary to examine documents and cases. And to prove the points, it is necessary to examine some of the sightings. Reports covered here include the Kelly-Hopkinville creature report, the Cash-Landrum injury case, the Bentwaters encounter, and the Belgium UFO sightings. Look at these cases, and the information that came from some of the "waves" of sightings reported in 1952 and 1957. By understanding these, we can begin to understand how the UFO phenomenon developed over the last five decades.

This book will examine a body of evidence and learn that the truth, as always, lies between two extremes. We will see that there has been government manipulation of the facts, but that is not all. UFO researchers and investigators are as guilty of manipulation as any government agency or agent.

When you have finished reading this book, I hope that some of the confusion will have vanished. Remember one thing: I have a definite point of view. My work is colored by my thinking, just as everyone's work is biased. Remember that well.

But also look beyond that. Look at the facts of the cases and the documentation for those cases. Documents are certainly open to interpretation, but the truth will shine through. When you finish, you will see that the UFO question is complicated and confusing. But, when you finish, some of the complication should be removed and simplified. When you finish, you might have a few of the answers about UFOs. If that is what happened, then I have done my job.

CHAPTER 1

The First of the Official UFO Investigations

It has been a matter of faith that we believe reports from the government regarding secret investigations that concluded UFOs were real. There have been spokesmen who have said that there were no secret studies and that the government and Air Force have been completely open with the American public. If they knew anything, they have claimed, they would have told us about it long ago.

It all sounds good, but it simply isn't the truth. There is a long history of secret studies that have concluded that there *is* something to the UFO phenomenon. Oh, they can weasel out of it because most of the studies have *not* concluded that UFOs are extraterrestrial, but that doesn't change the facts. Secret studies have been conducted and they have concluded that something real was happening.

One of the first, if not the very first, of these secret studies was requested in July 1947 by Brigadier General George F. Schulgen, the assistant chief of staff for air intelligence, when he sent detailed UFO sighting reports to the Air Materiel Command at Wright Field in Dayton, Ohio.

Schulgen was confused by the situation that was developing as more people were reporting flying saucers or, as they were sometimes called, flying disks. He, or members of his staff, had checked around inside the military, and learned that the reports were not of some kind of secret government project to develop a new fighter, bomber, or missile. No one, including Major General Curtis LeMay, then the head of research and development for the Army Air Forces, seemed to know what the flying saucers were.

Schulgen collected a number of the best cases, including those involving both military and commercial airline pilots, multiple witnesses, and those involving more than a single object. He asked the scientists, technicians, and other experts at the Air Materiel Command for their analysis of those reports.

The answer came on September 23, 1947 from then Lieutenant General Nathan F. Twining, the commanding general of AMC. Twining's letter said,

> "It is the opinion that: a. The phenomenon reported is something real and not visionary or fictitious. b. There are objects probably approximating the shape of a disc, of such appreciable size as to appear to be as large as man-made aircraft. c. There is a possibility that some of the in-

cidents may be caused by natural phenomena, such as meteors. d. The reported operating characteristics such as extreme rates of climb, maneuverability (particularly in roll), and action which must be considered *evasive* when sighted or contacted by friendly aircraft and radar, lend belief to the possibility that some of the objects are controlled either manually, automatically or remotely."

The analysis continued with Twining and his staff recommending that a priority project be established for the investigation of the sighting reports. This was the beginning of Project Sign.

Given the nature of our examination here, it is important to point out that the public was told that the project name was Project Saucer. Sign was a classified investigation operating as a "secret" project to determine what was being seen. From the very beginning the military was being less than candid about the situation.

It should be noted that it was what should be expected. In the summer of 1947 it was clear that military and government leaders had no more information than the rest of us. They were trying to determine what was happening and they didn't want to admit they had no real information on which to base their opinions.

I'm avoiding a discussion of the Roswell UFO crash here because it is not necessary to understand the situation. Twining had, in his report, mentioned the lack of crash-recovered debris, and that can be interpreted to mean that Schulgen, in his letter, mentioned nothing about it. Twining, in his response, didn't mention it because Schulgen hadn't included the data in his original request.

Instead, we're looking at the investigative situation. The Air Force found itself required to investigate reports of flying saucers. It was a task they took seriously in the beginning. Edward Ruppelt, onetime head of Project Blue Book (a descendant of Sign), wrote that in July 1947, the military took the idea of flying saucers very seriously. This was the environment in which Sign began its operations.

In 1948, the officers of Sign created an "Estimate of the Situation." There are no known copies of the report still in existence, but Edward Ruppelt, in his book *The Report on Unidentified Flying Objects*, provides us with clues about the document.

Ruppelt described the document itself, writing, "It was a rather thick document with a black cover and it was printed on legal-sized paper. Stamped across the front covers were the words TOP SECRET."

Ruppelt continued, "It contained the Air Force's analysis of many of the incidents I have told about plus many similar ones. All of them had come from scientists, pilots, and other equally credible observers, and each one was unknown.

"The document pointed out that the reports hadn't actually started with the Arnold incident. Belated reports from a weather observer in Richmond, Virginia, who observed a 'silver disc' through his theodolite telescope; an F-47 pilot and three pilots in his formation who saw a 'silver flying wing,' and the English 'ghost airplanes' that had been picked up on radar early in 1947 proved this point . . ."

According to Ruppelt, as well as others who have claimed to have seen the study, the report concluded that UFOs were "interplanetary." No one had found any evidence that the craft were manufactured on Earth, that any other country had the technical ability to create craft in the shapes described and that could perform as described. The only possible conclusion was that the flying saucers were from another world.

It is also interesting to note that Ruppelt, in the draft of his own book on the "Estimate" wrote, "It concluded that UFO's were interplanetary." So there was no question what the officers, scientists, and technicians who wrote the report believed.

When the "Estimate" was completed, it was signed and sent up the chain of command, ultimately arriving at the Office of the Chief of Staff, General Hoyt S. Vandenberg. He read it and, according to Ruppelt, "batted it back down." Vandenberg said that the evidence, in the form of sighting reports but no physical evidence, did not warrant the conclusions drawn.

Ruppelt, in his book, said that the report was declassified and then destroyed. Of course, from a military intelligence point of view that makes no sense. Why destroy it if it has been declassified? If, however, it remained classified, then it would have had to be destroyed.

At any rate, this marked a shift in the emphasis in the UFO project. The fire to learn the truth slipped away and apparently no one wanted to be caught expressing an opinion that had been rejected by the chief of staff. Project Sign began to disintegrate.

The report seems to have adversely affected the careers

of many of the men who were involved with it. They apparently believed in their conclusions and traveled to the Pentagon to defend their positions. Dr. Michael Swords reported that these men were probably Lawrence H. Truettner, A. B. Deyarmond, and Alfred Loedding. The military officers were Captain Robert Sneider, Colonel Howard McCoy, or possibly Colonel William Clingerman.

What is important about this, and what makes the history of the investigation clearer, is that after the unsuccessful defense, everyone was reassigned. Swords wrote, "So great was the carnage that only the lowest grades in the project ... were left to write the 1949 Project Grudge report about the same cases."

The point, however, is that a top secret report had been written by the men investigating flying saucers. They had concluded, based on the evidence they reviewed, that flying saucers were from outer space. It makes no real difference that the report, was rejected by a single officer at the very top of the Air Force. It was created and it was classified. For Air Force spokesmen to say that no such study had ever been made was, I suppose, technically correct, but it certainly wasn't accurate.

There is, however, another report written in that general time frame which was originally classified as Top Secret. Published on December 10, 1948, by the Air Force Directorate of Intelligence and the Office of Naval Intelligence, "The Analysis of Flying Object Incidents in the U.S." did draw some interesting conclusions. While they did not say that flying saucers were of alien origin, they did suggest that the reports were of something very real.

The problem, according to the report, was "TO EXAMINE

pattern of tactics of 'Flying Saucers' (hereinafter referred to as flying objects) and to develop conclusions as to the possibility of existence."

So what we're looking at is another top secret report on flying saucers that would try to determine if they really existed. They were not necessarily trying to determine that flying saucers were extraterrestrial, or in the case of early studies, interplanetary, but to discover if they were something more than illusions, misidentifications, and hoaxes, as the military was telling the public they were.

Under "Facts and Discussion," they wrote:

"A DETAILED discussion of information bearing on the problem as set forth above is attached as Appendix 'A'. The main points established therein are summarized below.

"THE FREQUENCY of reported incidents, the similarity in many of the characteristics attributed to the observed objects and the quality of observers considered as a whole, support the contention that some type of flying object has been observed. Approximately 210 incidents have been reported. Among the observers reporting such incidents are trained and experienced U.S. Weather Bureau personnel, USAF rated officers [meaning pilots and other flight crew], experienced civilian pilots, technicians associated with various research projects and technicians employed by commercial airlines.

"THE POSSIBILITY that reported observations of flying objects over the U.S. were influenced by previous sightings of unidentified phenomena in

Europe, particularly over Scandinavia in 1948 [the ghost rockets], and that observers reporting such incidents may have been interested in obtaining personal publicity have been considered as possible explanations. However, these possibilities seem to be improbable when certain selected reports such as the one from U.S. Weather Bureau at Richmond, Virginia, are examined. During observations of weather balloons at the Richmond Bureau, one well-trained observer has sighted strange metallic disks on three occasions and another observer has sighted a similar object on one occasion. The last observation of unidentified objects was in April, 1947. On all four occasions the weather balloon and the unidentified objects were in view through the theodolite. These observations at the Richmond Bureau occurred several months before publicity on the flying saucers appeared in a U.S. newspaper.

"DESCRIPTIONS of the flying objects fall into three configuration categories: (1) disk-shaped (2) rough cigar-shaped (3) balls of fire. Varying conditions of visibility and differences in angles at which objects have been observed rather than three different types. This possibility is further substantiated by the fact that in the areas where such objects have been observed the ratio of the three general configurations is approximately the same.

"THEREFORE, IT appears that some object has been seen; however, the identification of that object cannot be readily accomplished on the basis of information reported on each incident. It is possible that the object, or objects, may have been domestically launched devices such as weather balloons, rockets, experimental flying wing aircraft, or celestial phenomena. It is necessary to obtain information on such domestic activity to confirm or deny this possibility. Depending upon the degree with which this may be accomplished, foreign devices must then be considered as a possibility.

"THE PATTERN of sightings is definable. Sightings have been most intense throughout the states bordering the Atlantic and Pacific coast lines, and the central states of Ohio and Kentucky . . .

"THE ORIGIN of the devices is not ascertainable. There are two reasonable possibilities: (1) The objects are domestic devices, and if so, their identification or origin can be established by a survey of all launchings of airborne objects. Domestic flying-wing type aircraft observed in various aspects of flight might be responsible for some of the reported flying objects, particularly those described as disks and rough cigar shapes . . . Among those which have been operational in recent years are the XF5U-1 ('Flying Flapjack') developed by Chance-Vaught, the Northrup B-35, and the turbo-jet YB-49. The present existence of any privately developed flying-wing type aircraft has not been determined but one such aircraft, the Arup tailless monoplane, was operational at South Bend, Indiana, prior to 1935. (2) Objects are foreign, and if so, it would seem most logical to consider that they are from a Soviet source. The

Soviets possess information on a number of German flying-wing type aircraft such as the Gotha P60A, Junkers EF 130 long-range, high-speed jet bomber and the Horten 229 twin-jet fighter, which particularly resembles some of the description of unidentified flying objects . . . As early as 1924 Tscheranowsky developed a 'Parabola' aircraft, an all-wing design, which was the outcome of considerable Soviet experimentation with gliders of the same general form. Soviet aircraft based on such designs might have speeds approaching transsonic speeds attributed to some flying objects or greater overall performance assuming the successful development of some unusual propulsion device such as atomic energy engine.

"THAT THE Soviets have a current interest in flying-wing type aircraft is suggested by their utilization of Dr. Guenther Bock who, at the end of World War II, was in charge of the flying-wing program in Germany . . . Achievements satisfactory to the U.S.S.R. are indirectly indicated by the personal recognition he is reported to be receiving in the U.S.S.R. Recently it has been reported that the U.S.S.R. is planning to build a fleet of 1,800 Horten flying-wing aircraft. Information of low evaluation has been received stating that a regiment of jet night fighters, Model Horten XIII, is at Kuzmikha, an air base two miles southwest of Irkutsk. Kuzmikha is identified as one of a number of airfields for the protection of an atomic energy plant at Irkutsk. The Horten XIII as developed by Germany was a glider.

"ASSUMING THAT the objects might eventually be identified as foreign or foreign-sponsored devices, the possible reason for their appearance over the U.S. requires consideration. Several possible explanations appear noteworthy, viz:

"a. To negate U.S. confidence in the atom bomb as the most advanced and decisive weapon in warfare.

"b. To perform photographic reconnaissance missions.

"c. To test U.S. air defenses.

"d. To conduct familiarization flights over U.S. territory."

There were also two paragraphs of conclusions that brought the whole thing into perspective.

"SINCE the Air Force is responsible for control of the air in the defense of the U.S., it is imperative that all other agencies cooperate in confirming or denying the possibility that these objects have a domestic origin. Otherwise, if it is firmly indicated that there is no domestic explanation, the objects are a threat and warrant more active efforts of identification and interception.

"IT MUST be accepted that some type of flying objects have been observed, although their identification and origin are not discernible. In the interest of national defense it would be unwise to overlook the possibility that some of these objects may be of foreign origin."

Some comment on this document must be made. We have the luxury of looking back on it after half a century. We know things about the state of the world in 1947 that might have been known only to a few in the highest levels of intelligence then. For example, we know that Soviet plans to build a fleet of Horten Brothers flying wings never bore fruit. The flying-wing design is inherently unstable and it is only since the development of small, powerful, onboard computers that the instability problems have been mostly corrected.

We also know by an examination of the once-classified records that none of the domestic flying-wing type aircraft can account for flying disk sightings in 1947. The Northrup XB-35 had been grounded in November 1946 and had only flown briefly out of Muroc Army Air Field (later Edwards Air Force Base) in California on a single day in June 1947. The YB-49, the jet-powered version, didn't fly until October 1947, so it can be ruled out as a culprit during the summer of 1947. The flights of the aircraft were limited and well documented, allowing us to trace its flight path and rule it out of later flying saucer reports.

The same can be said for the Flying Flapjack. It only flew near Bridgeport, Connecticut, and only for short periods of time. There is no evidence that any flying saucer report was ever "solved" as being the Flying Flapjack.

And, we know now that overflights of U.S. territory by Soviet aircraft were not made in that time frame. In fact, I used the Freedom of Information Act to review the records of the Air Force, CIA, DIA, and other agencies, searching for any evidence that there was any penetration of our coastal defense zones by Soviet aircraft from

January 1, 1946 through December 31, 1947. All the responses I received were negative.

Skeptics have suggested that this document, classified originally as Top Secret, proves there are no UFOs and more specifically no crash of a flying saucer outside of Roswell in early July 1947. They argue that the men writing it had access to all the top secret information and yet they make no mention of Roswell, or of some of the other highly important UFO cases.

The argument against that is simple to make. Clearly they didn't have access to all areas classified as Top Secret. They speculated that domestic research projects might explain the flying disk reports, though they have nothing to point in that direction. Since they were forced to speculate rather than report, it meant that some doors were closed to them.

And finally, there are those who have suggested this might be the long-lost "Estimate of the Situation." However, Ruppelt's description of that document, based on his own claimed observation of it, rules this one out. It is clearly too short and too small.

But what it does show us is that at the beginning of 1949, some eighteen months after the first of the flying saucer reports came to public attention, the Air Force was still taking the subject seriously. It also shows that the officers creating this report believed that flying saucers were something real. They might have hedged their bets by suggesting foreign manufacture as opposed to extraterrestrial, but the point is, they believed in the reality of the situation.

They were advocating that the situation was serious

enough that the Air Force should continue to investigate. They were suggesting that the Air Force, because of its mission, was required to investigate. To do otherwise, without firm evidence that flying saucers were illusions, hallucinations, and hoaxes, would be to violate the public trust.

It is splitting a very fine hair to point out that the report doesn't say extraterrestrial or interplanetary. What it says is that there is a very real possibility that the objects are of foreign manufacture. Foreign manufacture could mean that they were extraterrestrial.

It must also be noted that this report was written after the alleged closure of Project Sign by Air Force Chief Vandenberg. Those writing it were certainly aware of what happened to the others who suggested the extraterrestrial idea. They suggested foreign rather than something from another world perhaps in self-defense.

The Air Force in the meantime was continuing its research and investigations of flying saucers. The name of the project was changed from Sign to Grudge, according to some, because the original code name had been compromised. That means that those without the proper clearances had learned of it.

However, there is another, more sinister explanation. When the final report by Project Sign officers was completed, the Air Force announced the conclusions, saying as they would many times, that flying saucers posed no threat to national security. They announced that the investigation had been completed. The flying saucer project was dead.

A report entitled, "The Findings of Project Sign," was eventually written. It outlined the motivation behind

Project Sign, who the players were, and the results of their research. In the "Summary," it was noted that the data in the report were "derived from reports of 243 domestic and thirty (30) foreign incidents. Data from these incidents is being summarized, reproduced and distributed to agencies and individuals cooperating in the analysis and evaluation ... The data obtained in reports received are studied in relation to many factors such as guided missile research research activity, weather and other atmospheric sounding balloon launchings, commercial and military aircraft flights, flights of migratory birds, and other considerations, to determine possible explanations for sightings."

The authors of the report wanted to make the situation clear. They wrote:

> "Based on the possibility that the objects are really unidentified and unconventional types of aircraft a technical analysis is made of some of the reports to determine the aerodynamic, propulsion, and control features that would be required for the objects to perform as described in the reports. The objects sighted have been grouped into four classifications according to configuration:
> "1. Flying disks, i.e., very low aspect ratio aircraft.
> "2. Torpedo- or cigar-shaped bodies with no wings or fins visible in flight.
> "3. Spherical or balloon-shaped objects.
> "4. Balls of light."

The authors also reported that:

"Approximately twenty percent of the incidents have been identified as conventional aerial objects to the satisfaction of personnel assigned to Project 'Sign' in this Command. It is expected that a study of the incidents in relation to weather and other atmospheric sounding balloons will provide solutions for an equivalent number . . . Elimination of incidents with reasonably satisfactory explanations will clarify the problem presented by a project of this nature.

"The possibility that some of the incidents may represent technical developments far in advance of knowledge available to engineers and scientists of this country has been considered. No facts are available to personnel at this Command that will permit an objective assessment of this possibility. All information so far presented on the possible existence of space ships from another planet or of aircraft propelled by an advanced type of atomic power plant have been largely conjecture."

They provided a number of recommendations, writing, "Future activity on this project should be carried on at the minimum level necessary to record, summarize, and evaluate the data received on future reports and to complete the specialized investigations now in progress." They then added a phrase that too many UFO researchers have overlooked in the past.

They also wrote, "When and if a sufficient number of incidents are solved to indicate that these sightings do not represent a threat to the security of the nation, the assignment of special project status to the activity could be terminated."

This is a theme that would be repeated in one official UFO investigation after another. They would mention this aspect again and again. Each of the investigations, from Sign forward, had national security as its main concern. If national security wasn't threatened, then the question of reality became unimportant. And, as time passed, it became more likely to all those military investigators that no threat to the nation was posed.

The authors also wrote, "Reporting agencies should be impressed with the necessity for getting more factual evidence on sightings such as photographs, physical evidence, radar sightings, and data on size and shape."

The conclusions of the report are interesting. "No definite and conclusive evidence is yet available that would prove or disprove the existence of these unidentified objects as real aircraft of unknown and unconventional configuration. It is unlikely that positive proof of their existence will be obtained without examination of the remains of crashed objects. Proof of the nonexistence is equally impossible to obtain unless a reasonable and convincing explanation is determined for each incident."

They then wrote, "Many sightings by qualified and apparently reliable witnesses have been reported. However, each incident has unsatisfactory features, such as shortness of time under observation, distance from observer, vagueness of description or photographs, inconsistencies between individual observers, and lack of descriptive data, that prevents conclusions being drawn."

This one paragraph would also become important in understanding the UFO investigations of the future. Time and again those in the government would suggest that there were no good photographs, that eyewitness testimony was unreliable, and that the sightings were of nothing more spectacular than a fuzzy object in the distance. Those arguing against the reality of the phenomenon would often make these same claims.

The reason for the recommendation for a continuation of the project had nothing to do with research into the phenomenon. The authors write, "Evaluation of reports of unidentified objects is a necessary activity of military intelligence agencies. Such sightings are inevitable, and under wartime conditions rapid and convincing solutions of such occurrences are necessary to maintain morale of military and civilian personnel. In this respect, it is considered that the establishment of procedures and training of personnel is in itself worth the effort expended on this project."

About a year earlier, the personnel assigned to Sign had concluded that flying saucers were extraterrestrial. Now, using the same cases and the same evidence, those who survived at ATIC were claiming that there was nothing to the UFO phenomenon. More importantly, they were saying there was no threat to national security, but that the project should be continued for training proposes.

Ruppelt, in his book, tends to reinforce the idea to a limited extent. He wrote, "Officially the military uses the term 'flying saucer' on only two occasions. First in an explanatory sense, as when briefing people who are unacquainted with the term 'UFO': 'UFO—you know—flying saucers.' And second in a derogatory sense, for purposes of ridicule, as when it is observed, 'He says he saw a flying saucer.' "

The documentation suggests that the failure to find the truth was just a case of incompetence and bungling, but we must look beyond it. The clue is in the "Estimate of the Situation." If the document was so poorly drawn, if the conclusions didn't hold up, why order it destroyed? Why deny its existence at all?

What the facts show, what the documents show, what the actions of the men at the top show, is that a conspiracy of silence was born in the summer of 1947, and it was operated from the very top. Threats to the silence were eliminated ruthlessly, and those who didn't want to see their careers ended had better pick up the clues. When the chief of staff of the Air Force suggests that your report is in error, you had better listen. And, when those summoned to Washington to defend that report find themselves looking for new jobs, the message is unmistakable. No one is to talk about flying saucers in a positive light. Those who see flying saucers are drunk or crazy, and those who believe in them are uneducated and quickly out of a job.

That was the attitude that existed when the code name of the UFO project was compromised and the name was changed to Grudge. It might have been a coincidence, but that seems unlikely. The Air Force had been trying to keep the lid down since the summer of 1947.

Proof of this is seen in some of the earliest magazines and books about flying saucers. All talked of the military's Project Saucer. This was the public name for Project Sign. Everyone seemed to know that an investigation existed, but they didn't know the proper name, nor could they track the extent of that investigation.

After the true name leaked into the press, apparently sometime in 1949, the name was changed to Grudge, but it still had a 2A priority. That is interesting because, after

Vandenberg had "batted back" the 1948 "Estimate," everyone was recommending that the project be reduced in scope and importance.

In a Project Sign report prepared in February 1949, it was recommended that, "Future activity on this project should be carried on at the minimum level necessary to record, summarize, and evaluate the data received on future reports and to complete the specialized investigations now in progress. When and if sufficient number of incidents are solved to indicate that these sightings do not represent a threat to the security of the nation, the assignment of special project status to the activity could be terminated. Future investigations of reports would then be handled on a routine basis like any other intelligence work."

They also recommended, "Reporting agencies should be impressed with the necessity for getting more factual evidence on sightings . . . Personnel sighting such objects should engage the assistance of others, when possible, to get more definite data . . ."

They concluded, "No definite and conclusive evidence is yet available that would prove or disprove the existence of these unidentified objects as real aircraft of unknown and unconventional configuration. It is unlikely that positive proof of their existence will be obtained without examination of the remains of crashed objects . . ."

That would seem to suggest that Roswell did not represent the crash of an extraterrestrial craft. Who would be more likely to know about such an event than those involved in the investigation of the flying saucers? What it actually demonstrates is the extent of the conspiracy of silence. Those in the trenches, conducting the investigations, were not privy to all the data held at the top. Military security regulations demanded that the Roswell crash information be compartmentalized so that the men working on Project Sign were unaware of its existence.

How else to explain the appalling lack of any information about Roswell in the Project Blue Book files? As mentioned in my previous book, *Conspiracy of Silence*, the only reference is a single, short clipping contained in a file that has nothing to do with the Roswell event. It is clear that the military investigators in that time frame were collecting data from the newspapers. Since the military was heavily involved in the Roswell case, and the sources of the information were military officers, there should have been a military source file. There was not.

Even when it seemed that everyone in the Air Force, from the top on down, believed that the flying saucer project should be reduced in scope, if not eliminated altogether, it continued at a high priority. In the Sign report of February 1949, there is a page that notes the title of the project is now Grudge, the authority for it is "Hq, USAF, Deputy Chief of Staff, Materiel, Washington 25, D.C., dated 30 Dec. 1947." The project retained its 2A priority, and the purpose was, "To collect, collate, evaluate and interpret data obtained relative to the sighting of unidentified flying objects in the atmosphere which may have importance on the national security, and to control and effect distribution of all objective information as requested to interested governmental agencies and contractors."

That sounded good, but it wasn't the case. According to Ruppelt, "Everything was being evaluated on the premise that UFOs couldn't exist. No matter what you hear, don't believe it."

In August 1949, another report was issued and again recommended, "That the investigation and study of reports of unidentified flying objects be reduced in scope." Interestingly, the authors of the report suggested, "That Psychological Warfare Division and other governmental agencies interested in psychological warfare be informed of the results of this study."

Just a few months later, on December 27, 1949, it was announced that Project Grudge had been closed. The final report would be available to the press. It was a large document, hundreds of pages long, and filled with the type of jargon that identified it as a strictly military report.

The Grudge Report, as it became known, studied 237 of the best UFO sighting reports. Hynek and his staff were able to explain some of them as astronomical phenomena. The Air Force Air Weather Service and the Cambridge Research Laboratory had been able to reduce the number of unexplained sightings. Weather balloons and huge Skyhook research balloons accounted for some sightings, including that of Thomas Mantell.

Captain A. C. Trakowski, from the Cambridge facility, also reviewed the records of then-classified Project Mogul. Reviewing the data provided in the sighting reports, Trakowski found none that could be explained by the project.

When all the sightings had been carefully studied, the Grudge Report explained all but twenty-three percent. In twenty-three percent of the sightings, no explanation was found. The Psychology Branch of the Air Force's Aeromedical Laboratory took the final shot at eliminating that percentage.

They wrote, "There are sufficient psychological explanations for the reports of unidentified objects to provide plausible explanations for reports not otherwise explainable . . . [some witnesses] have spots before their eyes."

Ruppelt, in his book, elaborated, writing, "They pointed out that some people are just plain nuts."

Ruppelt noted that the media grabbed the appendix labeled, "Summary of the Evaluation of Remaining Reports." After they read it, finding it impossible to believe, they didn't report on the findings of Grudge. Ruppelt elaborated by interviewing a long-time Washington correspondent, writing, "He said the report had been quite impressive, but only in its ambiguousness, illogical reasoning, and very apparent effort to write off all UFO reports at any cost. He, personally, thought it was a poor attempt to put out a 'fake' report, full of misleading information, to cover up the real story. Others, he told me, just plainly and simply didn't know what to think—they were confused."

The final conclusions of Grudge were:

1. Evaluation of reports of unidentified flying objects constitute no direct threat to the national security of the United States.

2. Reports of unidentified flying objects are the result of:

a. A mild form of mass hysteria or "war nerves."

b. Individuals who fabricate such reports to perpetuate a hoax or seek publicity.

c. Psychological persons.
d. Misidentification of various conventional objects.

Ruppelt seemed puzzled by this situation. After all, he had, on orders from the highest levels of the Air Force, reevaluated the UFO project. He knew that there was no break in the investigation of the objects, yet here was this confusing report.

What we have then, are a series of reports, many classified at the highest levels, dealing with flying saucers. Some of them concluded that UFOs were extraterrestrial in origin and others let it go, just saying there was evidence that they were of foreign manufacture. What is interesting, however, is that those early arguments did not center around the reality of the situation, only the final identity of it. In other words, everyone seemed to believe that the flying saucers were real, they just didn't know who, or what, had manufactured them.

The situation, however, seemed to have stabilized. There was periodic interest in flying saucers from the press, and there was a growing interest on the part of one segment of the public, but for the most part, no one cared about flyings saucers. That was the situation until the summer of 1952. After that summer, the whole situation would change permanently.

CHAPTER 2

Summer of 1952

To fully understand what happened to the UFO investigations conducted by the United States government and the U.S. Air Force, it is necessary to understand the motivation behind it. The situation in the world of UFOs changed radically in 1952, and the outgrowth of that change was a policy that has prevented us from seeing the whole truth. It was all the result of a situation that developed during the middle of the summer of 1952 when flying saucers again exploded on the scene.

By 1952, the UFO phenomenon was five years old. It had started, officially, in late 1947, when the Air Force formed a classified, priority project to investigate sightings of flying saucers. Originally called Project Sign, it eventually developed into Project Grudge and finally into Project Blue Book.

During those early years, opinion swung from a belief that flying saucers were extraterrestrial to the idea that all sightings could be explained if enough information had been provided and a proper investigation was conducted. By the early 1950s, the investigation was staggering along with no one caring about it. As we have already seen, the opinion at the top was that flying saucers were unimportant and probably nothing more than hallucinations. With that sort of opinion held by the generals, the lower-ranking officers and the enlisted men were going through the motions, but nothing was being accomplished.

About that time, General Cabell asked Lieutenant Jerry Cummings what was happening with the flying saucer project. Told that nothing was being done, Cabell ordered it revitalized, assigned new officers to take charge of it, and made sure that the investigations were being conducted.

First Lieutenant Edward Ruppelt, later Captain, was put in charge. He envisioned a solid investigative team that would rely on the expertise of the scientific community, a staff of military experts to help in the investigation, and equipment stationed around the country for monitoring the skies. Ruppelt, given the task of learning the truth about flying saucers, set out to do exactly that, apparently with the blessings of the generals at Wright-Patterson Air Force Base and at the Pentagon.

In the fall of 1951, as the investigation was just beginning to roll, Ruppelt and members of the Office of Special Investigation studied sightings and photographs taken in Lubbock, Texas. Although the majority were written off as migrating birds, the five photographs of a V-formation of UFOs taken by Carl Hart, Jr. have never been satisfactorily explained. Ruppelt himself believed he had found a solution for the sightings, but never made his opinion public. Years after his untimely death, through reading his personal files, I learned that he thought lightning bugs were responsible. That explanation didn't cover the photographs, and it didn't seem to explain the lights seen by many others in west Texas. In fact, I spoke to Carl Hart in 1992. I wondered if he had figured out what he had photographed in 1951. He told me that he wasn't sure if flying saucers were real, but still didn't know what he had seen or what he had photographed. He asserted that he certainly had done nothing to fake the pictures as some researchers had claimed.

Ruppelt was not only investigating UFO reports, but he was attempting to reorganize the files collected during the first five years. When he arrived at ATIC, after Grudge was disbanded, he found everything dumped together in boxes or file cabinets. As he put the new Project Grudge into effect, he tried to find a way to improve the filing and collection systems. He noticed that a number of scientists, some of them well known, were available as consultants to his project. For the most part, he couldn't reveal their names because of promises of confidentiality, but that didn't matter. He had the use of the scientific knowledge which he believed would benefit the entire UFO investigation.

The UFO situation, at that time, was one that rarely found its way into the public arena. There were localized reports, and the Lubbock Lights sighting, because of the spectacular photographs, had received some national publicity, but for the most part, flying saucers had slipped from public scrutiny.

In April 1952, however, *Life* magazine published an article about UFOs. To many civilians, that meant the subject was something to be taken seriously. Many suspected the Air Force had a hand in it. Ruppelt even suggested an "unofficial" connection. Ruppelt, in his book, *The Report on Unidentified Flying Objects*, wrote, "I knew the Air Force had unofficially inspired the *Life* article." He went further, pointing out that "maybe they're interplanetary with the 'maybe' bordering on 'they are' was the personal opinion of several very high-ranking officers at the Pentagon."

Ruppelt then made a distinction that is important to the understanding of the summer of 1952. He wrote, "Oddly enough, the *Life* article did not cause a flood of reports." It has been suggested that the article triggered the wave of sightings in 1952, but Ruppelt, from his position on the inside of the investigation, asserted that such wasn't the case.

Because of what Ruppelt had written in his book, and because other researchers had pointed to the *Life* article, a natural course seemed for me to try to find a copy of it. I learned that shops that sell old magazines rarely, if ever, have a copy of that particular magazine because Marilyn Monroe's picture was on the cover. It is a collector's item.

Bound periodicals at a university library seemed the natural alternative. The University of Iowa library had three copies of *Life* March through June 1952. The covers of all had been taken by "collectors," but that mattered little to me. Unfortunately, the same type of people have been searching for the flying saucer story. The pages from all three copies had been cut or torn from the magazine. Copy machines that still only cost a nickel a sheet were close, but apparently not close enough because the articles were stolen anyway.

The Reader's Guide to Periodic Literature told me that the article, in a condensed form, had been reprinted in the May issue of *Reader's Digest*. While not as complete as the *Life* article, it would have to do. The idiots with the razor blades had not made it to the *Reader's Digest*.

The article was a recap of the history of flying saucers, starting with Kenneth Arnold's sighting in June 1947, and even mentioning the sighting by Dr. Clyde Tombaugh, the man who discovered Pluto, outside his home in Las Cruces, New Mexico.

A survey of the *Reader's Guide* showed that articles about flying saucers had been printed in 1951 and early 1952. Many of them were negative in tone, such as Dr. Donald H. Menzel's "New Theory of the Flying Saucers," printed in the September 1952 *Science Digest*. Others were picture essays about the special effects used to create the Martian invasion for the 1953 production of *War of the Worlds*.

None of the articles, whether skeptical, objective, or supportive, can be seen as the cause of the wave of sightings during the summer of 1952. What did cause a sharp rise in the number of reports, again according to Ruppelt, was the publication of Air Force Letter 200-5. The letter, signed by the Secretary of the Air Force, reinforced the idea that flying saucers were not jokes. The Air Force was making a serious study of the problem. Because the letter outlined a specific reporting criterion requiring the commander of every Air Force installation to forward all reports of flying saucers to ATIC (Air Technical Intelligence Center) by teletype, with a copy going to the Pentagon, the number of sightings increased. This was not because there were necessarily more sightings, but now there was a regulation requiring the reporting of those sightings to a specific location. Note that Ruppelt's revitalized Project Blue Book was stationed at ATIC headquarters at Wright-Patterson.

Ruppelt also pointed out that the reporting channels allowed him to contact, directly, any Air Force unit anywhere in the world. This directive, which allowed him to bypass the normal chain of command, was something that was almost never done in the Air Force. It provides a clue about the importance of UFO investigations in 1952.

The result of these new directives, as said previously, was an upswing in the number of UFO sighting reports being made. Ruppelt, as mentioned, did not blame the interest generated by the *Life* article, but did blame the new reporting orders. In March (before the *Life* article) and April there had been an increase in sightings reported to the Air Force. By May, the number was down, and Ruppelt believed, at that time, things were about to return to normal.

By June 1952, Project Blue Book was operating under the plan that had been set up in January. Ruppelt had a staff of four officers, two enlisted men, two civilians, and three scientists employed on Project Bear, which was designed for a scientific analysis of UFOs. He had set up a clipping service so that newspaper reports would be forwarded to Blue Book headquarters. The stage was now properly set for what would happen during the summer.

Ruppelt noted that, in early 1952, the newspaper clippings would arrive in a thick envelope. They would be sorted and those that demanded an investigation were separated from those that were little more than interesting or anecdotal. According to Ruppelt, it was in June that the newspaper clippings began to arrive in cardboard boxes. It was clear that the flying saucers had returned.

Ruppelt and his staff were suddenly very busy with flying saucers. The investigative techniques that he had started just months earlier began to pay dividends. A series of spectacular sightings came in the middle of the month. Ruppelt, in his book wrote, "I had this build-up of reports in my mind one Sunday night, June 15 to be exact, when the OD [Officer of the Day] at ATIC called me at home and said that we were getting a lot of reports from Virginia."

This was a series of sightings beginning at 3:40 in the afternoon when a woman in Unionville, Virginia, said she saw an shiny object high in the sky. Forty minutes later the men at a CAA [later the FAA] radio facility spotted a round, shiny object south of Unionville. Over the next four hours, an airline crew would see the object and a Marine fighter pilot would attempt an intercept. An hour after the Marine failed to catch the object, the Air Force tried, and also failed. At 8:00 P.M., jets from Langley Air Force Base in Virginia tried still another intercept. Five minutes later, the round, shiny UFO disappeared.

Ruppelt wrote that it was a good series of sightings

and noted that it was the first time that his team had received a series of reports about the same object. Ruppelt wrote, "There was no doubt that all these people had reported the same object."

Ruppelt did some research into the balloon launchings from various weather stations that could account for the sightings. He decided that the information he gathered was good enough to label the case as a "probable balloon." After all, the object wasn't moving very fast, certainly no faster than ninety miles an hour, and it had been in sight for just under five hours.

But the explanation of one sighting didn't explain all the others that were pouring in. The numbers of sightings, and the media attention directed at them, was such that the brass in Washington took notice. It was about this time, mid-June 1952, that Ruppelt was alerted by Colonel Dunn that he, Ruppelt, would be needed to brief a number of Pentagon staff officers, including Major General John A. Samford, the Director of Intelligence, on the current state of the UFO investigation.

What is important to understand is that in the middle of June, with the number of sightings increasing rapidly, there were those in the Air Force who were still searching for legitimate answers. Ruppelt wrote that one of the colonels who attended his Pentagon briefing began asking penetrating questions about the status of the current investigation. The colonel wanted to know, for example, why all assumptions made by the Blue Book staff were in the negative. Why not make some of the assumptions in the positive?

Ruppelt's answer to the colonel made sense. They selected a conservative point of view because the evidence that he had seen himself was basically just eyewitness testimony. Ruppelt had seen nothing in their files, or in the reports, that was one hundred percent conclusive. Because of that, they tended toward negative conclusions.

The colonel then asked, according to Ruppelt, "Why not simply believe that most people know what they saw?" That began a lively discussion among the officers present.

The problem, one that Ruppelt ignored, is that most people did not know what they saw or believe what they saw. When I first had an opportunity to read the Project Blue Book files in the spring of 1975, before they were sanitized and relocated to the National Archives, I noticed some very strange notations. There was a "joint military and civilian observation of the moon." What it meant was that one multiple witness case involving both military personnel and civilians was solved by saying it had been a sighting of the moon.

To me, at that time, it didn't make sense. I assumed, along with others, that everyone knows what the moon looks like. It smacked of the Air Force merely writing off cases so that they could claim a smaller number of unidentified sightings. I learned the truth about that several years later in Grant County, Wisconsin. While investigating a series of sightings in that area, I was in the sheriff's office and a report came in. An excited man called, screaming that a flying saucer was landing in his backyard. The deputies asked if I wanted to go and I said, "Sure."

The hysterical man led us through his house, into the backyard, and pointed at a brightly lighted, round object that seemed to be flashing through the low-hanging clouds. There was no doubt in my mind. He was looking at the moon. Granted, the clouds were being whipped along by a strong wind and there was an appearance of motion for the object, but the bright "UFO" was the full moon.

So, when the colonel asked Ruppelt if they couldn't simply assume that people knew what they were looking at, the answer should have been, "No." Even trained people, pilots, police officers, and weather observers could be fooled if the conditions were unusual enough.

The meeting, however, resulted in a directive that more effort be made to obtain positive identification of UFOs. Ruppelt and his staff began to try to develop ideas that would allow them to gather the type of information they wanted. The plan seemed sound, but it was not put into effect, as far as we civilians know. At least there is nothing in the various reports, documents, and files that I have reviewed to show they followed up on this decision.

At the end of June, the UFO sightings became more frequent. According to Ruppelt, "In Massachusetts, New Jersey, and Maryland jet fighters had been scrambled almost nightly for a week. On three occasions radar-equipped F-94s had locked on aerial targets only to have the lock-on broken by the apparent violent maneuvers of the target."

Again early on the morning of July 1, fighters were scrambled when a Ground Observer Corps spotter reported an object traveling across the Boston area. Ground radar was unable to find the object, so the two F-94s were vectored into the general area. Neither of the fighter pilots was able to find the UFO.

The sighting would have become just another single witness case with no corroboration and no apparent solution, if not for another report made shortly after it. A man and his wife living in Boston reported that early in the morning they had seen the vapor trails of two jets and had looked to see what they were chasing. They saw a large, cigar-shaped object traveling to the southwest over Boston. Behind the first, some distance back, was a second, similar object. Neither was leaving a vapor trail of its own.

The man and his wife watched two objects, and the two jets that searched back and forth for the UFOs. The man said the objects were traveling a little faster than the jets and seemed to be much higher than the aircraft.

About the same time, an Air Force captain, leaving his home, saw the two jets, and like the other couple, looked up to see what they were after. He spotted the cigar-shaped object heading toward the south. His description matched that of the couple, but he saw only a single craft.

To Ruppelt, this was exactly the type of report he wanted to investigate. There were a number of witnesses, in widely separated areas of Boston, who had clearly seen the same object. Everyone had noted the time, and an investigator could get directions and elevations from the witnesses—a great deal of important data could be recovered. Most importantly, they were not dealing with "lights in the sky." A solid object had been reported.

Unfortunately, the dam had broken. Sighting reports

were coming from all over the country and Ruppelt had no one to send to Boston. Other cases, equally fascinating, were being reported almost daily, and sometimes more frequently than that.

One of the best of the new cases, because it involved not photographs but 16mm movie footage, occurred on July 2. The film, made by a Navy warrant officer named Delbert C. Newhouse, was in color. It would be carefully analyzed several times over the years. When all was said and done, the Air Force explained it to their own satisfaction, but that explanation did not impress many.

It was just after eleven in the morning, near Tremonton, Utah, when Newhouse's wife noticed a group of bright objects that she couldn't easily identify. Newhouse, a trained Navy photographer who was in the process of moving from one duty station to another, stopped the car to retrieve his 16mm camera from the trunk.

By the time he got the camera out, the objects had moved away from the car. Newhouse said later that when one object broke from the formation, he tracked it so that analysts would have something to work with. He let it fly across the field of view. He did that two or three times. When he turned back, the whole formation was gone.

The details of the story vary, depending on the source. Air Force files, based on the information supplied by others, show that Newhouse and his wife saw the objects at close range. By the time he got the car stopped and the camera out of the trunk, the objects had moved to a longer range. In an interview I conducted in 1976, Newhouse confirmed he had seen the objects at close range. He said they were large, disc-shaped, and brightly lighted. Dewey Fournet told me that Newhouse had said the same thing to him when Fournet spoke to him not long after the event.

After filming the objects, Newhouse stored his camera, got back into the car, and drove on to his new duty station. Once there, he had the film processed and sent a copy to the Air Force suggesting they might find it interesting.

The Air Force investigation lasted for months, including a painstaking analysis of the film. They tried everything to identify the objects but failed. When coupled to the report made by Newhouse, and the reliability of Newhouse because of his position as a Navy photographer, the Air Force was stuck. They had no explanation.

When the Air Force finished, the Navy asked for it. They made a frame-by-frame analysis that took more than a thousand man hours. They studied the motion of the objects, their relation to one another in the formation, the lighting of the objects, and every other piece of data they could find on the film. In the end, like their Air Force counterparts, they were left with no explanations.

But, unlike their Air Force counterparts, the Navy experts were not as restricted in their comments on the film. Their report included the details that the objects were internally lighted spheres which were not reflecting sunlight. They also estimated the speed at 3,780 miles an hour if the spheres were five miles away. At twice the distance, they would have been moving twice as fast. At half the distance, half the speed. If the objects were just under a mile distant, they were traveling at 472 miles an hour, according to the Naval analysts.

When the Robertson Panel reviewed the film in January 1953, Dr. Alverez said that the objects might be birds. Fournet told me, "Dr. Alverez suggested that as a possible solution to that Tremonton movie . . ."

The next morning, after the scientists on the panel had seen the film, "the Air Force, the CIA, has mysteriously produced this film of seagulls to show them and you just wonder," Dr. Michael Swords told me. "Wasn't that convenient? They just happened to have that seagull film handy in the stacks somewhere."

In the years that followed, the Tremonton movie's suggested explanation of seagulls became the solid explanation. Donald H. Menzel and L. G. Boyd, in their book, wrote of the Tremonton film: "The pictures are of such poor quality and show so little that even the most enthusiastic home-movie fan today would hesitate to show them to his friends. Only a stimulated imagination could suggest that the moving objects are anything but very badly photographed birds."

The Condon Committee (the University of Colorado UFO study) investigator on the Tremonton film, William K. Hartmann, reexamined the case years after the Robertson panel. After reviewing the evidence, Hartmann concluded, "These observations give *strong evidence that the Tremonton films do show birds* (emphasis in original), as hypothesized above, and I now regard the objects as so identified (sic)."

So a possible answer, suggested by the Robertson panel, became the final explanation for the film as the years passed. However, in the analysis that appeared after the Robertson panel and all the studies mentioned since, one important fact was left out. Newhouse saw the objects at close range. Fournet said, ". . . when you look at what Newhouse said when he was interviewed after that . . . When you put all that together, the seagull hypothesis becomes flimsier and flimsier."

Ruppelt, in fact, mentions that fact in his book. According to him, no one had asked Newhouse what the objects looked like because there were pictures of them. It was only later, after Ruppelt had gotten out of the Air Force, that he talked to Newhouse about what he had seen. According to what Ruppelt wrote, "He didn't *think* the UFOs were disk-shaped; he *knew* that they were."

When I spoke to Newhouse, I asked him the question that I always ask those who have had a UFO sighting. It had been nearly twenty-five years and I wanted to know if, during that time, he had come up with a solution for his sighting. He told me that he still didn't know what he had seen and photographed, except that they weren't birds or seagulls or any damned thing like that.

What is interesting is that the explanations offered by the various organizations that believe they have a solution all forget what Newhouse himself said. Clearly he had a sighting and he provided evidence of it. If we assume that he was not lying, and there is no reason to assume that he was, then the case must be marked as unidentified. No, it isn't sufficient, by itself, to prove that UFOs are extraterrestrial, but then, it does provide some interesting physical evidence that these objects *are real*, which is what the skeptics are always demanding.

The Newhouse sighting and his movie were only one of the important cases that would be examined by the Air Force in 1952. Many of them did turn out to have mundane explanations. With the newspapers of June and July filled with UFO reports, thousands were outside searching the skies. Weather balloons, drifting along at tremendous altitude, could reflect the sun, suggesting a flying saucer. High-flying jets, when the sun and clouds conspired, could fool almost anyone into believing he or she was looking at something from another world. There were hoaxes and jokes that fired another wave of sightings—and there were other things as well.

But about the middle of July came a series of sightings that caused a great number of problems for the Air Force. The headline, in the *Cedar Rapids Gazette* would be a classic. "SAUCERS SWARM OVER CAPITAL," the front page screamed.

What became known as "the Washington Nationals" began when, according to the CAA's logbook, two radarscopes at the Air Routing and Traffic Control Center (ARTC) picked up eight unidentified targets near Andrews Air Force Base at 11:40 P.M. on the evening of July 19. These were not airplanes because they were traveling too fast. First they moved along at only a hundred miles an hour, then suddenly would accelerate to fantastic speeds. One of the objects was tracked, according to the calculations made by an operator at the center, at about 7,000 miles an hour.

About twenty minutes later, or just after midnight on July 20, the tower at Washington's National Airport had five targets on their radarscopes. This means three radar facilities at three separate sites had shown solid targets that were not already identified as aircraft. That seemed to prove that there was no radar malfunction at one site, and that weather-related phenomena, such as a temperature inversion, were not responsible for the blip returns.

One of the controllers at the ARTC called for a senior

controller, Harry C. Barnes, who in turn called the National Airport control tower. They had unidentified targets on their scopes, as did the controllers at Andrews Air Force Base. They had already eliminated a mechanical malfunction as the cause, but with the objects on other scopes in other locations, there was no longer any question about their reality. All the men, including Barnes, were sure they were looking at solid objects based on their years of experience with radar. Weather-related phenomena wouldn't produce the same effect on all the radars at the widely scattered locations. In fact, if weather was the explanation, the targets would have varied from scope to scope.

Just after midnight, Airman Second Class (A/2c) Bill Goodman called the Andrews control tower to tell them he was watching a bright orange light about the size of a softball that was gaining and losing altitude as it zipped through the sky. It was one of the visual sightings that the Air Force would later discount as unimportant and unrelated.

During this time, Goodman talked to A/1c William B. Brady, who was in the tower. Goodman told Brady that the object was to the immediate south. Brady saw a ball of orange fire. There were discrepancies between the physical description given by Goodman and Brady, but the problems were relatively small. It can be argued that the discrepancies are the result of the points of view of the two observers.

Joseph DeBoves, who was also on the scene as a civilian control tower operator at Andrews, said that Brady became excited during one of his telephone conversations, yelling, "There one goes." DeBoves believed that

Brady was watching nothing more interesting than a meteor.

About two in the morning on July 20, the Radar Officer, Captain Harold C. Way, at Andrews Approach Control learned that the ARTC had a target east of Andrews. He went outside and saw a strange light which he didn't believe to be a star. Later, however, he went back out, and this time decided that he was looking at a star. At least, that is what the Air Force reported after their investigation into the sightings.

Bolling Air Force Base became involved briefly about the time Way went outside. The tower operator there said that he saw a "roundish" object drifting low in the sky to the southeast of Bolling. There were no radar confirmations of the sighting, and that was the last of the reports from that base.

This report would later become important simply because it brought in another set of observers and another set of equipment. While it might be argued that hysteria was overtaking the other locations, since Bolling was a separate facility, the argument lost persuasion. Instead, the Bolling sightings added another level of corroboration, one that would be ignored as the Air Force worked to explain away the sightings rather than investigate them.

The ARTC again told the controllers at Andrews that they still had the targets on their scopes. There is conflicting data because some of the reports suggest that the Andrews radar showed nothing, while other reports claim they did. Now DeBoves, and two others in the tower, Monte Banning and John P. Izzo, Jr., swept the sky with binoculars but could see no lights other than points of light they recognized as stars.

The sightings lasted through the night, and during that time, the crews of several airliners saw the lights right where the radar showed them to be. Tower operators also saw them, and jet fighters were brought in for attempted intercepts. Associated Press stories written hours after the sightings claimed that no intercepts had been attempted that night, but those stories were inaccurate. Documents in the Project Blue Book files, as well as what eyewitnesses told me in later interviews, confirm the many attempted intercepts.

Typical of the sightings were those made by Captain Casey Pierman on Capital Airlines flight 807. He was on a flight between Washington and Martinsburg, West Virginia, at 1:15 A.M. on July 20, when he and the rest of the crew saw seven objects flash across the sky. Pierman said, "They were like falling stars without trails."

Capital Airline officials said that National Airport radar picked up the objects and asked Pierman to keep an eye on them. Shortly after takeoff, Pierman radioed that he had the objects in sight. He was flying at 180 to 200 mph and reported the objects were traveling at tremendous speed. Official Air Force records confirm this.

One of the most persuasive sightings came early in the morning when one of the ARTC controllers called the Andrews Air Force Base control tower to tell them that there was a target south of the tower, over the Andrews Radio range station. The tower operators looked to the south where a "huge fiery-orange sphere" was hovering. This again was later explained by the Air Force as a star.

The radar contact reported by the ARTC, according to the Air Force, was mere coincidence.

Just before daylight, about four in the morning, after repeated requests from the ARTC, an F-94 interceptor arrived on the scene, but it was too little too late. All the targets were gone. Although the fighter's flight crew made a short search of the local area, they found nothing unusual and returned to their base quickly.

During that night, apparently the three radar facilities only once reported a target that was seen simultaneously by all three. There were, however, a number of times when the ARTC radar and the Washington National tower radar had simultaneous contacts. It also seems that the radar blips were displaying the same targets that were seen by the crews of the Capital Airlines flights. What it boils down to is that multiple radar detection and multiple eyewitnesses, both on the ground and in the air, were showing and seeing objects in the sky over Washington.

Air Force intelligence, including ATIC and the officers assigned to the UFO project, had no idea that these sightings had taken place. They learned of the Saturday night–Sunday morning UFO show when the information was published in several newspapers on Monday.

During the day, Ruppelt, in Washington on other business, was briefed on the various episodes of the Saturday night sightings. He knew what had to be done, what questions should be asked, and where to go to get the statements and evidence he needed for a complete investigation. Bureaucracy, however, was no more interested in flying saucers than the Pentagon seemed to be.

His orders had called for him to return to Dayton after

his scheduled meetings at the Pentagon. Ruppelt was also told, when he suggested he remain the night, that his orders didn't cover an overnight stay in Washington. If he didn't get his orders amended, or return to Dayton that day, he wouldn't collect his expense money (per diem) and would be, technically, at least, AWOL (Absent without Leave). There was nothing that could be done and Ruppelt had to return. Bureaucracy had won out over investigation.

But that wasn't the end of the Washington Nationals. There were other sightings including a good one from New Jersey and one from Massachusetts in which F-94s tried, unsuccessfully, to intercept unidentified lights. According to what I read in the Project Blue Book files, in both cases the pilots reported radar locks on the objects, but within seconds those locks were broken by the evasion maneuvers of the UFOs.

Ruppelt, in his book, reports that during the week following the first round of sightings at Washington National Airport, he spoke to Captain Roy James, a radar expert based at Wright-Patterson. James suggested that the sightings sounded as if the radar targets had been caused by weather. Later, Ruppelt wrote, "But Captain James has a powerful dislike for UFOs—especially on Saturday night."

The Saturday night on which James professed his dislike was the second time, a week later and almost to the hour, that the UFOs visited Washington National Airport. About 10:30 P.M. the same radar operators who had been on duty the week before again spotted several slow-moving targets. This time the controllers carefully marked each of the unidentifieds. When they were all marked, they called the Andrews AFB radar facility. The unidentified targets were on their scope too.

An hour later, with targets being tracked continually on radar, the controllers called for jet interceptors. Al Chop, the Pentagon spokesman for the UFO project, told me in a later interview that he was in communication with the main basement command post at the Pentagon. He requested that interceptors be sent. As a civilian, he could only make the request and then wait for the flag officer (general or admiral) in command at the Pentagon to make the official decision.

As happened the week before, there was a delay, but by midnight, two F-94s were on station over Washington. At that point, the reporters who had assembled to observe the situation were asked, by Chop, to leave the radar room at National Airport because classified radio and intercept procedures would be in operation.

Although that fact was well reported, Ruppelt in his book, wrote, "I knew this was absurd because any radio ham worth his salt could build equipment and listen in on any intercept. The real reason for the press dismissal, I learned, was that not a few people in the radar room were positive that this night would be the big night in UFO history—the night when a pilot would close in on and get a good look at a UFO—and they didn't want the press to be in on it."

With Chop and later Dewey Fournet watching, as well as the controllers at various facilities using various radars, the F-94s arrived. And the UFOs vanished from the scopes immediately. The jets were vectored to the last known position of the targets, but even though visibility was unrestricted in the area, the pilots could see nothing unusual. The fighters made a systematic search of the area, but since they could find nothing, there was nothing they could do but return to their base.

Chop told me, "The minute the first two interceptors appeared on our scope all our unknowns disappeared. It was like they just wiped them all off. All our other flights, all the known flights were still on the scope ... We watched these two planes leave. When they were out of our range, immediately we got our UFOs back."

Later, Air Force officers would learn that as the fighters appeared over Washington, people in the area of Langley Air Force Base, Virginia, spotted weird lights in the sky. An F-94 in the area on a routine mission was diverted to search for the light. The pilot saw it and turned toward it, but it disappeared "like somebody turning off a light bulb."

The pilot continued the intercept and did get a radar lock on the now unlighted and unseen target. That was broken by the object as it sped away. The fighter continued the pursuit, obtaining two more radar locks on the object, but each time the locks were broken.

The scene then shifted back to Washington National. Again the Air Defense Command was alerted and again fighters were sent. This time the pilots were able to see the objects, vectored toward them by the air traffic controllers. But the fighters couldn't close in on the lights. The pilots saw no external details, other than lights where the radar suggested that something should be seen.

After several minutes of failure to close in on a target, one of them was spotted loping along. A fighter piloted by Lieutenant William Patterson turned, kicked in the afterburner, and tried to catch the object. It disappeared before Patterson could see much of anything.

Interviewed by newspaper and radio reporters the next day, Patterson said, "I tried to make contact with the bogies below one thousand feet, but they [the controllers] vectored us around. I saw several bright lights. I was at my maximum speed, but even then I had no closing speed. I ceased chasing them because I saw no chance of overtaking them. I was vectored into new objects. Later I chased a single bright light which I estimated about ten miles away. I lost visual contact with it . . ."

Al Chop remembered this intercept, as did Dewey Fournet. Chop told me, "The flight controllers had directed him to them [the unknowns]. We had a little cluster of them. Five or six of them and he suddenly reports that he sees some lights . . . He said they are very brilliant blue-white lights. He was going try to close in to get a better look . . . he flew into the area where they were clustered and he reported they were all around him."

Chop said that he, along with the others in the radar room, watched the intercept on the radar scope. What the pilot was telling them, they could see on the radar.

Patterson had to break off the intercept, though there were still lights in the sky and objects on the scope. According to Chop, the pilot radioed that he was running very low on fuel. He turned so that he could head back to his base.

Chop said that the last of the objects disappeared from the scope about the time the sun came up. Ruppelt later quizzed Fournet about the activities that night. According to Ruppelt, Fournet and Holcomb, the radar expert, were convinced the targets were solid, metallic objects.

Fournet told Ruppelt that there were weather-related targets on the scopes, but the controllers were ignoring them. Everyone was convinced that the targets were real.

At 4:00 P.M. on the day following, in Washington, D.C., Major General John A. Samford, Chief of Air Intelligence, held a press conference. Of that conference, Ruppelt writes, "General Samford made an honest attempt to straighten out the Washington National Sightings, but the cards were stacked against him. He had to hedge on many answers to questions from the press because he didn't know the answers. This hedging gave the impression that he was trying to cover up something more than just the fact his people fouled up in not fully investigating the sightings. Then he brought in Captain Roy James from ATIC to handle all the queries about radar. James didn't do any better because he'd just arrived in Washington that morning and didn't know very much more about the sightings than he'd read in the papers. Major Dewey Fournet and Lieutenant Holcomb, who had been at the airport during the sightings, were extremely conspicuous by their absence..." As was the Pentagon spokesman on UFOs, Al Chop.

Ruppelt notes that the press decided that Samford's suggestion, of a weather-related explanation for the sightings, was the final solution. Ruppelt reported in 1956 that the sightings were still carried as unknowns in the Project Blue Book files.

Ruppelt wrote, "Some people said, 'Weather targets,' but the chances of a weather target's making a 180-degree turn just as an airplane turns into it, giving a radar lock-on, then changing speed to stay just out of the range of the airplane's radar, and then slowing down when the airplane leaves is as close to nil as you can get."

Others argued that the situation was created out of the hysteria in the ARTC, at Washington National Airport, and Andrews Air Force Base. Many times, according to some radar experts, when there is a visual sighting, there are "uncollateral" targets on the radarscope. It was suggested that the excitement of the night, coupled with that fact, produced the frightening results reported by the men at the various radar locations in the Washington, D.C., area. In other words, with the weather the way it was, pilots seeing unidentified lights in the sky would have those sightings confirmed by radar if they had initiated them. Of course, in this case, it was the radar operators who started it by asking pilots to search the sky for those "uncollateral" targets.

There were reports that tower operators at Andrews Air Force Base, who said they had seen a fiery orange color sphere over the radio range when told by National Airport radar controllers that an object was there, weren't quite as sure of their facts later. They completely changed their story, according to some later investigators, saying they had seen nothing more spectacular than a bright star. They said that they had been excited by all the reports of flying saucers being called to them by the radar operators at other facilities.

Ruppelt reported that no exceptionally bright stars were in the sky in a position to be seen over the radio range. He then wrote, "And I heard from a good source that the tower men had been 'persuaded' a bit." Persuaded by their superiors to suggest that they might have been looking at the nonexistent bright star.

A series of sightings, over two separate nights, over the nation's capital, had to be explained by the military. To leave them labeled as unknowns was to admit that something strange was going on. It was to admit that the Air Force couldn't do its job properly. After all, if flying saucers can flash through the sky at will, what good is an Air Force charged with keeping our skies free of the "enemy," whatever that enemy might be. So the answer began to evolve from "it sounds like a temperature inversion" to "it definitely was some kind of temperature inversion."

Joe Zacko, who had been in the tower at National Airport, told me he had seen the lights in the sky. As had some of the Air Force personnel, who later changed their stories. In other words, it is clear that there is a body of testimony from a number of different witnesses in different locations who saw lights where the radars showed objects were located. Temperature inversions do not explain these sightings, no matter how the information is twisted around to make it fit.

Interestingly, the two Pentagon personnel I interviewed, Major Dewey Fournet and Al Chop, disagreed with the weather-related phenomenon explanation. Both were sure, based on their own observations in the radar room, that the returns showed solid objects. Both were listening to Holcomb, the acknowledged military expert in radar. Chop told me he was unimpressed with the analysis made by men who were not in the radar room that night and who made their analysis some fifteen or twenty years after the event.

The Washington National event alerted those who had somehow missed it that the flying saucers, now called

UFOs, had returned. The Washington National sightings might be said to have marked the peak of the wave, but they did not signal the end of it. On August 1, for example, more radar facilities, these in Bellefontaine, Ohio, picked up a high-speed target moving to the southwest. Two fighters from a squadron stationed at Wright-Patterson Air Force Base were scrambled. This one, however, turned out to be nothing more than confusion by the radar operator and a weather balloon reflecting bright sunlight.

One of the most spectacular cases, which Ruppelt himself couldn't label, began on August 20. A Florida scoutmaster, J. D. Desvergers, claimed that he had been burned by a close-approaching UFO. Three boy scouts with him, though uninjured, had also seen the flying saucer and seemed to corroborate his story.

According to the story, Desvergers, while taking the boys home, noticed some lights through the trees. He believed that it might be a plane in trouble. Because he was a scoutmaster, he felt he had to check it out. He told the boys to wait for him in the car while he searched the thicket off the road.

He moved along, using his flashlight, and entered a clearing a hundred yards or so from the road. He noticed that the environment around him changed. There was a different odor and it had become oppressively hot. He looked up, and thirty feet over him was a dark shape.

He was suddenly overcome with anger, later telling the Air Force investigators that he wanted to destroy the object, whatever it was. There was the sound of a vault-like door opening. A ball of red mist was ejected through the opening. Desvergers dropped the machete and flashlight he was carrying and covered his face with his arms as the mist engulfed him. Moments later he passed out.

The boy scouts saw what happened to Desvergers and ran to the nearest house. They called the Florida State Highway Patrol. A few minutes later a deputy sheriff responded. He arrived in time to see the scoutmaster stumble from the thicket. According to Ruppelt, the deputy had never seen anyone as scared as Desvergers.

The investigation revealed that some of the things said did not reflect reality. Although the boy scouts said they had seen the ball of mist engulf their leader, Ruppelt and the investigators learned that even by standing on the car, they couldn't have seen anything.

And, it turned out that the scoutmaster's background was anything but sterling. Though he had been in the Marines, as he had claimed, he had been thrown out for stealing a car and going AWOL. He had a reputation around the town for telling tall tales. According to Ruppelt, one man said that if Desvergers told him the sun was shining, he would go look.

But, there were things that puzzled Ruppelt as well. The roots of the grass samples taken from the clearing where Desvergers had fallen had been burned. No one was sure how that was accomplished without heavy equipment and disturbing the soil.

To make it worse, the story told by Desvergers appeared in the local newspapers, complete with a notation that "high" brass from the Pentagon had arrived to investigate. Ruppelt writes that off as "literary license" by the reporters. But the scoutmaster also said that he couldn't tell what he knew because it would start a national panic. That seemed, to Ruppelt, to fall outside of literary license.

In the end, Ruppelt wrote the case off as a hoax. Given the background of Desvergers, it is not an unreasonable conclusion for him to have drawn. After all, the stories told by the boy scouts, who were probably being as honest as they could be, did not reflect the physical evidence. Given the background of Desvergers, Ruppelt was right, without additional evidence, to claim the case was a hoax.

Then on September 12, 1952, one of the few reports to mention alien creatures was made. Kathleen May, one of the witnesses, and the oldest of them, was quoted as saying, "It looked worse than Frankenstein."

It began when three boys saw a ball of slow-moving red light descend behind a hill near Flatwoods, West Virginia. As they headed toward what might have been the landing site, they were joined by May, her sons, and a seventeen-year-old member of the National Guard named Eugene Lemon.

As they walked up the hill, Lemon's dog ran ahead, found something, and began barking. A moment later it ran back down the hill, clearly frightened. About the same time, the group ran into a foul-smelling mist that stung their eyes and noses.

They pressed on, and at the top of the hill, Lemon and one of the boys spotted a large ball of light that was as big as a house. To the left were two smaller lights. Lemon turned his flashlight on it, and the hideous face of the creature was visible. It began to move toward them and then turned, floating toward the ball of light.

Thirty minutes later, after all them had gotten down the hill, a reporter for one of the local newspapers tried to interview some of the witnesses. The reporter convinced Lemon to accompany him back to the area. The foul-smelling odor was still there, but the creature was apparently long gone. In the dark, neither Lemon nor the reporter could see anything of importance.

The next morning the reporter returned to the area and found some skid marks on the ground. They led down the hill to an area where the grass was matted in a circle about fifteen feet in diameter. Investigation revealed a greaselike residue on the plants in the area.

The Air Force, as per usual in 1952, wrote the case off as hysteria resulting from a bright meteor and the ongoing wave of UFO sightings. In 1952, anyone who saw "extraterrestrial creatures" was not to be trusted as a reliable observer. Besides, it was clear from those who interviewed the witnesses right after the sighting that they were all badly frightened by something. Their opinions about what they had seen couldn't be trusted because of their immediate fear.

By September, however, the UFO wave was beginning to fade. The number of sightings reaching Project Blue Book was down, though still higher than the "average" when compared to other years. One of those new sightings included photographs and came from a sighting reported during a NATO exercise. While the military could mostly control the publicity surrounding the NATO case, some of the information, including the pictures, were leaked to the press.

Operation Mainbrace was a series of maneuvers conducted by eight NATO countries and New Zealand.

More than 80,000 men, 1,000 aircraft and two hundred ships were involved. It was the largest NATO operation held until that time.

On the first night of the maneuvers, Lt. Commander Schmidt Jensen on the Danish destroyer *Willemoes* saw a triangular-shaped object that moved at high speed. A number of the crew also saw a strange craft that moved at a speed estimated by Jensen at 900 miles an hour.

During the next several days, there were more sightings of objects over the Mainbrace fleet. The important sighting occurred on September 20, when the crew of the U.S.S. *Franklin D. Roosevelt* saw a spherical, shiny object. Reporter Wallace Letwin managed to take three pictures of it.

Although the Navy intelligence officers examined the photographs, they were eventually passed on to the Air Force. Ruppelt wrote, "[The picture] turned out to be excellent . . . judging by the size of the object in each successive photo, one could see that it was moving rapidly."

An explanation was quickly offered. Someone suggested that the photographs were of a weather balloon launched from one of the vessels during the exercise.

That possibility was checked, but no one in the fleet admitted to having launched a balloon. The Air Force records, however, show something different. Ten years later, in April 1962, Colonel Edward H. Wynn, the Deputy for Science and Components, wrote to Headquarters, USAF, SAFOI-3b [Secretary of Air Force Office of Information] (Major Hart). He identified the pictures for Project Blue Book: "The pictures were of a weather balloon . . ." It must be noted that the Air Force was contradicting itself here.

Although there were a couple of other sightings during the Mainbrace operation, it was clear that the summer wave was slowing. Sightings during the remainder of the year would drop until they returned to normal. Ruppelt wrote that about twenty percent remained unidentified, even under the new investigative activities of Project Blue Book.

What is important about the wave of 1952 isn't necessarily the number of sightings but some of the specifics. Those inside the Pentagon might not be concerned with media coverage of flying saucers, or with civilian response to them, until it happened in their backyard. The most important sightings of 1952 are those from Washington National Airport. The military was heavily involved in them, fighters had been scrambled on a number of occasions, and the pilots found the UFOs. To make it worse, radar sites in three different locations spotted the objects.

Had there been no other sightings, or had the wave built to its impressive level without media attention, the results might have been the same. The Air Force began to change the way it was handling the UFO situation. For five years, from 1947, it had bounced around Wright-Patterson Air Force Base. It had been hoped that the flying saucers would just quietly disappear. That was not going to happen and something else had to be tried.

CHAPTER 3

Aftermath of the Summer of 1952

What the wave of sightings during the summer of 1952 demonstrated to everyone was that flying saucers were not going away. After the storm during the summer of 1947, little had been heard about them. When reporters inquired, they were usually told that the official investigation had concluded there was nothing to flying saucers and it had been terminated. That, as we now know, is not what happened.

After the summer wave, after the spectacular sightings that had been reported throughout the country, it was clear that something had to be done. The situation, as it stood, was intolerable. During the fall, Air Force officers and governmental officials began to review the situation to determine a new course. All this for a phenomenon that they claimed didn't present a threat to national security, didn't officially exist, and was a waste of time.

As mentioned, the UFO situation had changed a number of times. It went from a priority program that was interested in learning the truth to one that barely functioned and didn't care about evidence. Edward Ruppelt was brought in so that by the summer of 1952 the Air Force had an organization in place that was prepared to investigate flying saucers. Ruppelt had fixed the original problem and by doing so inadvertently created a number of new ones for the brass in the Pentagon.

There is one interesting point to be made and its importance is confusing. Project Blue Book had an organizational structure that called for a lieutenant colonel. When Ruppelt took over, he was a lowly first lieutenant and was promoted, sometime later, to captain. Even with the promotion, Ruppelt was still two grades below that suggested rank for the officer in charge as listed by the table of organization.

This could be interpreted to mean that the Air Force didn't take the investigation of UFOs seriously, even in 1952. Or, it could mean that the requirements of the Korean War, then in full swing, had diverted other qualified officers into that environment, leaving Ruppelt as the highest-ranking officer qualified for the position of chief of Blue Book.

Whatever the reason, there was maneuvering behind the scenes, most of which can be considered an outgrowth of the wave of sightings during the summer months. Ruppelt, in his book, mentions plans that he had for acquiring the data and proof needed to solve the riddle of the flying saucers. In fact, he wrote about the problems with proof, explaining that some officers required more than others. The reasons for the various standards is irrelevant. The point is that it existed and Ruppelt was trying to find the sort of evidence that could convince those with the highest standards. He, as well as others, realized that proof beyond the testimony of credible witnesses was going to be necessary, otherwise the evidence would be called anecdotal and dismissed out of hand.

All his plans were overwhelmed by the number of sightings that started to pour in early in the summer of 1952. Manpower was lacking and good sightings had to be ignored simply because there were not sufficient assets to investigate them all. And, it seemed from Ruppelt's point of view, that nothing was being done to remedy the situation. In other words, Ruppelt received neither the approval of his investigative plans nor an increase in his staff to accommodate the number of sightings being reported around the country.

In the fall, as the number of sightings dropped off, Ruppelt began to brief other commands such as the Air Defense Command about the flying saucer situation. Ruppelt made several trips to the various commands with Major Dewey Fournet, an officer assigned to the UFO project but who was stationed at the Pentagon in Washington, D.C.

Ruppelt also pointed out that by August 1952, not that long after the sightings and attempted intercepts at Washington National airport, there were several groups of high-ranking officials in Washington "following the UFO situation very closely."

This was confirmed in late September 1952 when H. Marshall Chadwell sent a memo to General Walter Bedell Smith, writing, "Recently an inquiry was conducted by the Office of Scientific Intelligence [which was part of the CIA] to determine whether there are national security implications in the problem of 'unidentified flying objects,' i.e. flying saucers; whether adequate study and research is currently being directed to this problem in its relation to such national security implications; and what further investigation and research should be instituted, by whom, and under aegis."

Chadwell further wrote, "It was found that the only unit of government currently studying the problem is the Directorate of Intelligence, USAF, which has charged the Air Technical Intelligence Center (ATIC) with the responsibility for investigating the reports of sightings . . . and major Air Force bases have been ordered to make interceptions of unidentified flying objects . . ."

Chadwell then made the claims that so many other have since echoed: ". . . [P]ublic concern with the phenomena indicates that a fair proportion of our population is mentally conditioned to the acceptance of the incredible. In this fact lies the potential for the touching-off of mass hysteria . . . In order to minimize risk of panic, a national policy should be established as to what should be told to the public regarding the phenomena."

The letter, dated September 24, 1952, from the CIA had suggested part of the conclusions that would be reached by the Robertson panel some five months later. Chadwell was wondering what the public should be told and was suggesting that the information be managed by responsible agencies inside the federal government. I take this to mean that Chadwell was suggesting that we, as the American public, couldn't be trusted to understand the situation without hysteria and they were trying to figure out what to tell us.

Although Ruppelt should have been aware that such discussions were going on at the highest levels, there is no indication that he was. Dewey Fournet, whose role was also as liaison between the Pentagon and Blue Book at Wright-Patterson, told me, "[Frederick Durant] asked me to make a presentation to the CIA which I did. I gave them a few of my opinions based on what I had observed . . . from that idea the Robertson panel spawned. And Fred, through his superiors, convened it."

If, however, we examine the story told by Major Donald Keyhoe, one-time director of the National Investigations Committee on Aerial Phenomenon (a privately funded civilian UFO investigation organization), there is a suggestion that Fournet, with Ruppelt and Al Chop, who was the senior public relations man handing UFO-related press releases, were conspiring to end the cover-up.

But my conversations with Fournet did not bear this out. Rather, Fournet believed that the upcoming Robertson panel, though sponsored by the CIA, was an honest attempt to straighten out the UFO situation. Clearly, to Fournet's mind, as well as Ruppelt's, something was going on. UFOs were not figments of the imagination of unsophisticated people, nor were they a technological jump by a foreign power. Ruppelt, in his own work, pointed out over and over that military pilots were making reports and many of them were corroborated by radar.

In fact, Ruppelt had tried to use that argument as one of the proofs that UFOs were something other than mirages or hallucinations. In an informal discussion held with other military officers, the question of proof arose. They had talked of radar sightings, but one of the officers pointed out that every one of those radar cases could be explained as weather phenomena. The question turned to radar visual sightings, which would seem to rule out weather as the culprit.

Ruppelt pointed out that there were cases where an object was seen in the sky in the approximate location where the UFO was reported on radar. But, more importantly, there were other radar sightings where interceptors had chased UFOs and those watching the scopes had seen the UFO performing the same maneuvers as the jet. In other words, the target couldn't be weather related simply because it was maneuvering just as the jet fighter was.

Of course, this overlooked the incredible string of sightings at Washington National in July 1952. Fournet had told me of one intercept that got rather hairy, but didn't want to discuss the details. It was Fournet's opinion, based on his personal observations that night at Washington National Airport, that the UFOs were something other than weather targets. Fighters scrambled had actually spotted the UFOs, had their onboard radar lock on to the targets, and had given chase to them.

And Al Chop, who had also been present, told me the tale of the "hairy" intercept. The pilot had arrived in the area, seen the UFOs, and had given chase. At one point his aircraft had been surrounded by the blue-white balls of light. While the Air Force would later claim that the UFO sightings made in connection with the radar sightings could be explained as stars, it is difficult to envision a situation where a pilot would become convinced that these stars had surrounded his fighter. Or in which radar would corroborate the tale of the UFOs surrounding him.

Because of those sightings, the wave of the summer months, and because of the Operation Mainbrace UFO photographs taken during NATO maneuvers in Sept. 1952, it was decided that a panel of scientific experts would review the data. Ruppelt, from Blue Book, and Fournet, from the Pentagon, would brief the scientists on the situation as it stood at the beginning of 1953.

But this doesn't mean that Fournet didn't provide a briefing to the CIA sometime earlier. It simply means that by the time he got there, Chadwell had decided to form an advisory panel. Chadwell, with Durant and H. P. Robertson, who would head the panel, had gone to Wright-Patterson to review the situation with UFOs as well as the files held at ATIC. Ruppelt doesn't mention this visit, and in fact says little about the Robertson panel. It happened about the time he left Blue Book for other military assignments.

Even with all the trouble we've seen in the UFO arena—that is, people suggesting one thing and doing another—and attempts to suppress the information about the reality of the phenomenon, Fournet told me that he believed the panel was legitimate. He believed that they were searching for the truth and if their conclusions suggested otherwise, it was because the data had led them there.

Dr. Michael Swords, reviewing the history of the UFO phenomenon, had a slightly different opinion. According to him, the panel was "another of these things that is a *fait accompli* before the panel actually meets. But it's not a *fait accompli* for all the guys who are meeting on the panel." In other words, Swords believed, based on his research, that Robertson and a couple of the others had already determined the conclusions to be reached before any panel meeting had been held.

So, under the auspices of the CIA, and headed by Dr. H. P. Robertson, the panel convened on January 14, 1953. According to Ruppelt, the first two days were made up of his review for the scientists of the findings of Projects Sign, Grudge, and Blue Book and the current situation at ATIC. The Blue Book team had analyzed 1593 reports and found explanations for all but 429. Confidence in the explanations ranged from known to possible, meaning that Ruppelt and his staff sometimes felt they had an answer but weren't positive about it or couldn't prove it to their satisfaction.

Swords provided additional details about the chronology of the proceedings. During the first half day no one was allowed into the meeting room except the panel members and a couple of CIA men, including Chadwell and Philip G. Strong. Dr. J. Allen Hynek, a scientific consultant to Blue Book, and Ruppelt were kept cooling their heels outside in case there were questions from the panel.

Records suggest that Chadwell and Strong had prepared a briefing for the panel. They had been to Wright-Patterson and Ruppelt supposedly briefed them on the findings of Project Blue Book. The briefing to the panel included the intelligence security concerns and a short history of the UFO project, though it would seem that Ruppelt could have provided a more comprehensive analysis of the situation at Wright-Patterson than the two CIA men who had only reviewed the data.

The panel did, finally, listen to the briefings prepared by the officers who had spent the last several months or years investigating UFOs. Both Ruppelt and Fournet presented information which they considered the best of the evidence available to Project Blue Book. Their briefings might have been the most persuasive ever given, but they weren't going to convince the panel. According to Mike Swords, the conclusions, as well as the final report, might have been written before the panel ever met.

Swords said that during the last afternoon, Friday, while Hynek was invited to stay, Robertson was given, or took, the task of writing the final report. Swords said, "I can't imagine that H. P. Robertson, a guy like him is going to sit down late into the evening and bang out a draft of the report on his own that somehow, mysteriously the next morning is already read by Lloyd Berkner and has already been taken by Marshal Chadwell to the Air Force directorate of intelligence and been approved. So when they show up on Saturday, Robertson presents this draft to the rest of the committee and the rest of the committee does minor revisions . . . There is some remarks that are out of line that they decided are not going to be included."

According to Swords, "It seems an amazingly cut and dried deal that by the time Saturday shows up, here's this mildly to be revised draft that has already been seen by one of the other committee members who wasn't even there for the first two and a half days. It's already been seen by Chadwell and the U.S. Air Force."

Fournet, who had a chance to review the data, who had been present during some of the sessions, and who now has a forty-year perspective, says that the scientists had no choice in their conclusions. The evidence, although somewhat persuasive, was not conclusive. There was little evidence other than the testimonies of witnesses.

It is here that the history of the UFO research becomes cloudy. Clearly the Robertson panel was a set-up. The CIA and the government were trying to make it look as if a legitimate scientific inquiry had been made, but what sort of inquiry was it if the conclusions were already drawn? The one conclusion that might have surprised most people, after the panel said there was nothing to the UFO reports, was that the investigation be continued. Project Blue Book would survive the Robertson panel. Of course, as we'll see, after the panel, the wheels were set in motion to strip Blue Book of its authority. It would be an investigatory project in name only, henceforth.

But at the same time, January 1953, other plans were in the works. The timing makes the changes suspect, but it does demonstrate one thing. Project Blue Book was changing from the official investigation of UFOs into a public relations outfit that did little real investigative work. That mission was quietly slipped out of ATIC and away from Blue Book, and was then given to the Air Defense Command.

On January 3, 1953, just a matter of days before the Robertson panel would begin its work, the Air Defense Command created the 4602d Air Intelligence Service Squadron (AISS). Other new regulations, such as Air Force Regulation (AFR) 200-2, dated August 1953, tasked the 4602d with the investigation of UFOs. Rather than delegate officers at each base with the job of investigating UFOs, or instead of sending men from Project Blue Book, the UFO reports would pass through the 4602d before transmittal to ATIC. In other words, Blue Book was, by the new regulation, cut out of the loop.

It was also at this time, in early 1953, that Ruppelt was beginning to change assignments. According to Ruppelt himself, "In December of 1952 I'd asked for a transfer. I'd agreed to stay on as chief of Blue Book until the end of February so that a replacement could be obtained and be broken in. But no replacement showed up . . ."

This is quite disturbing. Here was a plum assignment. It was a job that called for a lieutenant colonel but was held down by a captain. Any officer moving into it could expect to be promoted quickly. Yet no replacement for Ruppelt could be found. No one wanted the job, and that suggests that the priority for the investigation of UFOs was disappearing and those in the Air Force knew it. If nothing else, the Air Force could have found another captain to take over.

Instead, according to Ruppelt, he along with the other officers were moved out of Blue Book and into other assignments. Ruppelt wrote that when he left for temporary duty in Denver, command of Blue Book fell to Lieutenant Bob Olsson. He had a staff of one, an airman named Max Futch. By July, only Futch remained at Blue Book, and was, by default, in charge of the project which still called for a lieutenant colonel.

In about six months Blue Book had gone from an organization that called for a lieutenant colonel to be in charge, with a staff of several officers and enlisted personnel with a couple of civilian secretaries, to an organization of one low-ranking enlisted man who had no secretarial support. Plans that called for the expenditure of nearly a quarter of a million dollars on investigation and a search for evidence, were scrapped.

Ruppelt, when he returned to Dayton in July 1953, found that the investigation had collapsed. There would be an ongoing investigation, but it was centered with the 4602d and not Blue Book. Ruppelt, in describing how the 4602d entered into the UFO investigation business, seemed to think it was the result not of manipulation at the top but because of his pushing from the bottom. He wrote, "Project Blue Book got a badly needed shot in the arm when an unpublicized but highly important change took place: another intelligence agency began to take over all field investigations . . . the orders had been to build it up—get more people—do what the [Robertson] panel recommended. But when I'd ask for more people, all I got was a polite 'So sorry.' . . . I happened to be expounding my troubles one day at Air Defense Command Headquarters while I was briefing General Burgess, ADC's Director of Intelligence, and he told me about his 4602d Air Intelligence Squadron, a specialized intelligence unit that had recently become operational. Maybe it could help . . ."

Ruppelt explained that he didn't expect much from Burgess. Ruppelt expected to write memos and letters and seal "it in a time capsule for preservation so that when the answer finally does come through the future generation that receives it will know how it all started."

This time things were different. Ruppelt wrote, "But I underestimated the efficiency of the Air Defense Command. Inside of two weeks General Burgess had called General Garland, they'd discussed the problem, and I was back in Colorado Springs setting up a program with Colonel White's 4602d."

In Ruppelt's book, he implies that all this happened late in the summer of 1953. Ruppelt's tour at Blue Book was scheduled to end in February 1953, and he departed for two months of temporary duty in Denver. He writes, "When I came back to ATIC in July 1953 and took over another job, Lieutenant Olsson was just getting out of the Air Force and A1/c (Airman First Class) [Max] Futch was now it . . . In a few days I again had Project Blue Book as an additional duty this time and I had orders to 'build it up.' "

So, Ruppelt, at the end of the summer, was talking to General Burgess and within weeks, he was told that the 4602d was available to investigate UFOs. Documentation, however, doesn't bear this out.

On March 5, 1953, months before Ruppelt met with General Burgess, a letter headed, "Utilization of 4602nd AISS Personnel in Project Blue Book Field Investigations," was sent to the Commanding General of the Air Defense Command and to the attention of the Director of Intelligence at Ent Air Force Base in Colorado Springs. The plan of action, outlined in the letter, was approved on March 23, 1953.

In the letter, it was written, "During the recent conference attended by personnel of the 4602nd AISS and Project Blue Book the possibility of utilizing 4602nd AISS field units to obtain additional data on reports of Unidentified Flying Objects was discussed. It is believed by this Center that such a program would materially aid ATIC and give 4602nd AISS personnel valuable experience in field interrogations. It would also give them an opportunity to establish further liaison with other governmental agencies, such as CAA, other military units, etc., in their areas."

The interesting statement here, as in many of the other documents relating to the 4602d, is the idea that the field teams, by interrogating witnesses to UFO sightings, can gain valuable experience. Ruppelt pointed out that the 4602d had a primary function of interrogating captured enemy airmen during war. In a peacetime environment, all they could do was interrogate "captured" Americans in simulations. According to Ruppelt, "Investigating UFO reports would supplement these problems [wartime simulations] and add a factor of realism that would be invaluable in their training."

All this went on while Ruppelt was on temporary duty and someone else was heading Project Blue Book. It would seem that some correspondence between the ADC and ATIC would have been on file at Blue Book. Ruppelt, when he returned to ATIC, should have been aware that negotiations between the 4602d and ATIC were in progress. Yet his own book suggests he didn't know that or didn't understand it.

Upon publication of Air Force Regulation 200-2, in August 1953, a briefing about implementation of the regulation was held at Ent Air Force Base for members of the 4602d. Publication of a regulation suggests that the changes had been in the planning stage for a long time. It suggests that the implementation of ADC regulation 24-3, published on January 3, 1953, was part of a larger plan. All of it was probably an outgrowth of the wave of sightings from the summer of 1952.

This marks the shift in UFO investigations. Blue Book was stripped of most of its investigative functions and became little more than a public relations clearinghouse designed to answer reporters' questions and nothing more. The real investigations, the important cases, were reviewed by the 4602d. There was no publicity for it. Public questions about UFOs went to Blue Book, but no one knew to ask about the 4602d.

From the documentation available, it is clear that UFO investigative functions after 1952 rested with the 4602d. UFO sighting reports were transmitted electronically to the closest of the 4602d field units for investigation. The regulation suggested that once the investigation was completed, those sightings not readily identified would be transmitted to ATIC and supposedly provided to Project Blue Book.

The evidence, however, suggests that many of the unidentified sightings never made it to Project Blue Book. Dr. J. Allen Hynek, the Air Force scientific consultant in astronomy for Blue Book, told colleagues the really good, really hot reports never reached Project Blue Book. They were intercepted somewhere up the line.

What is most interesting in all of this is the timing. During the fall of 1952, the brass in Washington were clearly concerned about UFOs. Evidence, good solid evidence, had been found. This included the movies that had been taken by a Naval officer and the radar-visual sightings, the most impressive of which are those from Washington National Airport. Not only were there numerous ground-based radar involved, but eyewitnesses on the ground and the interceptor pilots in the air reported seeing the objects. Add to that the airline pilots, interceptor airborne radar that locked on to targets, an impressive array of evidence had been collected. Surely someone at the top realized the significance of that data. Surely those at the top would react to that data.

But now we look at the sleight of hand. The public and the press were asking the Air Force, and Project Blue Book, questions. Blue Book, finally a good, investigative unit, with a leader who had plans to obtain even better evidence, was too public. They couldn't be hidden behind a veil of secrecy and silence.

After the amazing summer, when thousands reported UFOs, when good evidence had been collected, the reaction of the Pentagon wasn't to increase funding and manpower for Blue Book. It was to allow it to wither away. What kind of sense does this make?

Clearly, from their reactions on the inside, they were concerned with the problem. It doesn't matter what we believe today. All that matters are the actions taken in late 1952 and corroborated by the available documentation. Here we see the contradiction in events.

We can now document what we have been saying all along. The Air Force did have another investigation of UFOs that was not public knowledge. It was the secret investigation claimed to exist by UFO researchers for years and denied by the Air Force and the Pentagon. It was conducted by the 4602d, headquartered originally at Ent Air Force Base but later moved to Fort Belvoir, Virginia. ATIC might have quietly monitored the situation, but Blue Book no longer had anything to do with it.

CHAPTER 4

The 4602d Air Intelligence Service Squadron

I t turns out that the history of the 4602d (or its various incarnations, including 1006th AISS and the 1127th Air Activities Group) is not as black and white as we could want it. I have reviewed the documentation (on microfilm) available at the Air Force Archives at Maxwell Air Force Base and learned a few interesting things about the unit.

The 4602d Air Intelligence Service Squadron was activated and organized under authority of the Air Defense Command, General Order Number 20 (ADC GO #20), dated February 28, 1952, at Peterson Field, Ent Air Force Base, Colorado Springs, Colorado, with an authorized strength of thirty-four officers and ninety-seven airmen. A reorganization of the 4602d was directed by the ADC GO #47, dated October 17, 1952.

During that time, according to the documents originally classified Secret, "Considerable time and effort was expended during this reporting period in the drafting and submitting of an Air Defense Command Regulation which would prescribe the mission, organization, functions, and responsibilities of the 4602d AISS and the responsibilities within the Air Defense Command for its control, support, and general deployment. Acceptance of this regulation was received from Headquarters, Air Defense Command at the close of this reporting period and its publication as Air Defense Command Regulation 24-4 was to be effected 3 January 1953."

What is important about this is that its inception—that is, when the 4602d's official history began—was *prior* to the summer wave of 1952, although interest in flying saucers was beginning to grow at the very top level of the Air Force. The mission of the 4602d, again, originally classified Secret, ". . . is to provide an organization within Air Defense Command which will: a. Collect positive air intelligence information, by overt means, from: 1. Downed enemy air crews, 2. Enemy material and 3. Enemy documents . . . b. Collect information for such Bomb Damage Assessment as may be be directed by Headquarters, United States Air Force."

What we see then, is that the original mission of the 4602d was normal intelligence-gathering activities designed to fill a hole. It was inspired in 1951, during the Korean War, when it was realized there was a need for a special unit to interrogate enemy pilots and air crews, and to examine captured enemy equipment. There was also a requirement for bomb damage assessments, but these would be accomplished through photo reconnaissance rather than actual, on-site viewing by trained 4602d officers and enlisted personnel.

During the next several months, that is, most of 1952 and early 1953, the group's emphasis was on defining functions of the unit and training the personnel. The records that I reviewed indicated that members of the 4602d learned parachuting, horseback riding and animal packing, skiing, mountain climbing, and various survival skills. Clearly, those at the top envisioned the 4602d as the type of organization that would parachute into a hostile area for the retrieval of enemy air crews and equipment. They would be trained to survive for extended periods in hostile environments, meaning both those of nature and of enemy design.

It is interesting to note that the 4602d also spent a good deal of time cultivating local organizations to help in their mission. These included both city and state police agencies, the Civil Air Patrol, Civil Defense, and even rural electric cooperatives. They apparently saw the possibility that sometime in the future they might have to search for enemy air crews shot down over the continental United States.

In a commander's conference held on June 22, 1953, with the majority of the officers assigned to the 4602d in attendance, there was a brief discussion of UFOs. This was, of course, as the summer wave was building, and before the explosive sightings over Washington, D.C., in middle and late July.

Lieutenant Colonel Richard C. Jones, the operations officer for the 4602d, said at that conference, "Investigation of unidentified flying objects is not presently part of the mission of this Squadron. Field units are not authorized to make investigations of this type unless so directed or prior approval is obtained from this Headquarters. If ATIC gets a report and feels that an investigation is necessary, they will notify this Headquarters and we in turn will then direct the proper field team to make the investigation."

He ended the two-paragraph statement, saying, "If you are asked by the D/I [Director of Intelligence] of your Division to make an investigation, let us know about it. If it is not going to involve too much time, you can go ahead and make the investigation based on your own judgment. Don't let this sort of thing get out of hand, but if it will assist you in your relationships with the D/I and you feel that you have the time, go ahead. Otherwise, notify this Headquarters for prior approval."

What is interesting about this statement is that it exists at all. Nothing in the original mission of the 4602d suggests that they would be involved in UFO investigations, yet the operations officer warned his troops about becoming involved in such investigations. Clearly some sort of inquiry had been made before June 1952, and the commanders of the 4602d were attempting to avoid being dragged into UFO investigation.

The situation changed, however, within six months of that commander's conference. In the unit history, there is a paragraph about the "UFOB Program." It says:

"On 4 December 1953 Colonel [John M.] White, Captain [Joseph A.] Cybulski and Captain [Milton] Bellovan attended a conference with General [Brigadier General Woodbury M.] Burgess for the purpose of discussing the role of the 4602d AISS in the Unidentified Flying Object (UFOB) Program, and an ATI [Air Technical Intelligence] course for the 4602d. It was proposed that in the future the 4602d will be the agency responsible to ATIC for the investigation of FLYOBRPTS in the ZI [Zone of the Interior or the United States]. Captain Cybulski was appointed FLYOBRPT Officer and departed on 5 December 1953 for Wright-Patterson AFB for the purpose of (1. Establishing the role of the 4602d in the collection and reporting of FLYOBRPT data and (2. Developing an ATI course to meet 4602d requirements. The course will be designated primarily to instruct our personnel in the latest technical developments in SLRA, ECM, and A-Bomb and Guided Missile techniques as applicable to our responsibilities."

Ruppelt had thought that the 4602d would be *assisting* Project Blue Book, but it is clear that others had something else in mind. The investigation was being taken out of Blue Book's hands and given to the 4602d. When AFR 200-2 was officially published in August 1954, the investigative responsibility had fallen completely into the hands of the 4602d. The regulation required that ATIC be notified by electronic means, but that does not translate into a requirement to alert the Blue Book staff. The unsolved cases were then transmitted to ATIC, but there is nothing in the regulation that demanded they be forwarded on to Blue Book.

As mentioned earlier, after the Robertson panel and the disastrous summer of 1952, the official, and publicly announced, investigation fell apart. It seemed natural, after the summer, when there had been so many sightings that Ruppelt and the Blue Book investigators had to pick only those that were most interesting, Blue Book would be given more support and more authority. Instead, in the spring, Blue Book was virtually dead with one man at the helm. Later, that situation was changed, but by then, the 4602d had taken over the reins.

In fact, in the 4602d Unit History for September 1955, it was reported, "Considering the nationwide press release, by the Secretary of the Air Force, of the 'UFOB Summary and Study' and the statement that 'the Air Force has closed its Project Blue Book,' one would judge that the UFOB program had fulfilled its goal." In other words, there were no UFOs and the Air Force had stopped investigating them.

Please note that here is an official document, originally classified Secret, that suggested Project Blue Book had been closed. It is interesting that one area of the Air Force believed that Blue Book was dead while in another it was still operating. There is no evidence of a break in the life of Blue Book until it was ended in 1969.

There is something else in that statement that is both interesting and disturbing. It says, "This was especially true if one considered that the primary purpose of the program was to allay hysteria by systematically squelching rumors and illusions. Reassuring the public mind that no tangible evidence existed to support fears of an 'invasion from outer space' . . . was imperative."

This was the attitude in 1955. It meant that the 4602d wasn't taking the UFO question seriously, and that their investigators, as well as the top officers, believed there to be nothing to the UFO problem. They were going through the motions because regulations dictated that they do so. The question is: Was this attitude a result of their work, or were they predisposed to believe UFOs were nonsense because of the attitudes of the officers or the Pentagon?

Again, the documents I reviewed, available at Maxwell Air Force Base, provide the answer. The attitude of the 4602d was not as unbiased as it should have been. In Volume II of the Unit History, there is a "UFOB Summary" that contains some disturbing remarks. The author of the report writes, "First recorded instances of genuine UFOBs occurred in 1948 [sic] with the appearance of the 'Flying Saucer' in different parts of the United States. Rapid diffusion to all parts of the world, including the Soviet Union and its satellites . . . Birth of a new literary genre 'Science Fiction' which in most cases is entirely fictitious and unscientific . . . Emotional stimulus of speculation on the fantastic . . . General Public not qualified to evaluate material propounded in science fiction. Absurd and fantastic theories given credence solely on the basis of ignorance . . . UFOB reports even though patently ridiculous receive undue attention through latent fear, etc."

Even with that attitude, something was getting done. According to their report, "The 4602d AISS had received a total of 306 preliminary UFOB reports from 12 August 1954 to 30 June 1955. Of this total, 198 reports were resolved by analysis at Squadron Headquarters; 48 were resolved from follow-up investigations. Sixty (60) reports were forwarded to Air Technical Intelligence Center as unresolved, 37 for lack of sufficient data for evaluation and 23 as unknowns."

What this shows is that, although Blue Book was stripped of its importance and had its staff limited, UFO investigation was still important to the Air Force. Although the 4602d supposedly had other missions, such as the interrogation of enemy flight crews, by 1954 that was a meaningless mission. The Korean War had been resolved and there would be no enemy flight crews to interrogate. The 4602d might be trained in bomb damage assessment, but without a war, there was no damage to assess. In other words, a large unit filled with highly trained specialists existed, but they had nothing to do other than train.

In 1953, the UFO investigation dropped into their laps. From the commander's conferences and other documentation available, it is clear that they didn't want it. And, as they went through the motions, it is clear from the statements in the unit histories, that they believed UFO investigation to be a waste of time.

At the Third Commanders' Conference, held in June 1954, Captain Cybulski provided a long discussion of UFOs. He started out by cautioning those present that the regulation (AFR 200-2) was only in draft form and that they were waiting for approval of it from headquarters, USAF.

Cybulski said, "The primary reason for our participation in this program is to solve a very perplexing problem for the Air Force and the country as a whole. To the Air Force the investigations of the UFOB is very important. In all but a few cases a satisfactory solution has been reached and the Air Force feels that adequate, thorough investigative procedures can solve the small percentage of unsolved sightings. This is where we come into the picture."

What is interesting in that statement is the fact that the Air Force had been working on UFO investigation for a number of years, nearly a decade, and were still concerned about the problem. Now, however, the conclusion seems to have been reached. There is nothing to them. They want an investigation that will clear the remainder of the cases. And, as we have seen, the apparent attitude of the 4602d was to explain the cases, ridicule the phenomenon, and make wild, unsupported statements.

Cybulski then said, "Due to our our strategic locations throughout the country, we can be available at a moment's notice, to investigate any legitimate sightings."

Cybulski described the circumstances that might surround the investigation of a UFO sighting. He suggested that if there was a call from fifteen or twenty miles away, with the object still in sight, the responding unit would use the telephone to call for permission to investigate. If the sighting was several hundred miles away, time wouldn't be as important. Regular channels for requesting permission would be satisfactory.

"Above all," Cybulski told the assembled officers, "the Air Force is sincere in its attempt to obtain proof one way or the other. When I went to Dayton [Wright-Patterson AFB], the scientist and the astronomer [probably J. Allen Hynek] they had hired, were ready to quit. But before they were permitted to say anything I was introduced and told them what I was there for and what I was going to do. They threw their resignations away and decided to stay. Because as the astronomer said, 'Put yourself in my position. I am being ridiculed by members of my profession for chasing these imaginary objects, and when I went into this, I went into it sincerely, because I thought that both from an astronomical stand-point and also from scientific value, I could disprove these things. In so doing I would be rendering my profession and my country some service. However, in the past, I have not been able to get support from the Air Force. It seems that they all think this is a hot subject, and they want to drop it. They don't want to have anything to do with it. No one wants to be quoted.' "

We learn quite a bit from that statement. The astronomer hired didn't believe UFOs to be real and thought he could "disprove" them. What sort of an investigation is that? Before coming to a conclusion, isn't a scientist supposed to look at the data? It does provide a clue about the mindset of those who are supposedly objectively investigating these things.

Cybulski said, "Now that the 4602d has entered the picture, we are assuming quite a serious role. The feeling is, both at Wright-Patterson and Washington, that we could be very, very instrumental in bringing this thing to a head once and for all. They feel that it *can* be done by personal contact, where a piece of paper fails, because in the past if they had a sighting somewhere, the people looking into it were the people at Wright-Patterson where there was only one officer and one airman available . . ."

At that point Cybulski began to detail various scenarios concerned with the investigations and the best way to handle them. He discussed how some cases simply couldn't be solved because there was not enough information to draw any sort of conclusions. He said, "The biggest files at ATIC are compiled of materials that stated insufficient evidence."

Remember, at the close of Blue Book in 1969, the Air Force claimed that only seven hundred sightings were unidentified, but four thousand were labeled as having insufficient data. It meant there was no explanation for them, but they didn't clutter up the unidentified category. Even in the mid-1950s that was the case.

But then Cybulski made the comment that underscores the whole attitude of the UFO investigations at this level: "Then there are cases, like that near Great Falls, Montana, where a Warrant Officer shot 40 feet of film. After you blow it up and look at it, you see it's a formation of high flying geese."

Of course, that is the Tremonton, Utah, case from the summer of 1952. Cybulski has it confused with that of the manager of the Great Falls baseball team who filmed two objects over that city two years earlier. And, in his acceptance of the birds explanation, he overlooked the testimony of the witnesses: both Newhouse and his wife saw the objects at close range. The Robertson panel, and other debunking efforts, called them seagulls, not geese.

The rest of what Cybulski said during the commanders' conference had to do with the precise methods of reporting the objects, who held the responsibility, and how the reports were to be completed. He also told the officers that sightings that weren't identified went to ATIC, but said nothing about Project Blue Book. It might have been his impression that Blue Book no longer existed, or would soon end, based on the statements made by other officers.

Then, buried at the end of his report, was a paragraph that dealt with evidence or, more specifically, photographs. Cybulski said, "The photographs go to Washington. In addition one copy of each print will be forwarded to ATIC, and one to us here at headquarters.''

What is interesting is that the photographs go to Washington, D.C. The question that arises from that is why? Shouldn't they go to ATIC, along with the reports? Who in Washington has the power to demand something like that? What it does is subtly demonstrate that Washington has more than a passing interest in UFOs.

Then Cybulski compounded that impressive piece of information by saying, "In almost every case where gun cameras or aircraft cameras have been used, the thing has been too small for identification and the photographs haven't been of much value.''

So now we've learned something else. Remember these are from documents that were originally classified as secret. They were part of the commanders' conference in which the officers assigned to the various units of the 4602d were briefed on their upcoming assignments in the new UFO project. Buried in it is a reference to a group in Washington that wants the original photographs of UFOs and a reference to gun camera films of those same objects. This is official confirmation that some kind of extra investigation is being conducted from somewhere in Washington and confirmation that gun camera films exist.

In his book, Ruppelt talks about gun camera films, but implies that they are all identified as mundane objects. He mentioned that they had some very good film, taken by a pilot who couldn't close in on the UFO. When the photo analysts figured the size of the object, at the distance they believed it to be, one of them believed that a standard weather balloon at that distance would be the size of the image on the gun camera film. Case closed, and probably rightly so.

In another case, a pilot made a short film of an object in the distance that experts labeled as a smoke trail from a meteorite. The pilot reported that the head of the object didn't seem to be moving faster than three hundred miles an hour, much slower than a meteor. The pilot wasn't convinced it was a meteorite, but the Air Force labeled it as such anyway.

But, what about the other cases? By the time Cybulski was briefing the officers at the 4602d commander's conference, Project Blue Book was out of the loop. Before long, it would be nothing more than public relations. So, who is the group in Washington that has access to the pictures and the gun camera films?

In both my earlier book, *The UFO Casebook*, and Timothy Good's *Above Top Secret*, there are discussions of gun camera films. Ruppelt, in his book, mentioned that the Air Force had a plan to outfit a squadron of planes with gun cameras and then station them around the country with orders to scramble when there was a UFO sighting in the vicinity. Ruppelt, however, reported that the plan was never implemented because it was too expensive.

During a 1993 radio interview I was involved in, a woman called to say that her husband had been one of the pilots who was assigned to participate in these intercepts. She claimed that they were successful on a number of occasions, providing close-up views of UFOs. The man finally joined the conversation, adding little detail, other than he had seen three domed discs in a tight formation outrunning the latest fighters. Gun camera film from a number of interceptors was made, but the pilots had no opportunity to see them and none of them knew what happened to the films after they were removed from the aircraft.

Admittedly, this is the worst sort of testimony, from a man who refused to identify himself. He could be someone merely having a good time fooling those listening to the radio. However, there is documentation to support the claim that the Air Force did run intercepts and did collect gun camera film—documented evidence available in formerly classified reports and briefings given throughout the Air Force.

We have seen the statement buried in the commanders' conference briefing of the 4602d. There is one other such statement, hidden in the Project Blue Book files. On one page there is a minor notation about a gun camera spectroscopic film furnished for analysis. This implies that the camera had been fitted with a special filter so that spectroscopic pictures could be taken. It implies that someone was thinking ahead. And it implies that an intercept was made.

Of course, there is nothing in the Blue Book files to explain this and no analysis of the film could be found. It does, however, provide us with clues about what was going on in those days. Someone with a great deal of authority was attempting to gather additional information.

The problem seems to be that too many civilians, and too many in the military outside the loop, had learned about the UFO investigations. The summer wave of 1952 made Blue Book too high-profile and something had to be done. That may have been one of the reasons the

4602d was tasked with UFO investigation. It moved the work, and the data, from Blue Book to another organization that had no real public image. It effectively concealed the level of the investigation and just how many resources were being devoted to it.

Let's examine this from a logical standpoint. Almost from the beginning, the Air Force had been saying there was nothing to UFOs. They reported, a number of times, that their official investigation had been concluded and the operation closed. When Project Sign turned into Project Grudge, the Air Force announced that Sign was over. They didn't bother to tell the public that the investigation, however, was continuing under a new name.

The UFO investigations had been headquartered at ATIC, at Wright-Patterson Air Force Base. It seems that each of those projects was compromised by clever reporters. The solution, then, was to keep the name Blue Book and change the organization responsible for the investigation. That is what they did, and the role of the 4602d was ignored in order to be concealed.

During those years, the 4602d evolved into the 1006th AISS, the 1127th Air Activities Group, and the 7602d Field Activities Group, and now is know by a new name, headquartered at Fort Belvoir, Virginia. What is important here is that they were doing UFO investigations, some of them under the code name of Project Moon Dust. Those activities transcended the end of Project Blue Book in 1969 and continued, under the name Moon Dust, until 1985. Then, apparently, the name was changed because it had been compromised. The mission, however, continued.

CHAPTER 5

Scientists and UFO Investigations

It is a matter of faith with those who believe UFOs are nothing more than illusion, misidentification, and hoax that scientists do not see flying saucers. Scientists are trained to tell the difference between what is and what is not. They are not easily fooled. But the truth is, and according to the government's own UFO studies, scientists *do* see flying saucers. There are many good sightings by scientists, many of which have not been satisfactorily explained.

Such is the report made by Charles B. Moore of his UFO sighting on April 24, 1949, in New Mexico. The report is one of the few still classified as "unidentified" in the Project Blue Book files. It seems a perfect case for reexamination.

It wasn't a very spectacular sighting. Moore, along

with a crew from General Mills, and a Naval officer, Douglas C. McLaughlin (misidentified in some reports as Robert or "R" McLaughlin according to an AFOSI document in the Project Blue Book file), were launching balloons near Arrey, New Mexico. They had "released a 350-gram balloon about 1020 MST and were following it with a standard ML-47 David White Theodolite." Moore made a reading at 10:30 A.M. and then took over at the theodolite.

According to his report, made to Project Grudge, he had looked up to acquire the balloon with the naked eye and spotted what he thought was the balloon. Moore wrote, "When the distance between the theodolite and the supposed balloon became apparent, I took over the theodolite and found the true balloon still there, whereupon I abandoned it and picked up the object after it came out of the sun. The object was moving too fast to crank the theodolite around; therefore, one of the men pointed the theodolite and I looked. The object was ellipsoid . . . white in color except for a light yellow on one side as though it were in shadow."

"The object," according to Moore, "was not a balloon and was some distance away. Assuming escape velocity, a track is enclosed which figures elevation above the station of about 300,000 feet over the observed period. If this is true, the flight would have probably gone over the White Sands Proving Ground [later White Sands Missile Range], Holloman Air Force Base, and Los Alamos."

They lost sight of the object in the distance, after watching it for about sixty seconds. They had made measurements using their equipment and a stopwatch, but took no photographs.

Dr. Donald H. Menzel, a Harvard astronomer and the debunker of all UFO sightings, later did what the Air Force couldn't in their investigation. He identified the object seen by Moore and his crew. According to Menzel, the object was a mirage. That is, Menzel believed it to be an atmospheric reflection of the true balloon, making it appear as if there were two objects in the sky instead of one. He was so sure of this that he told Moore about the solution.

Moore, however, is an atmospheric physicist. He is as qualified as Menzel to discuss the dynamics of the atmosphere, and according to him when interviewed on El Paso radio station KTSM, the weather conditions were not right for the creation of mirages. Since Moore was on the scene, and since he is qualified to make judgments about the conditions of the atmosphere at the time of the sighting, his observations are more important than Menzel's speculations.

When Moore spoke to Menzel, the Harvard professor would not listen to what Moore had to say. Menzel had found what to him was a satisfactory solution for the sighting, and he didn't want to discuss it seriously or have his conclusions challenged. Air Force investigators, however, left the sighting labeled as "unidentified."

What it boils down to is a lesson in UFOlogy. By studying the case, we can learn the mental gymnastics that debunkers use to explain any sighting, regardless of the facts. Here was a case where scientists and military officers saw something, tracked it, and used their instruments to measure the event. The object was believed to be 300,000 feet in the air and moving rapidly. Unfortunately it was too far away for any detail to be seen, other than that the craft was elliptical in shape.

The case, however, doesn't end there, with just a report of a high-flying elliptical UFO. In 1949 all the sighting reports were classified as secret by the military. They were not to be discussed with those who did not have the proper clearances. In August 1949, the Navy was conducting tests at White Sands, and during those tests one of the officers mentioned flying saucer sightings. Articles published in various newspapers including those in El Paso, Texas, and Los Angeles, California, reported, "U.S. Officers see flying saucers."

According to one of the articles, written by Marvin Miles, "Flying saucers—or at least mysterious flying 'objects'—have been sighted by service personnel at this vital center of America's upper air research."

The article claims that, "One officer believes, sincerely, that the objects seen are space ships and declared that a ballistic formula applied to one observation through a photo theodolite showed the 'ship' was 35 to 40 miles high—an 'egg-shaped' craft of fantastic size and traveling at incredible speeds of three to four miles a second."

Miles, in the article, wrote that, "In all, some five reports have been made in the last six months . . ." An officer told Miles, ". . . three officers saw a flying object with the naked eye, and at another time two smaller objects were observed to chase a test rocket. These may have been dual images on the telescopes, he said, although they were seen from several widely separated stations."

There was even discussion of either photographs or movie footage taken of one sighting. Naval officer Douglas McLaughlin, however, said that the film didn't turn out. That is an interesting aside, simply because there have been rumors of good UFO movies hidden by the government.

Because of the articles and a radio broadcast about the sightings, the Air Force Office of Special Investigation was required to review the situation to see if military regulations or federal law had been violated, or if classified information had been compromised. A number of agents from District Office #17 at Kirtland Air Force Base, Albuquerque, New Mexico, conducted the investigation. According to the documentation available in the Project Blue Book files, John F. Frampton and James B. Shiley were involved, as well as District Office #18 in Maywood, California, and District Office #12 at Scott Air Force Base, Illinois.

The investigation centered not on the sightings but on the possible compromise of classified information. AFOSI agents, as well as FBI agents, interviewed a number of reporters and military officers. Miles, for example, told the agents that he had been at the office of a naval officer at White Sands, a captain he believed was named Gorry, when he overheard another officer make a report of a sighting of a flying object in the sky on August 26, 1949. Later, Miles searched out the man and questioned him about the flying saucer sighting. Miles, according to the report, "strongly suggested that the officer in question was Commander Douglas C. McLaughlin."

Clete Roberts, a radio reporter for a Los Angeles station, also reported on the flying disk sightings and was also interviewed by the AFOSI. Roberts was the man who reported that photographs had been taken. When he asked Commander McLaughlin about the pictures, he was told, ". . . they didn't turn out."

Interestingly, as the AFOSI tried to find the source of the leak about the flying saucer sightings at White Sands, C. B. Moore (misidentified as C. D. Moore) was mentioned. The results of the AFOSI investigation was that none of the reporters had talked to him about the events near Arrey, New Mexico. The leak, then, came not from the civilians working at the military base but from high-ranking naval officers who made offhand remarks in the presence of some reporters. The reporters, always looking for a good story, had followed up on those remarks, publishing or broadcasting the results of their investigation.

In the Project Blue Book files, there is no real record of those other sightings. There is only the mention of them in the newspaper articles and investigation into who leaked what. The index from Project Blue Book for "20–30 April [1949] sightings" lists only the Arrey, New Mexico, report from Professor Moore.

There are some sightings from the vicinity of White Sands. On June 14, there was a sighting from the missile range, but it was labeled as an additional sighting, not a separate case. There is no reported source or observer.

On April 12, 1949, there was a sighting at the Sandia Base (near Albuquerque) that lasted for about eight seconds. An Army private said the object was round, white, and traveling at a high rate of speed. Air Force investigations suggested that he had seen a meteor. There is not enough data available to determine if the Air Force merely slapped an explanation on the file or if they had actually solved the case.

On April 22, 1949, a sighting was reported at Cliff, New Mexico. This was identified as a conventional aircraft. Cliff is on the western border of New Mexico, a hundred miles or more from White Sands.

On May 19, 1949, several witnesses at Fort Bliss (El Paso, Texas, and located next to the White Sands Missile Range on the southern side) reported an object identified later as an aircraft.

There were also a number of sightings reported at Los Alamos. These were all identified later as mundane objects, including a meteor shower on May 3, a meteor on June 2, a meteor on June 11, and a meteor on June 20. It would seem that the scientists at Los Alamos would be able to identify meteors when they saw them. It would seem that after one or two were embarrassed by reporting meteors as UFOs, others would figure it out and the reports cease.

What this demonstrates is that there was a series of sightings at White Sands Proving Ground, as well as other restricted areas in New Mexico in 1949. The sightings were made by military officers, civilian scientists, and technicians employed at the missile range. They were made by qualified observers who were as familiar with what is in the sky as those who later investigated the sightings. It is a series of sightings, if they were of flying saucers, that suggested that someone was watching our primitive attempts to step into space. And it suggests that not all is as the Air Force would have us believe.

Interestingly, however, the sighting that sparked the AFOSI investigation on August 26, 1949, doesn't appear in the Project Blue Book files. Neither are there any indications that photographs or movie footage had been taken. The sightings made by Naval personnel, and referred to in the newspaper articles, are not reported in the files. At the time, regulations in effect suggested that sightings were to be reported to the Air Force, even if those sightings were made by members of other branches of the military service.

In reporting on Moore's sighting, a note in the files said, "The consultants of the AMC [Air Materiel Command] Aero-Med laboratory state that reliable estimates of distance can only be made when the object is identified as some known object or type of object by the observer. It is interesting to note that the observers at first thought the object was the balloon which they had released . . . The questionable data in this incident, the extremely short time of observation and the *overwhelming evidence of misidentifications* in other cases, leads to the conclusion that the object seen was misidentified by the observers."

In other words, when a solution didn't present itself, the Air Force didn't mind just inventing one, regardless of the expertise of the witnesses and the availability of technical equipment. Moore's sighting is interesting, providing us, as it turns out, with some insight into the operation of the Air Force investigation, but in the end, proves nothing conclusive. It is just another of the "unidentifieds" that plagued the Air Force from the very beginning.

Not long after Moore's sighting, in August 1949, Dr. Clyde Tombaugh, the man who discovered Pluto, had his own sighting from his backyard in Las Cruces, New

Mexico. Here is a man who could easily be classified as an expert observer, especially of the night sky. (Tombaugh has since died.)

According to Tombaugh:

"I saw the object about eleven o'clock at night in August 1949 from the backyard of my home in Las Cruces, New Mexico. I happened to be looking at zenith, admiring the beautiful transparent sky of stars, when suddenly I spied a geometrical group of faint bluish-green rectangles of light similar to the 'Lubbock lights.' [It should be noted that his report was written *after* the Lubbock Lights case in September 1951.] My wife and her mother were sitting in the yard with me and they saw them also. The group moved south-southeasterly, the individual rectangles became foreshortened, their space of formation smaller, (at first about one degree across) and the intensity duller, fading from view at about 35 degrees above the horizon. Total time of visibility was about three seconds. I was too flabbergasted to count the number of rectangles of light, or to note some other features I wondered about later. There was no sound. I have done thousands of hours of night sky watching, but never saw a sight so strange as this. The rectangles were of low luminosity; had there been a full moon in the sky, I am sure they would not have been visible."

Naturally, Tombaugh's sighting, because of who he is, has caused a great deal of speculation. Donald Menzel wrote about it, praising Tombaugh as a scientist, but then, after a fashion, explained that Tombaugh had been fooled because of a thin atmospheric inversion layer over New Mexico that night.

Menzel, in his 1953 book, *Flying Saucers*, wrote, "But what were these mysterious lights? I can only hazard here the same guess I made about the Lubbock lights— that a low, thin layer of haze or smoke reflected the lights of a distant house or some other multiple source. The haze must have been inconspicuous to the eye, because Tombaugh comments on the unusual clarity of the sky." (Must I actually note that Tombaugh commented on the unusual clarity of the sky, but Menzel postulates a thin layer of haze? It seems to be a true contradiction.)

By 1963, when Menzel wrote, with Lyle G. Boyd, *The World of Flying Saucers*, his tone had changed. He pointed out that in a *Life* magazine article, which contained only ten sentences about the Tombaugh sighting, the writer had made six misstatements. But the majority of them were minor, such as suggesting the sighting took place at 11:00 P.M., when the real time was 10:45, or that the direction was traveling south to north, when they were moving northwest to southeast.

Menzel went on to write, "While keeping an open mind on the possibility of interplanetary travel, Tombaugh himself has never supported the spaceship interpretation so often attributed to him in print but has considered various possible explanations—insects or birds illuminated by ground lights, or reflections of ground lights against the boundary of an inversion layer in the air. Of these, the inversion theory seems the most probable."

But the truth of the matter is somewhat different. First and foremost, Tombaugh *did* consider "spaceships." According to the "official" report Tombaugh completed in his own handwriting and sent to Project Blue Book, of which I have a copy, Tombaugh wrote that he thought that spacecraft might be an answer.

Question 38 on the form asks, "In your opinion what do you think the object was and what might have caused it? Tombaugh wrote, "Projection of lights on the sky as a screen? Very high aircraft, or space ship? (No sound)."

Others have looked into the sighting carefully. In 1966, Dr. James E. McDonald, an atmospheric physicist, apparently after reading one of Menzel's somewhat biased accounts, did a little research himself. He spoke to Tombaugh, trying to learn more about the case.

McDonald wrote in a letter dated October 24, 1966: "The date is of interest because, even putting aside the impossibility of getting light reflections from 'inversions or haze layers' at high angles of elevation such as were involved in the Tombaugh observations, the radiosonde from El Paso for that P.M shows no inversions at all. By 10:45 P.M. a surface inversion would have begun to form, but that doesn't alter the argument."

Later in the letter McDonald wrote, "I was just a bit surprised that he [Tombaugh] did not seem fully aware that Menzel's explanation was physically absurd. To him it seemed significant that I pointed out that the El Paso radiosonde from the 20th had no sign of an inversion—

whereas, in fact, no inversion ever known in the history of meteorology could give a reflection at the near-normal incidence involved here."

Further, in the letter is a paragraph that becomes important only because Menzel seems to believe that Tombaugh doesn't subscribe to the idea of interstellar visitors. McDonald wrote, "I asked him if he knew Hynek, and knows him well. He seemed aware that Hynek had been changing his position on ufos. Tombaugh agreed that the problem 'deserves careful scientific investigation by reliable people,' but added that fanatics have scared most scientists off. Said he didn't think he could go along with Keyhoe's ideas on the problem, yet a few seconds later he was noting that perhaps we have to admit the possibility of visitations..."

Dick Hall, at one time a member of NICAP, but now the president of the Fund for UFO Research, asked Tombaugh if he had any comments on Menzel's theory that he had seen lights from the ground reflected by an inversion layer. Tombaugh responded to Hall's question, writing, "Regarding the solidity of the phenomenon I saw: My wife thought she saw a faint connecting glow across the structure. The illumination rectangles I saw did maintain an exactly fixed position with respect to each other, which would tend to support the impression of solidity. I doubt that the phenomenon was any terrestrial reflection, because in that case some similarity to it should have appeared many times. I do a great deal of observing (both telescopic and unaided-eye) in the back yard and nothing of the kind has ever appeared before or since."

That covers the controversy of Tombaugh's sighting.

Clearly, he didn't accept the theory published by Menzel. He thought of the object in terms of something very strange. And he did not reject the extraterrestrial hypothesis, though he clearly pointed out that he doesn't believe the craft are from a planet in our solar system.

And, as in Moore's case, Menzel attempted to explain a sighting by an extremely qualified observer as a temperature inversion. Tombaugh is an astronomer, not an atmospheric physicist as is Moore, but the point is the same. The man who made the observations was at odds with the man who believed them all to be explained as temperature inversions. The man who was on the scene was at odds with the man who wasn't there but had to rely on the man on the scene for his data.

Menzel, in his attempt to explain everything as inversions, was also at odds with another group of scientists. These men, all professors at Texas Tech, reported, first, the objects that would later become known as the Lubbock Lights.

It was late August 1951 when several college professors, while sitting on a porch in Lubbock, Texas, saw a formation of lights sweep overhead. The lights were in sight for only three or four seconds and none of the men managed to get a very clear look at them. Air Force investigators would later say that sightings of a short duration are virtually useless because everything happens too fast for accurate observations to be made. The human eye and brain do not have time to record the event.

The professors, W. L. Ducker, A. G. Oberg, and W. I. Robinson, were upset they had not seen more. They discussed what to do if the lights should reappear and laid out a plan. Before the night was over, they had their chance and made a series of quick and well-coordinated observations.

The lights were softly glowing bluish objects in a loose formation. The first group, they believed, had been in a more rigid and more structured formation than later groups.

Jay Harris, the managing editor of the *Lubbock Avalanche*, first learned of the lights when Ducker called the news desk to report the sighting. Harris wasn't interested at first, but Ducker convinced him that it was important. Ducker wanted a story written so that others who might have seen the lights could be found and comparisons with their information could be made. Harris finally agreed, but only if the newspaper could print Ducker's name. Ducker didn't like that condition and refused.

A few minutes later Ducker called back and said that he could print not only his name but also the names of Oberg and Robinson. The only condition was that Harris would have to get permission from Texas Tech's public relations department first.

There were at least four others who saw the lights on that first night. Mrs. Earl Mediock, Mrs. F. A. Rogers, Mrs. R. A. Rogers, and Professor Carl Henninger all reported seeing the lights at 9:10 P.M. That was the first sighting described by the professors.

Over the next two weeks, the professors saw the lights on several occasions, but were unable to obtain any useful data. Joined by Grayson Meade, E. R. Hienaman and J. P. Brand, they equipped two teams with two-way radios, measured a base line from the location of the original sightings, and sent the teams out to watch the night sky. They hoped that sightings along the base line would provide them with enough information to allow triangulation. They hoped to determine the size of the lights, altitude, and speed.

They did manage to make a few observations. The lights traveled through about ninety degrees of sky in a matter of seconds. They normally appeared forty-five degrees above the horizon and disappeared about forty-five degrees above the opposite horizon. During the first observation, the lights had been in a roughly semicircular formation. In subsequent sightings no regular pattern was noticed.

None of the teams ever made a sighting, though on one or two occasions, the wives of the men said they had seen the lights while the men were at the bases. That would suggest that the lights were much lower than the professors had originally thought.

Carl Hart, Jr., a young man living in Lubbock in 1951, and an amateur photographer, managed to take a series of pictures of the objects as they flew over his house. According to the story told by Hart, and as interviewed by me in 1991, he had heard of the lights and hoped to see them. When a formation flashed overhead, Hart realized that he might be able to take pictures. He got his camera and waited.

Two more formations flew over. Hart took two photographs of the first and three of the second. The lights were dim, but Hart was certain there was an image on the film.

What would become important about the photographs was not bright white circles of light they showed, but the formation of the objects. The lights were in precise V-shaped formations in each of the pictures. None of the formations were ragged in appearance. Those photographs would tend to eliminate the explanations offered by both scientists and the Air Force that the lights were birds.

Ed Ruppelt also interviewed the college professors. They provided signed statements about what they had seen and done. In addition to recounting several flights, they mentioned an unusual event on September 2. While the flight passed directly overhead, as had the others, and was made up of fifteen to thirty lights, one professor noticed an irregularly shaped yellow light at the rear of the formation.

By the end of 1951, the Air Force investigation of the Lubbock sightings began to wind down. Investigators had spoken to all the witnesses several times. After they interviewed Bryant, a man who had seen plover (a west Texas bird), and spoken to another west Texan, T. E. Snider, who reported he had seen the lights but identified them as ducks, the official answer became: they were birds.

In still another, later report, investigators wrote, "It was concluded that birds, with street lights reflecting from them, were the probable cause of these sightings. The angular velocity was less. In all instances the witnesses were located in an area where their eyes were dark-adapted, thus making the objects appear brighter."

Of course, that conclusion overlooks the fact there are no migratory birds in the Lubbock area at that time of year that fly in any formation. Loren Smith at Texas Tech told me when I visited him that there are ducks that fly in V-formations in the area in late August. But they aren't migratory.

The glossy iris, for example, inhabits west Texas and does fly in the proper formation. The problem, however, is that species is reddish maroon and has no white to reflect the street lights as postulated by Air Force investigators. The glossy iris is not satisfactory as the explanation. In fact, there are no birds in west Texas that are satisfactory as an explanation for all the sightings, a fact the Air Force and debunkers overlook in their rush to judgment.

But that wasn't the last of it. In June 1952, Menzel published an article in *Look* magazine claiming that the Lubbock Lights were not birds but reflections of the city's lights: "mirages caused by atmospheric conditions known as 'temperature inversion.'" Temperature inversion would become one of Menzel's favorite explanations, even when there was no meteorological evidence that inversions existed at the time of the sightings.

Menzel, using chemicals, was able to reproduce what he claimed were the Lubbock Lights in his laboratory. His pictures, taken of stationary objects in the lab, showed lights in a similar formation, but the lights were more diffused than the photographs taken by Carl Hart of the V-shaped formations which flew over his house.

Dr. E. F. George, one of the scientists who had seen the lights, also disagreed with Menzel. He said, "I don't believe what I saw was a reflection from street lights."

Ducker, who was involved in the original sightings, said that he and the others had never tried to explain what it was they had seen, but only that they had seen something unusual. He pointed out that a reproduction in the laboratory, such as Menzel's chemical experiment, would not mean that the original sightings were "trickery."

In 1977, Donald Menzel, in his book coauthored with Ernest H. Taves, *The UFO Enigma*, had given up the temperature inversion explanation. He devoted less than a paragraph to the Lubbock Lights, dismissing Hart's photographs by saying, ". . . we believe that some of the Lubbock photographs may have been hoaxes." He further wrote that this was in no way inconsistent with the conclusion reached by some of the Lubbock viewers themselves, that flying flocks of birds illuminated by city lights produced the apparitions.

Not a single shred of solid evidence has ever been presented to suggest that the photographs are hoaxes. No one in the Lubbock area has been able to reproduce them under the same conditions that faced Hart. The photo editor of the Lubbock newspaper tried on more than one occasion to photograph night-flying birds and was unable to do it, even though his equipment was better than Hart's and he had access to a faster film.

The various investigators, both military and civilian, were not able to break Hart's story and, in fact, threatened him from the very beginning. First, Harris, of the *Lubbock Avalanche*, told Hart of the consequences of perpetrating a fraud against the newspaper. Later, Air Force officers told Hart of his rights under the Fifth Amendment to the Constitution. In all those cases Hart maintained that his story was true and that he had not faked anything.

The lights began as a mysterious case with highly qualified witnesses. The college professors, given the diversity of their disciplines, were considered experts. They were familiar with the sky and the atmosphere around them. Yet they were unable to identify the lights.

Others, in widely scattered locations, saw the lights on the first night and on subsequent nights. Some of them identified the lights they saw as birds. There is no question that some of the reports were of birds, identified as such by the witnesses at the time they made their sightings.

When confronted with evidence that is difficult to explain, the philosophy seems to be to offer as many explanations as possible and to publish those explanations as if there is no question about their accuracy, even if there should be. Public perception, then, will be that the case has been solved even when it has not. It doesn't matter if part of the public believes it was birds, or temperature inversions, or even a hoax. An answer has been offered and some of the people believe it. It also confuses the issue, and that is sometimes exactly what the Air Force and its investigators want.

As we have seen, Menzel was very good at this. He wrote many articles about UFOs. He explained UFOs in all his articles and books, but paid no attention to the facts. His dismissal of the Lubbock Lights, and his explanations in the Moore and Tombaugh cases, demonstrate his lack of scientific analysis. When he failed to explain a case as atmospheric phenomenon, or birds, he resorted to labeling a case as a hoax with absolutely no evidence that it was. Clearly, he was not interested in the truth, but in finding explanations for all sightings.

What we have seen here is that scientists, who are trained observers, who have spent their professional lives as observers, have seen things that they can't explain. They are not willing to have those observations ignored, and concede that extraterrestrial spaceships might . . . *might* . . . explain what they have seen.

Flying saucers should not be relegated to the dust heap simply because we find it hard to believe that an alien civilization has visited us. The evidence, here as elsewhere, is based on the testimony and the abilities of the observers. The point in these cases, however, is that these men, who were trained in science, were unable to produce solid explanations for their sightings.

What we are left with is the destruction of one of the myths of the flying saucer mystery. It is not true that scientists don't see flying saucers. Not only do they see them, they report them.

CHAPTER 6

August 22, 1955: the Kelly-Hopkinsville Case

The attitude of the military and the government can be easily seen in the UFO occupant case from the Hopkinsville, Kentucky, area in late summer 1955. Although there is a thick folder in the Project Blue Book files about the case, the file itself suggests that it is not an official investigation, just an informational folder. That means, though there is information about it, officers with Project Blue Book did not officially investigate it. In fact, the Air Force denied any official interest in it in newspaper articles from the time.

The report began early on the evening of August 21, 1955, when Billy Ray Taylor, a young friend of Elmer "Lucky" Sutton, had gone to the well behind the farmhouse and came running back telling all that he had seen a flying saucer. The object, described as bright with an exhaust that contained all the colors of the rainbow, passed over the house. It continued over the fields, finally came to a hover, and then descended, disappearing into a gully.

No one in the Sutton house, including Glennie Lankford, Lucky Sutton, Vera Sutton, John Charley (J. C.) Sutton, Alene Sutton, three Sutton children, June Taylor, and O. P. Baker, believed the story of the flying saucer. None of them considered walking out to the gully to see if something might be down there.

Not long after Taylor told his tale, the dog began to bark. Taylor and Lucky Sutton went to investigate, but the dog ran under the house, not to reappear that night.

Out in the fields, away from the house, was a strange, hovering glow. As it approached, they could see a "small man" inside it. He was about three and a half feet tall, with a large head that looked to be round, and long, thin arms that extended almost to the ground. The creature's hands were large and out of proportion with the body, and were shaped more like a bird's talons than a human hand. The two eyes were large and seemed to glow with a yellow fire.

As the creature continued to move toward the house, the two men retreated, found a rifle and a shotgun inside, and then waited. When the creature was within twenty feet of the back door, both men fired at it. The creature flipped back, regained its feet and fled into the darkness.

The two men watched for a few minutes, then walked into the living room where the others waited. The creature, or one just like it, appeared at one of the windows and the men shot at it, hitting it. This one also did a back flip and disappeared.

Now the men decided it was time to go out to learn if they had injured or killed the creature. Taylor was the first out, but stopped on the porch under a small over-hang. A clawlike hand reached down and touched his hair. Alene Taylor grabbed Taylor to pull him back into the house. Lucky pushed past him and fired upward at the creature on the roof. It was knocked from its perch.

Someone, probably Taylor, shouted, "There's one up in the tree."

Both Taylor and Lucky shot at it, knocking it from the limb, but it didn't fall to the ground. Instead, it seemed to float. They shot again, and it moved off, into the weeds.

At the same moment, another of the creatures ap-peared around the corner of the house. It might have been the one that had been on the roof or one of those seen in the backyard. Lucky whirled and fired. The buck-shot sounded as if it hit something metallic, like an empty bucket. Just as had the others, the little creature flipped over, scrambled to its feet, and fled, moving rap-idly into the darkness.

Having failed to stop the creatures with either the shot-guns or the .22 caliber rifle, Lucky decided to leave them alone. Someone noticed that the creatures only ap-proached from darkened areas. It seemed that they were repelled by the light.

At some point they heard noises on the roof and went out the back door to investigate. One of the creatures was back on the roof. They shot at it, knocked it off the roof, but it floated to a fence some forty feet away rather than falling to the ground. Hit by another shot, it fell from the fence and ran away, seeming to use its arms to aid its locomotion.

Some of the others in the house were still unconvinced, believing that the boys were playing some sort of a prank on them. Glennie Lankford, who was fifty at the time, asked Taylor what he was seeing. With the lights in the house turned out, they had taken up a position close to one of the windows. Taylor told her to wait and she would see for herself.

After twenty minutes or so, one of the creatures approached the front of the house. According to Lankford, it looked like a five-gallon gasoline can with a head on top of two thin, spindly legs. It shimmered as if made of bright metal.

Lankford, who had been crouching quietly near the window for a long time, tried to stand, but fell with a thud. She shrieked in surprise and the creature jumped to the rear. Taylor fired at it through the screen door.

Although they thought they had driven the creatures off a number of times that night, they kept returning. The people in the house were becoming more frightened. The children were beginning to panic. No one was sure what was happening.

About three hours after the first creature had been seen, approximately 11:00 that night, they decided to get out. Everybody ran to the cars. One of the kids was screaming and had to be carried. They raced to the Hopkinsville police station for help.

At the police station, there was no doubt that the people had been frightened by something. Police officers, and the chief, interviewed after the events, made it clear they believed the people had been scared by something. That doesn't mean they were "attacked" by strange little metallic men, but does mean they were relating what they believed to be the truth to the assembled officials.

Within minutes, the police were on their way back to the house with some of the Sutton men in the cars. The police also called the Madisonville headquarters of the Kentucky State Police. A call was even made to the chief, Russell Greenwell, at home. He was told that a spaceship had landed at Kelly. Greenwell then told the desk sergeant that it had better not be a joke.

There were now Kentucky state police, local police, the chief, and a sheriff's deputy either heading out to the Sutton house or already there. One of the state troopers, who was only a few miles from Hopkinsville, on the road to Kelly, said that he saw what he called several meteors flash over his car. They moved with a sound like artillery, and he looked up in time to see two of them. They were traveling in a slightly descending arc, heading toward the Sutton house.

The yard around the Sutton house was suddenly filled with cars, and more importantly, light. The men tried to point out where the various events had taken place. The chief searched for signs that anyone or everyone had been drinking, but found nothing to indicate that anyone had even a beer. Glennie Lankford later said that she didn't allow alcohol in the house.

Once the police arrived, the situation changed radically. Although the atmosphere was tension charged, and some of the police were nervous, they began to search for signs of the invasion from outer space. There were apparent bullet and shotgun blast holes in the screens over the windows, and there was evidence that weapons had been fired, but there were no traces of the alien creatures. The hard-packed ground did not take footprints.

The search of the yard and fields around the house revealed little, except a luminous patch where one of the creatures had fallen earlier, which was only visible from one angle. The chief said that he saw it himself and there was definitely some kind of stain on the grass. There is no record that anyone took samples for later analysis.

With no real evidence to be found, no alien creatures running around, and no spacecraft hidden in the gully, the police began to return to their regular duties. By two in the morning, only the Suttons were left at the house.

A newspaper photographer and his wife, who had accompanied the police to the Sutton house, also left. The wife had said that she hoped to see one of the creatures but was disappointed. A half hour or so after the last of the police left, and with the lights in the house down, Glennie Lankford saw one of the creatures looking in the window.

She alerted her son, Lucky, who wanted to shoot at it, but she told him not to. She didn't want a repeat of the situation earlier in the night. Besides, the creatures had done nothing to harm anyone during the first episode.

Lucky didn't listen to her. He shot at the creature, but the shot was no more effective than those fired earlier in the night. Other shots were fired with no apparent effect. The little creatures bounced up each time they were hit and then ran away.

The little beings kept reappearing throughout the night, the last sighting occurring just a half an hour before sunrise. That was the last time any of the beings were seen by the Suttons or their friends.

The next morning the men scattered on various errands, but the women remained home. The various police and private investigators began to arrive early that morning as well, interviewing as many of the witnesses, including the children, as they could. They searched the area again in a hope of finding some physical evidence in the daylight that might have been missed in the dark, but there was none.

Other investigators, some of them official and some of them from the UFO community, began their research as well. As mentioned, Project Blue Book, the public Air Force investigation, reported that they did not investigate. They had no real interest in the sighting, although the Blue Book files do contain documents that suggest one active duty officer, and possibly more, did some sort of "unofficial" investigation.

The curious also began to arrive. One night the yard was filled with little men from outer space, or so the witnesses claimed, and the next there were dozens of human sightseers. By Tuesday, it began to get seriously out of hand. People approached the house from all directions. Some people wanted to set up stands to sell hot dogs, soda, and souvenirs to make a little money, though the Suttons weren't among those with a monetary motive. And, as if that wasn't enough, reporters, some from the local radio station, also arrived demanding interviews. Some of those interviews were later broadcast over WHOP. Those tapes, which would have been important to follow up investigations, were saved for about a year, then erased and used again.

By the afternoon, the Suttons had had enough. They called the state police to ask for help, and the troopers cleared out all the cars. The NO TRESPASSING signs erected by the Suttons had done no good.

Without any sort of physical evidence, most people were quite skeptical. The media reflected that attitude. The Air Force, though still claiming there was no investigation, issued two statements on Tuesday. The Air Force told all that they were not investigating the case and that there was no basis for investigating it. In other words, the case was so unimportant that the Air Force wasn't going to waste its time or resources.

When the NO TRESPASSING signs again failed to stop the crowds, the Suttons erected one that demanded an admission to be paid to enter the property. A second sign told of a charge of one dollar for information and ten dollars for photographs. To the public, the police, and the Air Force, this was proof that the case was a hoax. Obviously the Suttons invented the tale as a way of making a little money.

Although it seems that military personnel from Fort Campbell, Kentucky, did visit the house, and interviews with the witnesses were conducted in 1955, an investigation by the Air Force didn't take place until two years later. Project Blue Book files, now available at the National Archives, show interest in the case apparently beginning in August 1957, prior to the publication of a magazine article about the incident.

In a letter from the Air Technical Intelligence Center at

Wright-Patterson to the commander of Campbell Air Force Base, Wallace W. Elwood wrote: "1. This Center requests any factual data, together with pertinent comments regarding an unusual incident reported to have taken place six miles north of Hopkinsville, Kentucky on subject date [21 August 1955]. Briefly, the incident involved an all-night attack on a family named Sutton by goblin-like creatures reported to have emerged from a so-called 'flying saucer.' "

Later in the letter, Elwood wrote: "3. Lacking factual, confirming data, no credence can be given this almost fantastic report. As the incident has never been officially reported to the Air Force, it has not taken official cognizance of the matter."

The matter was apparently assigned to First Lieutenant Charles N. Kirk, an Air Force officer at Campbell Air Force Base. He spent about six weeks investigating the case before sending the material on to ATIC on October 1, 1957. He researched the story using the Hopkinsville newspaper from August 22, 1955, and September 11, 1955. He also had a letter from Captain Robert J. Hertell, a statement from Glennie Lankford, and a statement given to Kirk by Major John E. Albert and a copy of an article written by Glennie Lankford.

Albert's statement provides some interesting information. Remember, the Air Force was claiming that the case had not been officially reported and therefore had not been investigated. It seems that here we get lost in the semantics of the situation.

It sounds like a police officer who, seeing a robbery in progress, then ignores it because it hadn't been reported to the station and he wasn't dispatched by headquarters.

A police officer can't ignore the crime, and it seems reasonable to assume that the Air Force shouldn't have ignored this. The sighting was reported in the media, including radio reports, and newspapers from various locations around the country were reporting it as well. Although the Air Force officers at Blue Book or ATIC must have known that the sighting had been made, they chose to ignore it. Why?

Ruppelt, when he had been the head of Blue Book, made an effort to find UFO sightings. He subscribed to a clipping service so that they would learn of sightings in other parts of the country via newspapers. Leads came to him through official channels, including the classified message center. Ruppelt searched out UFO sightings so that he could get a complete picture of what was happening.

Less than three years later, during the summer of 1955, the attitude at ATIC had apparently changed. If the sighting wasn't reported through official channels, then it didn't exist. Since no one reported this case through official channels, the sighting was ignored.

Or is that the case? Lieutenant Kirk, in his report in 1957, sent a copy of the statement made by Major John E. Albert on September 26, 1957, on to ATIC. The first paragraph seems to suggest that notification was made to Campbell Air Force Base which should have, according to regulations in effect at that time (1955), reported it in official channels. The regulation is quite clear on the point, and it doesn't matter if everyone in the military believed the sighting to be a hoax; it should have been investigated.

That investigation would not have been conducted by

ATIC and Project Blue Book, but by the 4602d Air Intelligence Service Squadron. AFR 200-2 tells us exactly what probably happened to the report. It went on to the 4602d and apparently disappeared there.

In the statement, Albert said, "On about August 22, 1955, about 8 A.M., I heard a news broadcast concerning an incident at Kelly Station, approximately six miles North of Hopkinsville. At the time I heard this news broadcast, I was at Gracey, Kentucky, on my way to Campbell Air Force Base, where I am assigned for reserve training. I called the Air Base and asked them if they had heard anything about an alleged flying saucer report. They stated that they had not and it was suggested that as long as I was close to the area, that I should determine if there was anything to this report. I immediately drove to the scene at Kelly [for some reason the word was blacked out, but it seems reasonable to assume the word is Kelly] Station and located the home belonging to a Mrs. Glennie Lankford [again the name is blacked out], who is the one who first reported the incident. (A copy of Mrs. Lankford's statement is attached to this report)."

Albert's statement continued,

> "Deputy Sheriff Batts was at the scene where this supposed flying saucer had landed and he could not show any evidence that any object had landed in the vicinity. There was nothing to show that there was anything to prove this incident.
>
> "Mrs. Lankford was an impoverished widow woman who had grown up in this small community just outside of Hopkinsville, with very lit-

tle education. She belonged to the Holy Roller Church and the night and evening of this occurrence had gone to a religious meeting and she indicated that the members of the congregation and her two sons and their wives and some friends of her sons' were also at this religious meeting and were worked up into a frenzy, becoming emotionally unbalanced and that after the religious meeting, they had discussed this article which she had heard about over the radio and had sent for them from the Kingdom Publishers, Fort Worth 1, Texas, and they had sent her this article with a picture which appeared to be a little man when it actually was a monkey, painted silver. This article had to be returned to Mrs. Lankford as she stated it was her property. However, a copy of the writing is attached to this statement and if it is necessary, a photograph can be obtained from the above-mentioned publishers."

There are a number of problems with the first couple of paragraphs of Albert's statement, but those are trivial. As an example, it wasn't Glennie Lankford who first reported the incident, but the whole family who had traveled into town to alert the police.

The third paragraph, however, is filled with things that bear no resemblance to reality. Lankford was not a member of the Holy Rollers, but was, in fact a member of the Trinity Pentecostal. Neither she, nor any of the family had been to any religious services the night of the "attack." She couldn't have heard about any article on the radio because there was no radio in the farmhouse. And there was no evidence that Lankford ever sent away for any kind of article about flying saucers and little creatures. In other words, Albert had written the case off, almost before he began his "investigation," because of his false impressions. Apparently he was only interested in facts that would allow him to debunk the case and not learning what had happened.

Further evidence of this is provided in the next paragraph of his statement. "It is my opinion that the report Mrs. Lankford or her son, Elmer Sutton [again the name is blacked out, but it seems reasonable to assume the name is Elmer Sutton], was caused by one of two reasons. Either they actually did see what they thought was a little man and at the time, there was a circus in the area and a monkey might have escaped, giving the appearance of a small man. Two, being emotionally upset, and discussing the article and showing pictures of this little monkey, that appeared like a man, their imaginations ran away with them and they really did believe what they saw, which they thought was a little man."

It is interesting to note that Albert is not suggesting that Lankford, the Suttons, and the Taylors were engaged in inventing a hoax. Instead, with absolutely no evidence, Albert invented the tale of a monkey. That does not explain how the monkey was able to survive the shots fired at it, especially if it was as close to the house as the witnesses suggested. In other words, with shotguns and rifles being fired, someone should have hit it, and there should have been bits of monkey all over the farm land. And, remember, the various witnesses talked of a number of little men, not an individual.

But Albert wasn't through with the monkey theory.

"The home that Mrs. Lankford lived in was in a very run down condition and there were about eight people sleeping in two rooms. The window that was pointed out to be the one that she saw the small silver shining object about two and a half feet tall, that had its hands on the screen looking in, was a very low window and a small monkey could put his hands on the top of it while standing on the ground."

The final sentence said, "It is felt that the report cannot be substantiated as far as any actual object appearing in the vicinity at that time." It was then signed by Kirk.

What is interesting is that Albert, and then Kirk, was willing to ignore the report of the object because there was nothing solid to substantiate it. They were willing, however, to buy the monkey theory, though there was nothing to substantiate *it*. They needed a "little man," and they created one because a "monkey might have escaped."

Glennie Lankford might have inspired the little monkey story with her own statement. A handwritten letter signed on August 22, 1955, said:

"My name is Glennie Lankford age 50 and I live at Kelly Station, Hopkinsville Route 6, Kentucky.

"On Sunday night Aug 21, '55 about 10:30 P.M. I was walking through the hallway which is located in the middle of my house and I looked out the back door (south) and saw a bright silver object about two and a half feet tall appearing round. I became excited and did not look at it long enough to see if it had any eyes or moved.

I was about 15 or 20 feet from it. I fell backward, and then was carried into the bedroom.

"My two sons, Elmer Sutton aged 25 and his wife Vera age 29, J. C. Sutton age 21 and his wife Alene age 27 and their friends Billy Taylor age 21 and his wife June, 18 were all in the house and saw this little man that looked like a monkey.

"About 3:30 A.M. I was in my bedroom and looked out the north window and saw a small silver shinning (sic) object about 2½ feet tall that had its hands on the screen looking in. I called for my sons and they shot at it and it left. I was about 60 feet from it at this time. I did not see it anymore.

"I have read the above statement and it is true to the best of my knowledge and belief."

It was signed by Glennie Lankford and by John E. Albert. The copy in the Blue Book file was also signed by Charles Kirk.

This does tell us one thing. Albert was sure that the family had been frightened by something. He was busy trying to find what to him was a rational explanation. To do so, he had to convince himself that the religious services of the Holy Rollers would induce the hysteria of the witnesses even if the witnesses hadn't attended those sorts of religious services. He wanted to find anything to explain the sighting to his satisfaction. He would do anything but accept the idea the Suttons might have been accurately reporting what they had seen.

The file contains other documents that are somewhat confusing. There is a letter from the Civilian Saucer Intelligence of New York, a private group interested in flying saucers, sent to Dr. J. Allen Hynek in Cambridge, Massachusetts, on July 4, 1956, in which they described the Kelly (Hopkinsville) sighting. They wrote, "I believe you will be interested in Isabel Davis's data on the Hopkinsville landing, which includes two versions, with witness-checked drawings, made by two independent investigators on the day after the event. Thus we learn not only that the case is indubitably 'solid' (which Isabel's own investigation establishes), but also a good deal of information of interest to comparative biologists. Of course, the behaviour [sic] of the creatures was disconcertingly weird and incomprehensible, but we are faced with the fact, however much we might wish that it did not deviate so *markedly* from the sort of thing we are accustomed to on this planet. Probably you have not had this information before, as it appears that the Air Force investigators showed little interest in the drawings when offered them: quite probably they 'evaluated' the case as a hoax, which is what a biased person would naturally do on superficial examination."

Because the letter was in the Air Force file, it means that some information about it was known to the Air Force prior to the mysterious article that started Kirk on his belated investigation. It mentions the Air Force investigated in 1955, but everyone, including Kirk, suggests that no investigation was made at the time.

It seems that everyone is forgetting that Major Albert, after checking in with Campbell Air Force Base, was told to drive over to learn what he could. He confirms that he did go to the farmhouse, but apparently spoke to few people, including one of the sheriff's deputies.

There were other military personnel at the site within hours of the reports. These included an Army PFC Hodson, who wrote an article for the Clarksville, Tennessee, *Leaf Chronicle*. There is no evidence that Hodson was there in any sort of official capacity.

It seemed reasonable to me, after what I had read and heard about the 4602d Air Intelligence Service Squadron, that any reports might have been forwarded to them. But the records that I reviewed gave no indication that the 4602d conducted any sort of investigation of the case. While I don't have any of the reports of their investigation, I do have several maps produced by the 4602d that detail where sightings had been made over a given period. The map for August 1955 shows no reports or sightings from anywhere in Kentucky. The map for September contains a sighting in Ohio, close to the Kentucky border, but it is obviously something else. If Albert wrote a report and filed it prior to the 1957 investigation, it apparently went somewhere other than ATIC, Blue Book, or the 4602d.

This is just another sighting filled with things that make no sense. The logic of it argues that it was some kind of hoax, mistaken identity, or hysteria. The descriptions of the beings fit only, very generally, into the reported types of "aliens" that we know of today. No one has reported anything like this since.

The assault on the farmhouse was ridiculous. Although it is clear that the shotguns and rifles had no effect on the little creatures, there is no reason for them to return to be shot at again. They kept at it for several hours, reacting to the situation like teenagers who have managed to arouse and irritate a neighbor.

But what is important about this case is not the details of the sighting or the description of the little men—it is the way it was handled by the military. They wanted nothing to do with it, but had representatives there anyway. It sounds extremely haphazard, and I see nothing in the files to suggest that some kind of covert investigation was mounted. Albert drove over, took a few minutes to look around, then returned to his regular duties after making his decision about the case.

We cannot forget the Air Force attitude: this case doesn't count because it wasn't reported through normal channels. We'll just ignore the whole thing and hope that it goes away.

Air Force interest was rekindled when the head of Blue Book, in 1955, learned that an article about the sighting was going to be printed in a magazine. Unfortunately, there is nothing in the files to indicate if the article was ever printed, or if the Air Force reacted to nothing more than rumor.

What we are left with, then, is an interesting case of a farm family who believe they were attacked by aliens. Unfortunately, that is probably all that we are ever going to know for sure, despite all the discrepancies of this story.

CHAPTER 7

The Fall of 1957

If Air Force Colonel George M. Mattingley, Jr. is to be believed, Project Moon Dust began in 1957, probably as a response to the Soviet launch of Sputnik and the wave of UFO reports that began near Levelland, Texas, in early November of that year. Of course, that point can be debated simply because we have evidence that the Air Force has lied about Project Moon Dust and admitted the truth only after being caught.

Mattingley also suggested that the history of the UFO investigation went back to 1953 when it was discovered that the mission of the 4602d AISS had been completed with the end of the Korean War.

Moon Dust itself had a number of missions, although they were all closely related. According to the documents, its main function was to recover returning space debris from foreign sources. In other words, according to the people who designed it, Moon Dust was to recover Soviet-manufactured equipment that fell back to Earth.

However, the point is that by 1957, Moon Dust did exist and part of the mission was to investigate "reliable" UFO sightings. It seems that the 4602d, now designated as the 1006th, was involved in the Levelland sightings. Air Force regulations demanded it. Project Blue Book, the official UFO investigation, however, has records of investigations at this time, or rather, collecting data on the sightings.

Many have suggested that the November wave was inspired by the announcement of the launch of Sputnik II by the Soviets. Just after the Soviets made their announcement, several people in widely separated parts of Levelland, Texas, reported they had witnessed something strange close to the ground that stalled their car engines, affected the electrical systems, and dimmed their headlights.

Although the number of sightings had been growing weeks prior to the Sputnik launch, the Levelland reports were the ones to receive the publicity. Project Blue Book files, newspaper reports, and other documentation show, however, that the wave had its antecedents in the months before November.

A study shows that UFO sightings were increasing throughout 1957, beginning in late August. The upswing was slow but steady. What is interesting about this is the number of accounts in which the presence of the UFO adversely affected machinery and electrical systems on the ground. Before 1957, there had been similar reports, but during November the numbers skyrocketed.

The first hints came on August 22 when a couple near the Cecil Naval Air Station in Florida reported a bell-shaped UFO with two white lights suspended over the top. The object descended toward the car and passed it, moving along the highway. Their car stalled as the UFO hovered in front of them. The UFO finally shot off, but the car refused to start. The battery had been discharged.

Just over a week later, on September 1, near Le Mars, Iowa, another couple saw a bright flash in the sky. At the same time, their car engine died and the headlights failed.

On October 15, Robert Moudy was in his fields near Foster, Indiana, when a large, flat oval shot overhead. There was a pinkish flame from the underside of the craft, which changed to blue as it departed. The engine on his combine died, but when the UFO disappeared, it sputtered back to life.

These sightings and others like them are important because of the physical effects. There were many other sightings during this time frame, and several pictures were taken in widely separated locations. One of those received wide attention because it was one of the few to have been taken in color.

Ella Louise Fortune, while traveling near the White Sands Missile Range, not far from Holloman Air Force Base in Alamogordo, New Mexico, saw a large, glowing white cigar-shaped object. She took a single photograph of it, which has been published dozens of times by a variety of researchers and writers. It is an interesting picture. It is, however, a lenticular cloud. There is no doubt about it. I have seen similar clouds in that area on many different occasions.

But the point is, UFOs were being seen and reported

prior to the launch of Sputnik II late in the fall. While the satellite might have inspired people to go out to look up into the night sky, there is nothing to suggest that the wave of sighting reports was caused by the satellite launch. In fact, the most impressive series of sightings from the 1957 wave happened about the time the news of Sputnik was being reported throughout the world.

The country learned of the wave in early November when the Levelland, Texas, sightings were widely reported. Pedro Saucido was driving toward Levelland when a glowing UFO swept across the highway in front of his pickup truck. As it landed, not far away, the headlights of the truck dimmed and died and the engine quit. Saucido dived out the door and rolled out of the way. His passenger, Joe Salaz, sat terror-stricken in the truck, his eyes glued to the UFO. The blue-green glow faded into a red so bright that Salaz could not look directly at it. During the three or four minutes the torpedo-shaped object sat on the highway, both men believed they could hear noises from inside it. Then, as suddenly as it appeared, the UFO leapt into the sky, vanishing in seconds.

Saucido was afraid to continue on to Levelland because he might run into the object again. Instead he drove to another west Texas town and called the police in Levelland. A deputy sheriff listened to the story but laughed it off.

About an hour later, around midnight, Jim Wheeler saw a glowing red UFO sitting on the road near Levelland. He described it as egg-shaped rather than torpedo-shaped, but that could be little more than a matter of perspective. As he drew near, the headlights and engine of his car failed. When he got out of his car, the object lifted to two hundred feet and then disappeared. When the object was gone, his headlights came back on and he was able to restart his engine.

Five minutes later, a student from Texas Tech in nearby Lubbock, Ronald Martin, noticed that his car engine was beginning to run poorly. The ampmeter fell to discharge and jumped back again. The headlights went out and the engine died. He got out to look under the hood but found nothing wrong. As he turned, he saw a red UFO sitting on the road. Unsure of what to do, he got into his car and tried to start the engine. After a few minutes, the UFO rose into the air and the car started again.

About the same time, at a point nine miles north of Levelland, another man saw an object sitting on the road. Like the others, as he approached, his car engine died and the headlights went out. After a short period, the strange object climbed to two or three hundred feet, stopped glowing, and vanished from sight.

Police in Levelland received a number of calls during the night. About the time Wheeler made his call, Jose Alverez reported that he had seen an egg-shaped object that killed his car engine. A few minutes after that call, Frank Williams walked into the office to report a red UFO.

Law enforcement agencies in the area had now received a number of calls about the flying saucer. Many of the witnesses, separated by several miles, were reporting, basically, the same thing. That is, they were telling of a glowing UFO that either landed or hovered close to the road, and that stalled the engines of their cars. A range of other electromagnetic effects, such as dimming headlights and jumping ampmeters, were also reported. It was either some kind of elaborate practical joke, or there was some kind of strange craft near the ground in the Levelland area.

While deputies in the sheriff's office were sitting around, either discussing or laughing at the strange reports, James Long walked in to tell them that he was driving near Levelland when he came upon a landed, red-glowing UFO on the highway. His truck engine died and the headlights winked out. As Long got out of the truck and began to walk toward the object, it lifted off. When it was gone, his truck engine started easily and his headlights brightened.

By now the sheriff, Weir Clem, decided it was time to find out what was happening. He didn't care for the idea of chasing lights in the night sky, and like his deputies had ignored the first couple of reports. But now it was getting ridiculous. Too many people from too many areas were telling him about the red UFO. According to much of the UFO literature, there is a suggestion that thunderstorms in the area might have been causing some trouble. But a thunderstorm doesn't translate into a glowing red UFO that kills engines and dims headlights.

Clem, with Deputy Patrick McCullogh, drove the back roads near Levelland when, about 1:30, they saw the glowing UFO. It was in the distance, so they didn't experience any of the relayed side effects. About the same time, two highway patrol officers and Constable Lloyd Bollen saw the UFO. In all that night, five police officers reported the object, but none of them got very close to it.

Project Blue Book was alerted shortly after the sheriff saw the UFO. He had called Reese Air Force Base in nearby Lubbock. They, in turn, relayed the information on to ATIC in Dayton, Ohio. A copy of the weather report was included. Officers in Dayton looked at the notation there were thunderstorms in the vicinity and decided they had the answer: the witnesses had all witnessed ball lightning. They were so excited about seeing this extremely rare phenomenon that they probably killed their engines themselves. Of course, when the engines died, the headlights dimmed—or so the Air Force officers reasoned.

But what is interesting to our story here is that Air Force regulation 200-2 was in effect in November 1957. According to the 1954 version, reports of UFO sightings were to be made to the 4602d AISS. About two years later, a new version of AFR 200-2 was published. ATIC was again the responsible agency, with reports made to them. ATIC was authorized to contact the 1006th Field Activities Group (which had once been the 4602d AISS) at Fort Belvoir, Virginia.

The new regulation also mentioned that photographic evidence should be handled in a specific way. What is important is that AFM (Air Force Manual) 200-9 is to be used as a reference. The manual is listed as a classified document and, therefore, I have not been able to obtain a copy of the manual.

If the old version of the regulation was in effect, and there is no reason to suspect it wasn't, then the original required that the report go first to the investigative agency and then on to ATIC.

All of this might be of no importance in understanding how the sightings in Levelland were reported to Blue Book. The sightings were news the next day. Before the Air Force could enter the case, the news went national. In fact, in more than one newspaper, the story of Sputnik

II was side by side with the stories of the Levelland UFO. The Air Force had no choice but to issue statements attributed to the officers at Project Blue Book or admit there was something else going on.

But the UFOs were not done. Although Air Force officers believed they had found an answer for the Levelland reports, there were other sightings that were difficult to ignore. At White Sands Missile Range, between Alamogordo and Las Cruces, New Mexico, more sightings were made. These, beginning about two hours after the Levelland reports, were made by military policemen who were assigned to guard the range.

According to the reports, the two men watched a bright, egg-shaped object that fell a short distance before the light went out and they lost sight of it. Just before it hit the ground, or landed, the light came back on. They reported what they had seen to their immediate superiors, but no one seemed to care.

The next night, however, a second patrol at the White Sands Missile Range reported the same thing. The second patrol had not heard of the first report and knew nothing of it. In neither case were the military police officers close enough for the craft to stall their vehicle engines or dim the lights.

The Air Force suggested that because these sightings followed so closely those in Levelland, the sightings themselves were the result of a renewed interest in UFOs. Although the patrols were to protect one of the most important and secret bases in the Southwest, the Air Force was suggesting that the men on the patrols were not the best and brightest available. The missile base, until recently, had signs posted restricting photography even from the highways outside it.

On November 4, on the highway between Alamogordo and El Paso, Texas, near the little town of Orogrande, New Mexico, the car driven by James Stokes began to sputter. As the radio faded and the engine finally quit, Stokes glided to the side of the road. Ahead of him was a group of people standing near their cars, staring up, into the bright, blue sky. Looking up, Stokes saw a large, oval-shaped object diving toward the road. It flashed over the cars, flew toward the northwest, reversed itself for another pass, and then disappeared.

As the object passed over, Stokes thought he could feel heat from it. He believed it to be about three thousand feet above the ground and traveling about 760 miles an hour.

While watching, Stokes saw one of the men from the other cars take several photographs of the UFO. Stokes reported the information to a number of investigators, both official and private, but Stokes hadn't gotten either the man's name or his address.

That evening, several hours after the sighting, Stokes noticed a burning and itching sensation on his face and hands. The areas that had been exposed to the UFO had turned red, as if he had been sunburned.

On November 5, Stokes made an official report to the Air Force. Someone, maybe Stokes himself, alerted the news media, and reporters from all over the country began to call him. Eventually he left his post at Holloman Air Force Base. It was obvious to those present that Stokes was agitated, both by seeing the UFO and from the interest by the media.

It was also on November 5 that a Washington news release explained the Levelland sightings as exaggerations or misinterpretations of natural phenomena. Interestingly, at Holloman, an Air Force spokesman said that Stokes was an employee of the Air Force Missile Development Center, had been in the Navy for twenty-four years and, most importantly, was believed to be a competent and reliable observer. The Air Force, or rather those officers stationed at Holloman, believed what he was saying.

November 5 brought more reports of flying saucers and strange effects from them. Near Playa del Rey, California, Richard Kehoe reported that his car's engine failed. Like Stokes, Kehoe got out of his car and saw other drivers had had the same problem. Kehoe reported that he saw an egg-shaped craft hovering in a blue haze. Two creatures, who had yellow-green skin, got out to ask questions of the men. Once the aliens returned to their craft and it took off, the cars all started easily.

In fact, there were almost as many reports of UFOs stalling cars on November 5 as there had been from Levelland on November 2. Again, the majority of them were from the desert Southwest, including reports from Hobbs, New Mexico, which is not all that far from Levelland, near El Paso, and some distance from San Antonio.

The most interesting, though not necessarily the most reliable, of the reports came from Kearney, Nebraska. Reinhold O. Schmidt walked into the police station to report what he had seen. He claimed that while he was inspecting grain in a field he found what he thought, at first, was a wrecked balloon. As he approached it, he was stopped, and paralyzed, by a beam of light from the object.

Two men from the UFO, which Schmidt now knew wasn't a balloon, searched him for weapons and then invited him onboard the craft. Inside he saw two women and three men working on some sort of instrumentation. He was told that the beings meant him no harm. They refused to tell him where they were from, or maybe they couldn't make him understand it, but they did reveal that they might make an announcement about their presence in the near future. Schmidt was escorted from the ship. There was a flash of light, and the object vanished.

Police originally thought enough of Schmidt's bizarre story to check it out. They searched the area but could find no landing gear imprints. They found a greenish, oil-like substance that they took to Kearney College for analysis.

Schmidt enjoyed fleeting fame as a "contactee," that is, someone who claimed to have contact with the alien creatures piloting the UFOs. *Time* magazine reported on the Schmidt sighting, suggesting that if he did see it, no one would believe him, and people would think him crazy. If, on the other hand, he didn't see it, then he would be crazy. Either way, Schmidt found himself being accused of insanity simply for making his report.

In fact, later in the month, Schmidt was examined by psychiatrists who found him unstable and very ill. After his release from the hospital, however, he joined the lecture circuit and made many more UFO contacts.

The Schmidt and Kehoe sightings began a rash of similar occupant reports. Everett Clark, near his home in Dante, Tennessee, claimed he saw a landed UFO in a field. Near the object were four men and a woman trying to capture an agitated dog. Clark talked to them briefly before they returned to the UFO, which then shot quietly into the sky.

Friends and neighbors described Clark as intelligent and honest. But a search of the field revealed little in the way of physical evidence. Searchers did find an area where the grass was matted and looked as if something heavy had rested there for a short period. It suggested there might be something to Clark's story.

In Everittstown, New Jersey, John Trasco claimed he saw a brilliant, egg-shaped object hovering over his barn. Underneath the UFO was a small, putty-colored humanoid trying to grab his dog. Trasco shouted at the creature, but it said that it only wanted the dog. Trasco responded by telling it to leave the dog alone and get the hell out of there. The creature dropped the animal and fled toward the object. Once on board, the craft lifted straight up, disappearing quickly.

With the whole country talking about UFOs, newspapers reporting them, and news broadcasts telling of them, the Air Force jumped in again. On November 6 came an official press release claiming that the Air Force, in the ten years it had studied UFOs, had investigated just over 5,700 sightings. Of those, none had been confirmed as a craft from another world. There was no physical evidence or footprints or anything else that proved any of the so-called flying saucers were anything more than imagination, hallucination, or illusion.

At the same time a report came from Wright-Patterson Air Force Base near Dayton, Ohio, claiming that no physical evidence had ever been recovered. Although three percent of the sightings had not been explained, officers believed that if full information had been presented, solutions would have been found. What the spokesman didn't mention was that more than thirty percent of the sightings had been stamped as "insufficient data for a scientific analysis." What this meant was that no solution existed to explain the sighting, but it had been labeled so that it wasn't in the "unidentified" category. That raised the number of unexplained sightings to over thirty-three percent.

Even with the negative publicity, the number of sighting reports continued to grow. What is interesting is the Air Force still claimed there was no physical evidence, even with the number of cases in which witnesses said there had been interference with electrical systems and car engines. While not direct physical evidence, it was certainly evidence of something interacting with the environment.

On November 6, for example, a taxicab company owner and one of his drivers saw an egg-shaped object approach them near Santa Fe, New Mexico. As it flew over their car, the engine died and the dashboard clock stopped. One of the men also said that his wristwatch was stopped by the object, which climbed suddenly and disappeared to the southwest.

Near Danville, Illinois, two police officers spotted a brilliant white light that changed color to amber and then orange. They gave chase, but their radio would not function. Eventually the light flew out of sight.

And, finally, on that same day, Rene Gilham saw a UFO hovering over his farm. After it disappeared, he began to itch and his skin reddened, just as had been reported by Stokes. Before the rash disappeared, he was hospitalized for eleven days.

The next day, both the occupant reports and the electromagnetic effects continued. Melvin Stevens was driving near Meridian, Mississippi, when he saw an object on the highway. As he approached, three men about four and a half feet tall got out of the object and walked toward him. Stevens said they wanted to talk, but he couldn't understand them. When it was clear that Stevens couldn't understand them, they returned to their object and Stevens, badly frightened, drove to the closest police station.

Orogrande, New Mexico, little more than a wide spot in the road, again hosted a UFO sighting. Mr. and Mrs. Linsey Trent, driving near the town, noticed the speedometer jumping wildly from one end of the scale to the other. In the southwest was a metallic-appearing, oval-shaped UFO that continued moving in that direction until it disappeared.

Other sightings continued, many of them producing some of the physical evidence the Air Force denied existing. In Madison, Ohio, a woman was cleaning out her garden when a bright, triangular-shaped object flew over her house. She watched it for thirty minutes, but finally had to look away because her eyes began to hurt. A few days later, a rash developed over her body. Her family doctor said that it was a result of the UFO sighting. She was the third American to report that she had been injured, though not severely, by watching a UFO.

On the fifteenth, the Air Force announced that the whole series of sightings, beginning with those in Levelland, were the result of misinterpretations of natural phenomena. Included in this blanket statement was the sighting by Stokes. Five days later, Air Force officers changed their minds about Stokes. Now they believed his story to be a hoax, suggested by the series of misinterpretations and other natural phenomena reported outside of Levelland. They said they had tried to find the other witnesses to the UFOs but had failed.

They should have been able to find, at the very least, one other witness. Highway 54, which runs through Orogrande, is the main drag north out of El Paso that leads to the White Sands Missile Range and various military activities which are a part of the Fort Bliss military reservation. In other words, there is a very good possibility that some of those other witnesses were employees of the federal government.

Coral Lorenzen, one of the directors of APRO, however, did find another of the witnesses. According to her, one of them had gone to the hospital for treatment of his burns. When it was suggested that he talk to the Air Force, he refused. Given the climate, and the Air Force's attitude, his reluctance isn't surprising.

The Air Force, in their report of November 20, mentioned that Stokes had admitted to them he had radio problems in that area before his UFO sighting. This, I suppose, was to suggest that the radio interference had some sort of mundane explanation. Of course, it didn't provide an explanation for the failure of his engine, or the failures of the other cars stopped by the highway.

It was about this time the wave began to subside. It might be that public interest had waned. Newspaper reporters often say that a good story has a life of about ten days to two weeks. Some stories transcend that, but most fade from the public mind in that period. The flying saucer sightings that began on November 2 had been in the newspapers for about eighteen days. The newness of the story, and the public interest in it, was over.

Air Force investigators officially suggested that the sightings were the result of the Soviet announcement of the launch of Sputnik II, and that the first of the Levelland sightings was nothing more than coincidence. In fact, the sightings began almost at the time the announcement was being made. The odds are that few, if any, of the people in Levelland had heard about Sputnik.

The real proof that the sightings were not the result of the Soviet launch can be found. The wave didn't begin in November 1957 as Air Force investigators would have us believe, but long before that, and in Asia. Pictures of a UFO were taken in Japan in September, and the numbers of sightings were building from that point. They peaked about November 6 or 7, then dropped off.

In January, 1958, a series of pictures were taken off the coast of Brazil showing a "saturn"-shaped object. There were, literally, dozens of witnesses to the sightings. No investigation has produced a viable explanation for the pictures. Skeptics claim they are faked, but have no evidence that such is the case.

Project Blue Book files provide us with few clues about the Levelland sightings, or about the others reported at the time. Of course, we know, based on the documentation available, that the investigation was no longer in the hands of Project Blue Book officers. The real investigations were being conducted by someone else. By late 1957, the 4602d had evolved into the 1006th and the investigations continued. The public was kept in the dark, believing that UFOs were being investigated by Project Blue Book. Such wasn't the case.

CHAPTER 8

The History of
Project Moon Dust

When United States Senator Jeff Bingaman asked the Air Force about a classified project called Moon Dust, Lieutenant Colonel John E. Madison of the Congressional Inquiry Division, Office of Legislative Liaison, wrote, "There is no agency, nor has there ever been, at Fort Belvoir, Virginia, which would deal with UFOs or have any information about the incident in Roswell. In addition, there is no Project Moon Dust or Operation Blue Fly. Those missions have never existed."

What the documentation, now available thanks in part to the Freedom of Information Act, and the pioneering work of Clifford Stone, tells us is that Madison's letter to a United States senator is, at best, inaccurate. The question can be asked was he merely uninformed, or was he purposefully lying to a senator?

Stone, a researcher living in Roswell, New Mexico, challenged Madison's response with a series of documents that had been obtained through Freedom of Information Act requests. He pointed out that documents, originally classified as secret, and since downgraded, mentioned the code name Moon Dust, and specifically as a project for UFO-related materials. It also established as fact the location of the parent unit being at Fort Belvoir, Virginia.

The response to this documented information was another letter to Senator Bingaman, apparently from Madison's boss in the Congressional Liaison Office. Colonel George M. Mattingley, Jr., wrote, "This is in reply to your inquiry in behalf of Mr. Clifford E. Stone on the accuracy of the information we previously provided to your office. Upon further review of the case (which was aided by the several attachments to Mr. Stone's letter), we wish to amend the statements contained in the previous response to your inquiry."

Is it necessary here to suggest that the Air Force had been caught in a lie (or misinformation) to Senator Bingaman because the documents were available to positively refute them? We can look at this as a simple mistake, based on the lack of information available to the Congressional Liaison Office and Lieutenant Colonel Madison. It can be suggested that nothing nefarious was going on here. Madison simply wasn't aware of the classified Project Moon Dust and responded without checking the information as he should have done.

We could believe that except for the response written by Mattingley after Madison had been caught. It would seem that once they had been caught, they would be sure their information would be as accurate as possible.

Mattingley, in his letter to Bingaman to correct the previous mistakes, wrote, "In 1953, during the Korean War, the Air Defense Command organized intelligence teams to deploy, recover, or exploit at the scene downed enemy personnel, equipment, and aircraft. The unit with responsibility for maintaining these teams was located at Fort Belvoir, Virginia. As the occasion never arose to use these air defense teams, the mission was assigned to Headquarters, United States Air Force in 1957 and expanded to include the following peace-time functions: a) Unidentified Flying Objects (UFOs), to investigate reliably reported UFOs within the United States; b) Project MOON DUST, to recover objects and debris from space vehicles that had survived re-entry from space to earth; c) Operation BLUE FLY, to expeditiously retrieve downed Soviet Bloc equipment."

Having access to the previously classified 4602d records, I know that Mattingley's statements are not accurate. By the end of 1953, after the wave of summer sightings in 1952, after Blue Book had virtually ceased to exist, the 4602d was involved in UFO sighting investigations. Mattingley suggested the change came in 1957, but Mattingley is wrong. The only question is if he was as ill-informed as Madison, or if he was deliberately trying to suggest something else.

Mattingley also wrote, "These teams were eventually disbanded because of a lack of activity; Project MOON DUST teams and Operation BLUE FLY missions were similarly discontinued. The Air Force has no information that any UFOs were ever confirmed downed in the United States."

Again, this simply isn't the truth. We know from released documents that Moon Dust wasn't discontinued. Its code name was changed after it was compromised. Robert G. Todd, in a letter from the Air Force dated July 1, 1987, learned that the "nickname Project Moon Dust no longer officially exists." According to Colonel Phillip E. Thompson, deputy assistant chief of staff, Intelligence, "It [Project Moon Dust] has been replaced by another name that is not releaseable. FTD's [Foreign Technology Division, headquartered at Wright-Patterson] duties are listed in a classified passage in a classified regulation that is being withheld because it is currently and properly classified."

And, we know, from documentation, much of it recovered from State Department records, that Moon Dust teams were notified and dispatched for various cases, some examples of which will follow here. It should be made clear that most of these cases deal with material and wreckage that is clearly of terrestrial origin. The point here is not to prove an extraterrestrial connection, but to confirm the use of Moon Dust teams, which contradicts the statements made by Colonel Mattingley to Senator Bingaman. The messages also confirm Moon Dust interest in UFOs and the involvement of the State Department.

On the night of March 25–26, 1968, four objects fell in an area of Nepal. The American embassy in Kathmandu, in a secret message dated July 23, alerted the 1127th USAF Field Activities Group, which had once been the 4602d, and the 1006th at Fort Belvoir, that they expected

Air Force investigators as well as civilian researchers agree that this picture offered as proof of flying saucers was a hoax.

One of the many gates leading to Wright-Patterson Air Force Base where part of the UFO investigation was housed.

A possible explanation for some flying saucer reports. This object, launched under balloons, was used to photograph rocket launches from White Sands in the 1950s.

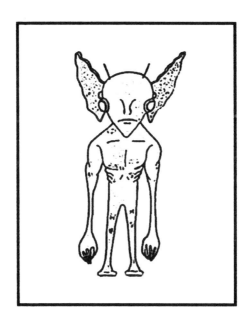

The creature as reported by those who were "attacked" during the Kelly-Hopkinsville siege of August 1955.

PROJECT 10073 RECORD CARD

1. DATE	2. LOCATION		12. CONCLUSIONS
☒ 21-22 Aug 55	Hopkinsville, Kentucky		☐ Was Balloon ☐ Probably Balloon ☐ Possibly Balloon
3. DATE-TIME GROUP Local 2000 - 0300	4. TYPE OF OBSERVATION		☐ Was Aircraft ☐ Probably Aircraft ☐ Possibly Aircraft
	☒ Ground-Visual	☐ Ground-Radar	
GMT	☐ Air-Visual	☐ Air-Intercept Radar	
5. PHOTOS	6. SOURCE		☐ Was Astronomical ☐ Probably Astronomical ☐ Possibly Astronomical
☐ Yes ☒ No sketch	civilian		
7. LENGTH OF OBSERVATION	8. NUMBER OF OBJECTS	9. COURSE	☐ Other UNIDENTIFIED ☐ Insufficient Data for Evaluation ☒ Unknown
12hours	multiple	L U/A	
10. BRIEF SUMMARY OF SIGHTING		11. COMMENTS	
LITTLE MEN. SEE CASE FILE.		UNIDENTIFIED	

ATIC FORM 329 (REV 26 SEP 52)

Official Project Blue Book card showing the Air Force considered the case to be "Unidentified."

Captain Gregory   September 10, 1956

J. A. Hynek

Hopkinsville Case

The Chief of Police in Hopkinsville is ▓▓▓▓▓▓▓▓▓▓▓▓. It was he
who stated that the affair was investigated by Air Force officers
from Fort Campbell. I understand that MP's and a Pfc from Fort
Campbell investigated at the farmhouse on late Monday afternoon.
The Pfc was a Mr. Hodson and his account and pictures were published in the Clarksville Tennessee Leaf Chronicle.

Chief ▓▓▓▓▓▓▓ also stated that the affair had been investigated by
two men from an unidentified agency at Standiford Field in Louisville,
a commercial field. The Kentucky State Police investigated the case
and their report and available sketches are on file with Trooper
Riley's case report at Frankfort, Kentucky. Attached is a list of
all people concerned in the case.

A Miss Isabelle Davis is preparing a full-scaled report, of which I
shall receive a copy, after it has been cross-checked by the people
involved.

Letter showing Air Force interest in the Kelly-Hopkinsville
case even though the Air Force denied that interest.

The sightings outside Levelland, Texas, in November 1957 that sparked the wave that would continue until December of that year.

Investigators from Reese Air Force Base in Lubbock were dispatched to investigate the Levelland sightings.

6 NOVEMBER 1957 SIGHTINGS

DATE	LOCATION	OBSERVER	EVALUATION
6	United States /21 Reports (FOLDER #3)		Astro (AURORA)
6	N of Seoul, Korea	Military	Balloon
6	Philippines	Military & Civilian	Astro (VENUS)
6	Kaisong, Korea (FOLDER #3)	Malti	Astro (METEOR)
6	Farmingdale, New York	Bahn	Insufficient Data
6	Milwaukee, Wisconsin	Military	Insufficient Data
6	Anaheim, California (FOLDER #3)	Lendford (PHOTO)	Other (HOAX)
6	Shiroi AB, Japan	Military	Astro (METEOR)
6	Whiteman AFB, Missouri (FOLDER #3)	Military (RADAR)	Other (FALSE TARGET)
6	Georgia, Florida, Alabama	Multi (6 cases)	Astro (METEOR)
6	New Orleans, Louisiana	Accardo	Insufficient Data
6	Denbigh, North Dakota (CASE MISSING)	Civilian	Astro (VENUS)
6	Lake County, Ohio	Markell	Insufficient Data
6	Robbins AFB, Georgia	Green	Other (UNRELIABLE REPORT)
6	Washington Island, Wisconsin	Eaton	Aircraft
6	Kogashima, Japan	Military RADAR & Vis	1. Aircraft
			2. Radar (WX Effects)
6	Danbury, Connecticut	Morzenski	Insufficient Data
6	Atlantic 43.20N 17.30W	Military	Astro (METEOR)
6	Atlantic 35.22N 74.14W	Civilian Ship	Astro (AURORA)
6	Laredo AFB, Texas	Military (RADAR)	Other (ANOMALOUS PROP)
6	Vassalboro, Maine	Pierce	Astro (VENUS)
6	Selma, North Carolina	Broadwell	Insufficient Data
6	Oak Tree, New Jersey	Lasko	Insufficient Data
6	Haverhill, Massachusetts	Chadwick	Aircraft
6	Harrisburg, Pennsylvania	Stewart	Insufficient Data
6	Columbus, Ohio (CASE MISSING)	Civilian	Aircraft
6	Buffalo, New York	Loghran	Astro (VENUS)
6	Abington, West Virginia	Booth	Aircraft
6	New York, Maine	Multi (6 cases)	Astro (VENUS)
6	Great Neck, New York	Frank	Aircraft
6	Ft Knox, Kentucky	Conway	Insufficient Data
6	St Albans, West Virginia (CASE MISSING)	COC	Astro (METEOR)
6	Rydal, Georgia	Bishop	Aircraft
6	Macon, Georgia	Multi (Brown)	Other (UNRELIABLE REPORT)
6	Englishtown, New Jersey	Silvio	Astro (METEOR)
6	Oconto, Wisconsin	Dedlette	Insufficient Data
6	Boerne, Texas	McGregor	UNIDENTIFIED
6	Montville, Ohio (FOLDER #3)	Olden, Moore	Astro (METEOR)
6	Cleveland, Ohio	Jetty	Other (Searchlight)
6	Hempstead, Long Island, New York	Merkle	Aircraft
6	Chilo, Ohio (CASE MISSING)	Civilian (COC)	Other (UNRELIABLE RPT)
6	Turner AFB, Georgia	Military	Astro (METEOR)
6	Bellmoor, Long Island, New York	Berger	Insufficient Data
6	El Paso, Texas	Dominguez, Flores	Astro (METEOR)
6	Greensboro, North Carolina	Bell	Aircraft
6	Lakewood, California	La Grande/Cole/Keane	Aircraft
6	Albuquerque, New Mexico	Military	Astro (VENUS)

The official index of the Project Blue Book sightings. This page is only for those reported on November 6, 1957.

Charles Moore and his team working near Array, New Mexico, not all that far from Socorro, sighted a UFO. Moore is one of the few people to report a UFO on more than one occasion and not be labeled unreliable.

George "Jud" Roberts of radio station KGFL reported that he received telephone calls from Washington and the FCC warning him not to broadcast an interview with UFO witness Mac Brazel. If they did, they would lose their license.

UFO researcher Clifford Stone sparked the interest of many in both the 4602d AISS and the Project Moon Dust.

One of the best repositories of information about the space age is located in Alamogordo, New Mexico.

full cooperation with the government of Nepal. The subject of the message was . . . MOON DUST.

It is clear from the message that the debris was readily identifiable to the staff at the embassy in Nepal. They had seen photographs of three of the items but had not been allowed to inspect the fourth. They noted that a "technical team should not be sent unless visual examination of the fourth object is felt essential."

This is, of course, a backward way of getting to the point. However, the embassy did prove that technical teams were available and that they were dispatched. The composition of those teams was described in another document that surfaced in the various Freedom of Information Act requests made.

Stone provided me with a copy of a document created in November 1961. It seemed to be directing the creation or the reinforcement of AFCIN Intelligence Team personnel. That document, however, is now wrapped in controversy because *two* versions have been discovered.

First, we must understand what this document is. The problem, according to the opening statement is, "To provide qualified personnel to AFCIN intelligence teams." The document has a section deleted and then, in paragraph 2, subsection C, says, "In addition to their staff duty assignments, intelligence team personnel have peacetime duty functions in support of such Air Force Projects such as Moon Dust, Blue Fly, and UFO, and other AFCIN directed quick reaction projects which require intelligence team operational capabilities (see Definitions)."

It should be pointed out that this document ties Moon Dust, Blue Fly and UFOs together. It points out that their assignments already existed, and they were already assigned personnel.

The definitions mentioned appear in paragraph 5. It covers not only those assigned to the teams, but also the terms used in the document itself. What is important here is the fact that "Moon Dust," "Blue Fly," and "UFO" are all parts of the definitions. Moon Dust is defined "As a specialized aspect of its overall material exploitation program, Headquarters USAF has established Project Moon Dust to locate, recover and deliver descended foreign space vehicles."

Although Mattingley defines Blue Fly as an operation to "expeditiously retrieve downed Soviet Bloc equipment," this document suggests that Blue Fly was "established to facilitate expeditious delivery to FTD of Moon Dust or other items of great technical intelligence interest." Certainly, Soviet Bloc equipment would fit into that definition, but it covers other items, including UFO-related debris, as well.

And finally, under definitions, it says, "Unidentified Flying Objects (UFO): Headquarters USAF has established a program for investigation of reliably reported unidentified flying objects within the United States. AFR 200-2 delineates 1127th collection responsibilities."

The second version of this document, one that I have seen, is exactly the same as the first, but contains a handwritten note that says it was a draft proposal and that it was never implemented. Robert Todd located this version. It is clearly the same as the first document, which I have in my possession, the difference being a handwritten note at the top. Barry Greenwood of Citizens

Against UFO Secrecy suggested to me that the version Stone has, a copy of which he supplied to me, is the same as the version Todd has, with the exception of the handwritten note. According to Greenwood, the two versions are the same, and the source is the same, but someone inside the UFO community removed the handwritten note before releasing it to other UFO researchers. Greenwood seems to suspect Stone of having altered the document for the purpose of advancing his belief in Project Moon Dust and the missions it carried out.

Stone, on the other hand, claims that he received his version from military sources without the handwritten note. His sources were not the same as those used by Todd, and he didn't receive his copy from Todd. Stone also makes the point that the handwritten note is irrelevant and refers only to the "Action Recommended" section at the end of the document. The other material, referring to "Factors Bearing on the Problem" and the "Discussion" reflects the situation as it already existed. In other words, the discussion about the composition of the teams and their missions was not a suggestion to develop those teams. The "not implemented" statement referred to adding, or tasking, additional Air Force personnel with Moon Dust.

So what we have, then, based on the documentation, including the disputed AFCIN intelligence team documents, are two letters from the Air Force to a United States senator that do not reflect accurate information. Even after being caught once, the Air Force came back with information that was less than perfect. And even if Todd and Greenwood are right in asserting that the November 1961 document was merely a draft, it provides information about the various projects and operations that were in existence at the time.

In fact, the information about the composition of the intelligence teams is corroborated by other documents I recovered through both the Freedom of Information Act and general research conducted through the Air Force Archives at Maxwell Air Force Base in Alabama.

As mentioned elsewhere, I learned that members of the 4602d and later the 1127th learned parachuting, horseback riding and animal packing, skiing, mountain climbing and various other survival skills. The November document, under "Criteria" notes, "Intelligence personnel can perform effectively only with an adequate background of training and experience. Inadequately qualified personnel in such assignment would be a liability rather than an asset to successful accomplishment of the mission."

The question that must be asked is if the Moon Dust personnel were ever used. Clearly, since the mission began in 1953 and continues today, as far as we can tell from the information available, we must answer, "Yes." This, too, is a contradiction to the letters from Madison and Mattingley.

Stone, in his response to the Madison letter, enclosed two debriefings of Soviet pilots in which UFO sightings were mentioned. If there was no interest in UFOs, Stone wondered what purpose was served by including that information. Mattingley replied, "Enclosures 3 and 4 of Mr. Stone's letter pertain to debriefings of two Soviet sources who were being interviewed for possible military information of interest. Their recounts of UFO sightings, even though they had occurred many years earlier, were included in the report for historical interest and were incidental to the main purpose of the report."

It is possible that Mattingley, in this respect, was being candid. But the question that can be asked is what historical interest can there be in sightings of objects that, according to the Air Force, do not exist? Why waste valuable time and effort recounting old UFO sightings? Just what was the historical context to which he referred?

Stone, in his rebuttal, argued, "Inclosures 3 and 4 were once classified Air Force Intelligence Reports. Inclosure 3 was IIR 1 517 0002 88, dated November 25, 1987, entitled UFO siting [sic] in Shadrinsk. This report deals with UFO sightings which took place in 1974. Inclosure 4 was IIR 1 517 0619 90, dated December 7, 1989, entitled Soviet Aircrew Sightings of Unexplained Phenomena. This report deals with UFO sightings that occurred in 1984 and later."

Stone asks, and rightly so, "What was the main purpose of these reports?? They deal directly with UFO sightings and make no reference to Soviet missiles, or MIGs, or tanks. So what was the main purpose of these reports to which UFOs were incidental???"

So exactly what was Project Moon Dust? Did the Air Force ever activate it? Did the team members ever participate in the retrieval of an alien spacecraft?

We have a time frame for the beginning of the project from Mattingley's letter: 1953. As we have seen from the project's history, this was apparently an outgrowth of the situation in the summer of 1952. If Moon Dust came into existence at that time, to take over the investigative duties that had formerly rested with Blue Book, we have one set of answers. Blue Book was too public and the military was afraid of what might be spilled into the public arena because of that.

We must remember that in that time, at least publicly, the Air Force was telling us that there was no evidence for the existence of UFOs. If they were convinced of the accuracy of that statement, then why form teams to recover the material?

Teams were formed. We've already seen the documentation about it. And I know they were deployed. Again, there is documentation, but there is also personal testimony. Brigadier General Arthur Exon was the base commander at Wright-Patterson Air Force Base in the mid-1960s. During an interview I conducted with him in May 1990, he said, "Well, the way this happened to me was that I would get a call and say that the crew or the team was leaving and they knew . . . There was such and such a time and they wanted an airplane and pilots to take X number of people to wherever . . . They might be gone two or three days or might be gone a week."

According to Exon, these were officers assigned to the Washington, D.C., area. They would fly into Wright-Patterson on commercial flights and then deploy on military aircraft. Their missions, according to Exon, were to investigate UFO sightings. He mentioned a case in Arizona where the craft had touched down and left a burned area.

These were, according to Exon, priority missions. He didn't ask questions, just alerted the proper facilities and scheduled the flights using their aircraft. It is clear, however, that these were Moon Dust teams engaging in the collection of UFO-related material.

Exon retired about the time that Project Blue Book was closed. His information doesn't suggest that any activity survived the end of Blue Book. However, it must be noted that Blue Book was based at Wright-Patterson, and if the officers coming into Ohio had been part of Blue Book, they would have already been there. In other words, it suggests an agency outside of Blue Book was interested in UFOs.

The other documents we've seen show that Moon Dust survived the end of Project Blue Book. There are, of course, the State Department records, and Colonel Thompson's letter telling Todd that the name, Moon Dust, had been changed.

Moon Dust became the real investigation of UFOs, the secret study that all of us claimed existed and that the Air Force denied. It was carried out by specially trained intelligence personnel. And, its existence was denied by the Air Force despite the facts.

Now we have all the data.

CHAPTER 9

Flying Saucers and Disappearing Airplanes

We are told that flying saucers are not real and that they pose no threat to national security. We are told that the few "scientific" studies that have been completed suggest there is no evidence that UFOs are real. Flying saucers are a myth, an illusion, or just misidentification. Flying saucers are no more real than the pools of water seen in the distance on the desert at high noon. Flying saucers simply do not exist.

Yet, when we study the history of the phenomenon, we learn that a number of aircraft have vanished when flying saucers were near. In some cases these were Air Force fighters that were sent up to intercept strange things seen on radar, but that never return. Sometimes aircraft were seen close to UFOs and the aircraft never landed. And sometimes there was radio contact between the plane and ground controllers when the aircraft vanished.

These are not the fighters that have crashed chasing UFOs, such as the Thomas Mantell case of January 1948. Mantell, a decorated pilot of World War II, chased a large object over the Godman Army Air Field–Fort Knox, Kentucky, area. At the time, it was believed that he, along with tower operators, had misidentified Venus. Further research, including a study of the Air Force file which I managed to obtain, suggest that Mantell was chasing one of the then-classified Skyhook balloons. Descriptions and drawings contained in the file seem to confirm this.

Though Mantell was killed during the attempted intercept, that seems to be a side effect of the incident. Mantell apparently climbed above safe levels, had no oxygen equipment on his aircraft, and then blacked out due to oxygen starvation. It is a tragic event, but it is not the result of extraterrestrial intervention.

There have been, however, other cases in which aircraft, either intercepting or flying near UFOs, have vanished. These cases are documented by official files and eyewitness testimony. These cases suggest that something other than misidentification of natural phenomena, or terrestrially manufactured objects, is the culprit.

In 1953, a jet interceptor with a crew of two disappeared while the jet and the unidentified object were being watched on military radar. It was on the evening of November 23, when the radar at Truax Air Force Base picked up an unidentified return over the Soo Locks area and in restricted airspace. Because of that, a fighter was scrambled from Kinross Field to intercept and identify the intruder.

The official accident report, made by Air Force investigators, said:

"F-98c, Serial No. 51-5853A, assigned to the 433rd Fighter-Interceptor Squadron, Truax Field, Wisconsin, was reported missing over Lake Superior at approximately 2000 Eastern Standard Time (EST) on 23 November 1953. The aircraft was scrambled from Kinross Air Force Base, Michigan to participate in an Active Air Defense Mission. The aircraft and air crew had not been located as of 1 January 1954.

"On 23 November 1953, F-89C, Serial No. 51-5853A, was scrambled by 'Naples' GCI [ground control intercept] to intercept and identify an unknown aircraft flying over Lake Superior. The interceptor became airborne from Kinross Air Force Base, Michigan, at 1833 EST. Original radar control of the aircraft was maintained by 'Naples' GCI and at 1841 EST control was transferred to 'Pillow' GCI. The aircraft was flying at 30,000 feet at this time. At 1847 EST, at the request of 'Pillow,' the aircraft descended to 7,000 feet to begin the interception. Location of the aircraft was then approximately 150 miles northeast from Kinross AFB and over northern Lake Superior. At 1851 EST, the interceptor pilot was requested to turn to a heading of 20 degrees to the cut-off vector. After the turn was completed, the pilot was advised the unidentified aircraft was at 11 o'clock, 10 miles distant. Radar returns from both aircraft were then seen to merge on 'Pillow's' radarscope. The radar return from the other aircraft indicated it was continuing on its original flight path, while the return from the F-89 disappeared from the GCI station's radarscope.

"The unknown aircraft being intercepted was a Royal Canadian Air Force Dakota (C-47), Serial No. VC-912, flying from Winnipeg to Sudbury, Canada. At the time of the interception, it was crossing Northern Lake Superior from west to east at 7,000 feet.

"The pilot [Lt. Felix Moncla, Jr.] and radar observer [Lt. R. R. Wilson] were assigned to the 433rd Fighter-Interceptor Squadron, Truax AFB, Wisconsin. They were on temporary duty at Kinross AFB, Michigan, while the base's regularly assigned personnel were firing gunnery at Yuma, Arizona. The pilot had a total of 811:00 hours of which 121:00 hours were in F-89 type aircraft. He had 101:00 instrument hours and 91:50 hours night time. The radar observer had a total of 206:45 hours of which 11:30 hours were at night.

"Search for the missing aircraft was conducted by both USAF and RCAF [Royal Canadian Air Force] aircraft without success. Although 80 percent area coverage was reported, heavy snows precluded effective land search. All civilian reports of seeing or hearing the aircraft were investigated with negative results."

The Air Force insisted then, and continues to insist, that the Canadian Air Force cargo plane was the UFO spotted on radar, despite denials by the Canadian government. The explanation also fails to account for the merging of the two blips with only the Canadian aircraft surviving. If the F-89 had hit the Canadians, surely the Canadians would have reported the incident. Surely there would have been damage to the Canadian aircraft. Instead, no physical evidence has ever been presented to suggest that such a midair collision took place.

For a year the Air Force stuck to the C-47 story before changing it to an RCAF jet. The Canadians, however, weren't going to take the blame. They again denied they had any aircraft in the area to account for the unidentified object. Whatever Moncla had chased, it hadn't been a Canadian aircraft of any type.

In 1976, before the Air Force transferred the Project Blue Book files to the National Archives in Washington, D.C., I had a chance to review them at Maxwell Air Force Base. This was before Air Force officers went through, taking out the names of all the witnesses. One of the first files that I asked to see was the Kinross case.

There was a note saying that the file had been opened because of all the inquiries to the Air Force about the crash. It made it clear that the file was an aircraft accident and not a UFO sighting, despite the radar case and the lack of a solid explanation.

I was surprised to see that the file itself contained only two sheets of paper. One of them was a single sheet that suggested Moncla had died chasing the Canadian aircraft. We've already seen what the Canadian government thought of that answer.

The other was a galley from a book by UFO debunker Dr. Donald H. Menzel. He suggested that many writers had used the case to prove that UFOs were extraterrestrial and possibly hostile to us. Menzel accepted the Air Force answers for the disappearance. All of them. Each time they were changed.

But the case doesn't end there. I had an opportunity to interview one of the officers who was at the base when Moncla disappeared. He told me that there were two schools of thought about the incident. One was that Moncla had crashed straight into the lake, the plane sinking intact. If that happened, there wouldn't be any surface wreckage for rescue crews to find, and probably no oil slick to mark its passage.

The second, larger school, according to the officer, seemed to think that the object, whatever it was, had "taken" Moncla, Wilson, and the jet intact. He told me that the two blips were seen to merge, just as the official documentation shows. To those on the scene in November 1953, it meant that the UFO had either somehow kidnapped the jet or had destroyed it, possibly by accident.

Before I went to Maxwell AFB to search the Project Blue Book records, the officer asked me about the Kinross case and told me a few other things. There had been a number of other UFO sightings in that area about the same time. In fact, according to him, a friend had been paced by a UFO for a short period of time. He and his wingman were concerned because they knew what had happened to Moncla a few weeks earlier. When the UFO did nothing but stay with them, the flight leader decided it was time for action. He called the break and they both turned toward the UFO. It disappeared in a burst of speed.

The officer told me that the report had been properly filed and he was interested in what the official conclusion was. He asked if I would look for it. I said that I would and I did. But it wasn't there. There was no indication of any UFO reports from either Kinross or Truax, and nothing from that area of the United States. The officer told me he was surprised because he knew that reports had been filed. He knew that other pilots had reported UFOs, as demanded by military regulation.

Although the Kinross sighting is the most famous of the cases of disappearing aircraft, it is not the only one to have been reported by the UFO community. Sometimes, in the course of one investigation, someone will say something that will lead in a different direction. While trying to learn more about the Roswell crash, I interviewed former Air Force Brigadier General Arthur Exon.

Exon had been at Wright Field in July 1947 and told me about some of the activities that went on there just after the Roswell crash. Later, he had been transferred and, during the mid-1950s, as a full colonel, had been working at the Pentagon. It was during this time that a flight of four aircraft disappeared.

According to Exon, they had been scrambled to chase something from a field in either Tennessee or Kentucky. He couldn't remember which. All four fighters neared the object, and all were lost.

Exon said, "And they don't know what happened. If they went out overseas or out over water . . ."

He was trying to say that if they had been lost over an ocean, then it might be understandable. The ocean hides many things, and four aircraft could easily disappear just as huge ships are sometimes swallowed whole. But over dry land it is extremely difficult to lose all trace of an aircraft. Or in this case, lose track of all four.

I asked, specifically, if any wreckage had ever been found. Exon said, "Not that I know of. That's been investigated before and it's a matter of record and it's kind of a mysterious thing."

Records of that kind of disaster would be interesting to review, but there was nothing that I could find. I did search the *New York Times Index*, but found no reference to a flight of fighters disappearing together at any time between 1953 and 1959. That, of course, didn't mean it didn't happen, just that it wasn't reported in the newspaper.

It was also in the mid-1950s that Eugene Metcalf of Paris, Illinois, reported the disappearance of a jet fighter. According to the information in my files, and the sworn affidavit by Metcalf, "On March 9, 1955, at approximately 5:50 P.M. I witnessed the 'plane-napping' of a jet plane while standing in my backyard at Paris, Illinois. The plane was coming toward me from the southwest and was traveling in a northeasterly direction. As I stood watching this plane, an odd-looking craft came from behind the plane and just swallowed it. The U.F.O. had an opening that was in my line of vision, and through the opening it took the plane. After this, the U.F.O. hovered and pulsated and churned up and down. Then it seemed to whirl and lift upwards.

"While going through these gyrations, vapor came

from porthole-like openings around the bottom part. The plane and the U.F.O. were in perfect view, and stood out clearly against the sky. The object was bright silver and I heard no noise. The U.F.O. was very big and bell-shaped."

The affidavit was signed by Metcalf on April 2, 1957, in Edgar County, Illinois. Of course, signing the affidavit doesn't mean that the event took place. However, going to that much trouble suggests that Metcalf believed it.

In fact, according to the documentation, Metcalf "... sent letters describing this action to the following: The Chicago *American* newspaper: Comment, none. *Newsweek*: comment, would like to print letter if room is found; Civil Air Patrol, comment, first said was American craft, then said they didn't know. Who does? Federal Bureau of Investigation: they thanked me for my information, so maybe some one of them will get their eyes opened."

Len Stringfield, a longtime UFO researcher who lived in Cincinnati, Ohio, did some investigation on the case in 1956. I have the notes of Stringfield's preliminary work, which were dictated on August 26, 1956. According to the notes, Len asked a friend, identified only as Fitch, of Cleveland, to investigate Metcalf. Fitch believed that Metcalf was sincere, and believed that he saw exactly what he claims to have seen. There is a note that Fitch is also considered to be reliable and intelligent.

There should be discussion about the reliability of the lone witness. Metcalf was alone in his report. Nothing else has ever surfaced about the disappearance of the aircraft and no one seems to have reported either the aircraft or the pilot missing. Maybe it was a vivid hallucination by Metcalf. Maybe he dreamed it and believed it to be real. Without additional information, the case is an interesting abnormality, but that is all it is.

A particular report from Australia, however, doesn't suffer from those problems. The pilot was in contact with a flight-following service when the UFO appeared. The pilot was on the radio when the UFO apparently decided that it was time to make him disappear.

On October 21, 1978, Frederick Valentich, a twenty-year-old instructor pilot, took off from Moorabin, Victoria, Australia, heading toward King Island, Tasmania. He was flying a Cessna 182 designated Delta Sierra Juliet, which was part of its registration number. The flight following was with the Melbourne Flight Service Unit and controller Steve Robey.

Just after 7:00 P.M., Valentich contacted Melbourne and asked if there was any traffic, that is, other aircraft below him at five thousand feet. The answer was, "No known traffic."

"I am—seems [to] be a large aircraft below five thousand," said Valentich.

"What type of aircraft?"

"I cannot affirm. It [has] four bright . . . it seems to me like landing lights . . . The aircraft has just passed over me at least a thousand feet above."

Flight following (Robey) said, "Roger, and it is a large aircraft? Confirm."

". . . Unknown due to the speed it's traveling. Is there any Air Force aircraft in the vicinity?"

"No known aircraft in the vicinity."

"It's approaching now from due east towards

me." Valentich was silent for several moments and then added, "It seems to me that he's playing some sort of game. He's flying over me two to three times at speeds I could not identify."

"Roger. What is your actual level?"

"My level is four and a half thousand. Four five zero zero."

"Confirm you cannot identify the aircraft," said Robey.

"Affirmative."

"Roger. Stand by."

Valentich then said, "It's not an aircraft. It is . . ." There was a brief silence.

"Can you describe the, er, aircraft?"

"As it's flying past, it's a long shape. [I cannot] identify more than [that it has such speed] . . . [It is] before me right now, Melbourne."

"And how large would the . . . er . . . object be?"

"It seems like it's stationary. What I'm doing right now is orbiting, and the thing is just orbiting on top of me. Also it's got a green light and sort of metallic. It's shiny . . . the outside . . . It's just vanished . . . Would you know what kind of aircraft I've got? Is it [a] military aircraft?"

Robey said, "Confirm that the . . . aircraft just vanished."

"Say again."

"Is the aircraft still with you?"

"Approaching from the southwest . . . The engine is rough idling. I've got it at twenty-three twenty-four, and this is . . ."

"Roger. What are your intentions?"

"My intentions are, ah, to go to King Island. Ah, Melbourne, that strange aircraft is hovering on top of me again . . . It is hovering, and it's not an aircraft . . ."

That was the last message that anyone received from Frederick Valentich. There were, according to a number of sources, an additional seventeen seconds of sound. There was no voice, just metallic scraping. And then there was just dead silence. Repeated attempts by Robey to raise Valentich failed. Valentich, and his aircraft, seemed to have vanished.

When Valentich failed to arrive at King Island at his estimated arrival time, other light aircraft began to make a visual search, but found nothing. Although Valentich's aircraft was equipped with a radio survival beacon, nothing was heard from it.

The Royal Australian Air Force (RAAF) Orion, a long-range maritime reconnaissance aircraft, conducted a tracking crawl following the course taken by Valentich's Cessna and continued searching all day Sunday. They continued their search on Monday and an oil slick was spotted. Samples of the slick, taken by ships dispatched to the area, showed that the material was marine diesel fuel and not aviation gas. Clearly it was not from Valentich's missing Cessna.

After several days, with no positive results, the search operations were quietly suspended. Although they had found debris in the general area of where Valentich and the aircraft would have disappeared, the material was identified as packing cases and plastic bags. It had nothing to do with Valentich or his missing aircraft.

Australia's Bureau of Air Safety released a report in May 1982, three and a half years after the event, explaining that they really knew nothing about it. They were unable to determine the location of the "occurrence," they didn't know the time that it happened, they believed it was fatal, but there was no body or wrecked airplane, and they had no opinion as to why the aircraft disappeared. In other words, they knew nothing and added nothing to the case.

Over the years, a number of explanations for the disappearance have been offered. Bill Chalker, an Australian UFO researcher, spoke to A. Woodward, who had signed the official Aircraft Accident Summary Report. Woodward stressed that the event was an aircraft accident and then gave a series of mundane explanations ranging from pilot disorientation and suicide to the idea that the aircraft had been struck by a meteorite and knocked out of the sky. Woodward did, however, concede that there was no positive answer. He was merely speculating.

Another Australian, Harley Klauer, suggested two explanations for the incident. He believed that Valentich had either been knocked down by drug runners or by an electrical discharge from a lenticular cloud. I assume this discharge is what we call lightning.

Later Klauer abandoned the drug smuggler explanation but did say he had direct evidence from a series of photographs taken of a sunset on October 21, 1978, that is, on the date Valentich disappeared. Klauer suggested the photographs showed the aircraft exploding. The problem, however, is that photographs were taken prior to Valentich's last radio transmission. An explosion also would have left debris scattered on the water.

More than four years after the disappearance, press reports surfaced that Valentich's aircraft had finally been found. An independent film producer, Ron Cameron, said that two divers had approached him claiming they had found the wreckage of Valentich's aircraft, deep underwater, during a salvage search. For $10,000, they would provide the location of the plane and other documentation.

Cameron, however, was never able to prove a thing or learn the truth about the claim. The Australian Department of Aviation told Cameron it was mandatory they be involved in any salvage because it was a still open aviation accident. They also claimed that they wanted to keep a low profile, afraid that the affair would turn into a media circus.

The divers backed away, claiming Cameron had insulted them on a radio broadcast. They suggested that he had told the radio audience they were less than honest. Although Cameron tried to assure them that he believed them, they would not speak to him again.

It could also be that the divers, by requesting the money, realized that they had or were about to engage in fraud if they hadn't really found the aircraft. Although Cameron tried to contact them later, he could never find them.

What it boils down to is that two men who claimed they had found Valentich's aircraft failed to produce any evidence that such is the case. The divers backed out at the thinnest of excuses. It suggests that the divers' tale, as so often happens under similar circumstances, was nothing more than a hoax.

Valentich's family, in an effort to learn what happened to him, employed a number of psychics. The information produced by them was contradictory and of little value. It ranged from Valentich disappearing on purpose to his being captured by space aliens and now living on a higher plane as a bundle of energy.

What we see, then, is a variety of things in these tales of disappearing aircraft. Thomas Mantell, a well qualified and trained military pilot, was probably killed chasing a then-classified balloon known as Skyhook. The descriptions and drawings of the object, from the official files, look like a Skyhook. Mantell, unfamiliar with the Skyhook project and huge balloons, because they were classified, could easily have been fooled. The incident is a tragic accident.

The others are disappearances of aircraft. Eugene Metcalf's story is interesting but uncorroborated. Metcalf was probably telling the truth about what he believed he saw, but without corroboration there is nothing more to be done with it.

Exon's story of disappearing aircraft is more substantial than Metcalf's simply because Exon was an Air Force general. Although I have been unable to corroborate the tale through various records and newspaper files, I am still intrigued by it. If we can corroborate it, the story would be of great importance. As it stands, it is from a single though reliable source, but with no corroboration.

The last two tales, the Kinross and Valentich disappearances, are more heavily documented. It can be established, through official records and files, that the aircraft in question did disappear. Both had been in radio contact with air facilities when they vanished. And no trace of either has been found to date.

While it could be said that Valentich's radio transmissions could be interpreted in a number of ways, only one of which is to suggest UFO involvement, the Kinross case is UFO related. Not only had the jet been scrambled to intercept a UFO, other officers assigned to the base told me about UFO sightings in the area at the time. The Air Force claimed they identified the UFO as a Canadian aircraft, but the Canadians denied it.

It should also be noted that both aircraft disappeared over water and the water can hide many things. Of course, searches failed to reveal any suggestions about the fate of either craft.

There are tales of aircraft disappearances related to UFO sightings and they are well documented by governmental sources. It can be said that such cases provide, indirectly, evidence for the existence of flying saucers. After all, an illusion or hoax can't be responsible for the disappearance of an airplane.

CHAPTER 10

December 26–27, 1980: Bentwaters AFB, England

There are those who give credit to Larry Warren for revealing the UFO activities at Bentwaters in December 1980. And it might be that Warren did provide the clues that allowed UFO researchers to learn that something had happened there. But, as we'll see, based on both audio- and video-taped statements, Warren's version of the events doesn't match those of the real participants.

The best documented of the sightings took place on the second night when Lieutenant Colonel Charles Halt, the senior officer present, made his observations. During the sighting, he made a tape recording of his impressions and later he would file a written report about the UFO event that he witnessed. Of the witnesses who have been identified, Halt is probably the most credible, given his military rank and his position at the air base in December 1980.

Halt learned of the events which took place the first night when he reported for work on the following morning. He heard the story of the lights in the woods the night before, and that some believed them to be UFOs, but Halt dismissed the idea. UFOs, after all, don't exist.

It was during that day that Halt presented the briefing about the events because the base commander, Colonel Henry Cochran, had been awake all night. Halt interviewed a number of the men and read the security police blotter, so that he was, at least, aware of what had been reported. He told the assembled security police officers about the base report, then going to search for what might have been something that crashed into the forest off the end of one of the runways at the base. There were indications that radar at one of the nearby British radar facilities had tracked something at about the time a light was seen dropping into the woods of Rendlesham Forest. Everyone seemed to accept the idea that the American airmen had seen something in the woods. No one was sure what it was, but something had been there.

There are reports that after the first night's sightings several men in civilian clothes were seen in the woods. A master sergeant and others accompanied Cochran into the woods to the location of the landing. Holes were found pressed into the soft, wet ground. According to one source, they formed a perfect equilateral triangle measuring about twelve feet on a side. It must be noted that one police officer, seeing the holes, dismissed them as having been dug by animals.

The first day, then, produced a report of a radar sighting, visual reports of lights close to the ground that might be linked to what was seen on radar, and some physical evidence. The story was somewhat confusing and could be dismissed as an aberration if it wasn't for the events that would follow.

Just before midnight the sightings began again. A number of the men on guard duty saw lights in the sky that didn't look like any aircraft they had ever seen. They talked about them until they vanished, winked out. But soon, there was a glow in the forest. It was in the same general location as the night before.

The security men radioed to base, telling them what was happening. The base contacted Colonel Halt, who authorized an investigation. That meant the men would be leaving the air base proper and moving out into the English countryside.

There was something going on in Rendlesham Forest. There was something that appeared to be hovering over a carpet of yellow. There was a red light on top and a series of blue lights around the middle. There was no definite shape behind the lights. There also seemed to be some kind of electrical field that affected the men.

They decided that they should radio to the base for more instructions. Halt, who was now back at the base, told the men to wait at the edge of the forest. "I'm on my way with more people," he told them.

It was just after midnight when Halt and his party arrived on the scene. They had a number of vehicles and other equipment including "light-alls." These are large, independent lights used in the field to light aircraft and other equipment for maintenance or for any other purpose that requires a great deal of light. These are smaller versions of the huge lights used in stadiums for night games.

Halt ordered the lights erected, but there were various malfunctions. Rather than use the trucks to pull the lights into the forest, they had to manhandle them because of the terrain. As they were set up near the area where the triangular marks had been found, the lights would switch on and then back off seemingly by themselves. In other words, they seemed to be malfunctioning.

The men were spread out, in pockets, through the woods. They were searching for anything that could explain the lights seen earlier that night. They wanted to take a close look at the area where the markings had been found and they wanted to see if they could find anything else.

One of the things that makes this sighting report different from all the others is that Halt carried a small tape recorder with him. He made notes throughout the night about what he was seeing and what he was doing. Other voices, providing their perspective, can also be heard on the tape at various times.

Now, rather than having to interview a witness about what he was feeling during the sighting, we have an audio record. It provides a unique look at this complicated case.

One of the first voices heard, at 1:48 in the morning, said, "We're hearing strange sounds out of the farmer's barnyard animals. They're very, very active, making awful lot of noise . . . You just saw a light? . . ."

Another voice said, "Right on this position. Here, straight ahead in between the trees . . . there it is again. Watch. Straight ahead off my flashlight, sir. There it is."

Halt then said, "I see it too. What is it?"

"We don't know, sir."

Halt said, "It's a strange, small red light. Looks to be maybe a quarter to a half mile, maybe further out. I'm gonna switch off. The light is gone now. It was approximately 120 degrees from our site. It is back again?"

"Yes, sir."

Someone said, "Well douse flashlights then. Let's go back to the edge of the clearing so we can get a better look at it. See if you can get the star[light] scope on it. The light's still there and all the barnyard animals have gone quiet now. We're heading about 110, 120 degrees from the site out through to the clearing now, still getting a reading on the [Geiger counter] meter . . . We're about 150 or 200 yards from the site. Everywhere else is just deathly calm. There is no doubt about it. There's some type of strange flashing red light ahead."

"Sir, it's yellow."

Halt responded, "I saw a yellow tinge in it too. Weird. It appears to be maybe moving a little bit this way? It's brighter than it has been. It's coming this way. It is definitely coming this way. Pieces of it are shooting off. There is no doubt about it. This is weird."

"Two lights," said someone. "One to the right and one light to the left."

"Keep your flashlights off," ordered Halt. "There's something very, very strange. Keep the headset on. See if it gets any . . . Pieces falling off it again."

"It just moved to the right."

Another voice said, "Yeah. Strange. Let's approach to the edge of the woods up there. Okay, we're looking at the thing. We're probably about two to three hundred yards away. It looks like an eye winking at you. Still moving from side to side. And when you put the star[light] scope on it, it's like this thing has a hollow center, a dark center, like the pupil of an eye looking at you, winking. And it flashes so bright in the star[light] scope that it almost burns your eye . . . We've passed the farmer's house and across into the next field and now we have multiple sightings of up to five lights with a similar shape and all but they seem to be steady now rather than a pulsating or glow with a red flash. We've just crossed a creek and we're getting what kind of readings [Geiger counter] now? We're getting three good clicks on the meter and we're seeing strange lights in the sky."

The next time check on the tape is at 2:44 A.M. Halt said, "We're at the far side of the second farmer's field and made [a] sighting again about 110 degrees. This looks like it's clear off to the coast. It's right on the horizon. Moves about a bit and flashes from time to time. Still steady or red in color. Also after negative readings in the center of the field we're picking up slight readings. Four or five clicks now, on the meter."

About twenty-one minutes later, Halt added, "We see strange strobe-like flashes . . . well, they're sporadic, but there's definitely some kind of phenomenon . . . At about ten degrees, horizon, directly to the north, we've got two strange objects . . . half-moon shape, dancing about with colored lights on them. That . . . guess to be about five to ten miles out, maybe less. The half-moons are now turning full circles, as though there was an eclipse or something there, for a minute or two."

Ten minutes later, at 3:15 A.M., Halt added, "Now

we've got an object about ten degrees directly south, ten degrees off the horizon. And the ones to the north are moving. One's moving away from us."

Someone corroborated Halt's observation, saying clearly, "It's moving out fast."

"This one on the right's heading away too," said another voice.

A third man said, "They're both heading north. Okay, here he comes from the south. He's coming toward us now. Now we're observing what appears to be a beam coming down to the ground. This is unreal."

Fifteen minutes later, Halt said, "And the objects are still in the sky although the one to the south looks like it's losing a little bit of altitude. We're going around and heading back toward the house. The object to the south is still beaming down lights to the ground."

Thirty minutes after that, Halt said, "One object still hovering over Woodbridge base at about five or ten degrees off the horizon. Still moving erratic, and similar lights and beaming down . . ."

If that was the end of it, just an audio tape of witnesses talking about strange lights in the forest near the base, it would still be an intriguing case. After all, it isn't often that an Air Force officer makes a recording as he's chasing unidentified lights and objects through the woods near a NATO airbase. But that wasn't the end of it. About two weeks after the event, Halt sent a letter to the Royal Air Force Commander, detailing the events of the day.

"1. Early in the morning of 27 Dec 80 (approximately 0300L [that is three in the morning, local time], two USAF security police patrolmen saw unusual lights outside the back gate at RAF Woodbridge. Thinking an aircraft might have crashed or been forced down, they called for permission to go outside the gate to investigate. The on duty flight chief responded and allowed three patrolmen to proceed on foot. The individuals reported seeing a strange glowing object in the forest. The object was described as being metallic in appearance and triangular in shape, approximately two to three meters across the base and approximately two meters high. It illuminated the entire forest with a white light. The object itself had a pulsating red light on top and a bank(s) of blue lights underneath. The object was hovering or on legs. As the patrolmen approached the object, it maneuvered through the trees and disappeared. At this time the animals on a nearby farm went into a frenzy. The object was briefly sighted approximately an hour later near the back gate.

2. The next day, three depressions 1½" deep and 7" in diameter were found where the object had been sighted on the ground. The following night (29 Dec 80) the area was checked for radiation. Beta/Gamma readings of 0.1 milliroentgens were recorded with peak readings in the three depressions and near the center of the triangle formed by the depressions. A nearby tree had moderate (.05-.07) readings on the side of the tree toward the depressions.

3. Later in the night a red sun-like light was seen through the trees. It moved about and pulsated. At one point it appeared to throw off glow-

ing particles and then broke into five separate white objects and then disappeared. Immediately thereafter, three star-like objects were noticed in the sky, two objects to the north and one to the south, all of which were about 10 [degrees] off the horizon. The objects moved rapidly in sharp angular movements and displayed red, green and blue lights. The objects to the north appeared to be elliptical through an 8-12 power lens. They then turned to full circles. The objects to the north remained in the sky for an hour or more. The object to the south was visible for two or three hours and beamed down a stream of light from time to time. Numerous individuals, including the undersigned [Lieutenant Colonel Halt], witnessed the activities in paragraphs 2 and 3."

So we have a good record of two nights of activities, including the statement of an Air Force lieutenant colonel (later a full colonel). There is no doubt that these events took place. In fact, no one disputes that. The questions concern the sightings and the evidence reported by Halt in both his recordings and his letter and the observations of the other Air Force personnel out there that night.

Skeptics have already dismissed the holes as dug by rabbits. The radiation found was nothing more than ordinary background radiation. And the lights are explained as either bright, low stars, or the flashing beacon of a lighthouse some distance away.

They suggested the men had become excited by the discussions of something strange in the fields in the hours before the sightings. Lights that had been there for years but unnoticed were suddenly interpreted as craft from another world. The flashing light was clearly, at least to the skeptics, the lighthouse some miles distant.

My first reaction in hearing something like that is to dismiss it out of hand. However, my own research has taught me that many people are not familiar with their environment. In Grant County, Wisconsin, during a minor wave of sightings, I heard of one man who believed that a flashing red UFO was landing in his backyard. We discovered it to be the red lights on a radio transmitter tower that had been there for years. He'd never noticed them until people began to talk of flying saucers.

But these men were security police whose job it was to guard the military base. They were, you might say, on the front lines. If the Soviet Union had launched an attack against Western Europe, these were the men who would have been buying time and trying to halt the invasion. They were responsible for the security of the installation. They should have been aware of stationary lights and other features of the terrain around them as part of their jobs.

And, in a time when a few people are willing to sacrifice themselves to make a big splash on the news, terrorism and sabotage were not unknown. Many military units were briefed on terrorist activities and heightened states of readiness were often ordered to prevent infiltration and destruction on all military bases. Those on NATO bases in Europe would have a proportionally higher readiness than those of us in the United States.

All this means is that I find it difficult to believe that the security police and the officers at the Bentwaters base would be fooled by something as mundane as a flashing light from a lighthouse that had been there for years. These were men who had to be aware of their environment because their lives might depend on it.

The skeptical answer, that the men were fooled by mundane lights, should be rejected. In doing so, we must remember a couple of things. First, it doesn't mean there was an extraterrestrial visitation. There might be another, equally mundane explanation. No one has offered it yet, but that doesn't mean it doesn't exist.

Some other facts are even more important, however. If all that was seen was a light flashing in the woods, then the lighthouse might make some sense. I had the opportunity to interview John Burroughs, one of the enlisted security men who finally talked publicly. He told me, as he had others, that a ball of red light seemed to come from high overhead, dropped down to close to where he was standing, and then flash away. It wasn't something seen in the distance, but something close to him.

It is clear from his description that he is talking of a ball of light without any metallic or solid shape behind it. I have no explanation for what he saw. It clearly was not an extraterrestrial craft, which is not to say that it wasn't a manifestation caused by the appearance of such a craft. It is one of those aspects of the case that seems to defy conventional explanations.

There are also discussions among those who were present that the military equipment was not working as it should. Yes, equipment malfunctions, especially that which is well and often used. However, it seems that the trucks and light-alls were functioning properly until they were moved closer to the location where the events were taking place. It was as if something about that specific area, while the lights and craft were being seen, affected the equipment.

Such electromagnetic effects are well known in the UFO field. The Levelland, Texas, sightings, as discussed earlier, are good examples of this. Many people reported that their cars, headlights, and radios were affected by the close passage of the UFO seen there. There are other good examples of these electromagnetic effects reported in the UFO literature.

The skeptical explanations don't explain the failure of the equipment except to suggest damp weather and co-incidence. So now we have the security police unable to identify a lighthouse, excitement that led to the hysteria of the second night so that stars were identified as being close to the ground, and electromagnetic effects that mean nothing.

Finally there is the radiation that Halt and others mentioned. Skeptics have suggested that it was normal background radiation and is therefore, insignificant. But once again, we're dealing with people who are not untrained. These men were familiar with Geiger counters and background radiation. By examining the written reports, it's obvious that the radiation detected is not normal, background radiation. They were familiar enough with the equipment and radiation to have realized that. After all, they weren't a group of UFO investigators trying to make a good case. They were military enlisted men and officers whose job it was to protect their base.

There is, however, one area of confusion that the skeptics didn't create. Each of those who have written about the Bentwaters/Rendlesham Forest case has mentioned confusion as to the date of the second event. A few researchers have postulated that there was a *third* day. Because the events on day three haven't been as thoroughly researched, because we're dealing with events that began before midnight and ended after midnight, there seems to be confusion.

Larry Warren, a teenaged airman in 1980 (and I should point out here that I was a teenaged helicopter pilot for the Army, having been sent to Vietnam as a pilot at nineteen), told all that he knew about the events at Bentwaters. He was first identified as Art Wallace and later under his own name. He told authors Barry Greenwood and Larry Fawcett about his observations at Bentwaters, and they published his account in their book *Clear Intent*, later rereleased as *The UFO Cover Up*.

According to them, Warren (Wallace) told them that he had been assigned to guard part of the flight line (on what he claimed was the third night), when a jeep roared up and he was ordered to get in. As they drove toward the motor pool, Warren claimed that he noticed the animals were all running from the woods.

At the motor pool, Warren and a sergeant were told to get the light-alls. They were hooked to a jeep and they drove to the main gate of the base. There they joined other vehicles already assembled and drove out into the Rendlesham Forest, stopping along a road in what Warren assumed was a staging area.

Now they were all ordered to turn in their weapons since they would not be taking them deeper into the forest, which was British land. Warren, along with four other enlisted men commanded by a captain, walked into the woods, heading in the general direction of a clearing.

Overhead were helicopters, and in front of them was an unidentified light source.

They passed an airman at the edge of the clearing. The man was crying and there was a medic with him. Warren couldn't understand what was happening, especially when he then saw a large movie camera and a number of military and plainclothes people who seemed to be watching something.

Warren, in many interviews conducted later, described the something as an object that looked like a transparent aspirin tablet that was hovering a foot or so above the ground. The object, again according to Warren, was about fifty feet in diameter and had a bright, pulsating yellow mist near it. Warren claimed that he walked to within ten feet of the object.

A red light then appeared in the distance, first behind a pine tree and then in front of it. It raced toward the object and flashed up to a position about twenty feet above it. After a minute, the red object broke apart, disintegrating into a shower of particles.

Then, in place of the red light and the original object, a domed disc appeared. Warren said that it was bright white in color and had a detailed surface like the ships in *Star Wars*. There were shadows on the object, cast by the surface detail. Warren also said that the men cast shadows on the disc, probably from the bright lights of the equipment the Air Force had brought in. Warren claimed there was some strange effect in which the shadows of the men seemed to be strangely out of sync with the bodies of the men creating them.

Warren said that he turned to talk to one of the other men, and the next thing he knew, he was in bed, fully clothed and muddy. It was several hours later and he had no idea as to how he had gotten back to the barracks.

As time passed, his story got better. Asked earlier by researchers if he had seen alien creatures, he said that he had the impression that he did. He also suggested that Air Force officers had communicated with the beings on the craft.

Later still, after undergoing hypnotic regression, Warren told Chuck deCaro of CNN that, "My impression was that [the aliens] were children . . . I thought they were children in snowsuits."

Others writing about the case, such as Jenny Randles, noted that Warren's story suggested clear evidence of missing time. She wrote, "Airmen cannot account for unknown periods of time . . ."

Warren has since claimed that he is an abductee, having been taken into alien craft on a number of occasions. He has been regressed by behavioral psychologist Fred Max and described the aliens at Bentwaters in greater detail for various UFO researchers.

According to Warren, three figures appeared, floating from the object toward the senior officer present, Charles Halt. Warren said that two of the creatures wore silver suits and the other a dark suit. The eyes were like an inverted cat's eye. According to Warren, something happened at the far side of the UFO and the alien eyes became large and round. When their eyes returned to normal, the aliens began to float toward Warren and he remembered nothing more until he woke up in the barracks several hours later.

It must be remembered that Halt created a tape of his encounter, if that is the proper word for it, and there is nothing on the tape to suggest aliens or contact. Halt also wrote a letter about the two nights of lights near Bentwaters and never suggests there were aliens involved.

There is one other important piece of evidence. While I was recently in California, I had the opportunity to review a series of interviews that had been videotaped of Larry Warren. Russ Estes, a documentarian and independent producer, had interviewed Warren on a number of occasions. When I happened to mention to Estes that I was looking into the Bentwaters case, he said that he had something I needed to see.

What was interesting was that almost the first thing that Warren said, on the tape, was that he had not been at Bentwaters on the first two nights. It wasn't clear if he had been on a "weekend" pass to Germany, or if he had been on assignment there, but when Halt and the boys were trooping through the woods, Warren was not in England.

It was obvious that he had been assigned to the base in early December 1980, but that he was not physically present on the critical days. It was Warren who began to talk of a *third* day that seemed to mirror some of the events on the *second* day.

What became clear to me as I watched the tapes was that the confusion expressed by others who wrote about Warren and his experiences was created by Warren himself. He changed the dates around so that he could suggest that he had been involved. If the dates weren't altered, and someone found the records, then he would be left trying to explain the discrepancy. Now, it was the writers such as Greenwood and Fawcett who were trying to explain a problem that didn't exist until Warren entered the picture.

Halt, in fact, confirmed the problems in a conversation he held with Warren on February 16, 1993. Warren explained that he wanted to set the record straight because of the distortion. He said, beginning with Fawcett's book, he had seen the distortion, apparently forgetting that the distortion is a result of his telling the story several different ways on many different occasions.

Halt was asked during the conversation if he knew what Warren had alleged were his experiences. Halt, in answering, explained that he had agreed to help Fawcett understand the Bentwaters case. Halt said, "All I know is what I have gained from two or three tapes that Larry [Fawcett] and somebody, I don't even remember now who, shared with me. In fact, one time I agreed to co-operate with Larry [Fawcett] . . . I provided him a lot of information and then he sent me a tape . . ."

Warren then began to explain that he was working on a book and that he just wanted to tell the story. Halt interrupted him and said, "You're aware that the story you've told or the stories you've told through the years don't fit in with what I recollect and other witnesses recollect . . ."

Warren responded by saying, "Oh yes." But added, "I have statements from other guys that were right next to me in certain elements of this thing and . . . It's like being at the scene of the accident where all the different people say some variation of [the] thing . . ."

Warren then changed the conversation to talk about the problems he had with his military records. He mentioned that he had been working with his congressman, apparently trying to locate his records.

Halt interrupted and asked, "Have you taken a polygraph examine relative to what you recall as the events that occurred related to you?"

"You mean a lie detector test?"

"Yeah."

"Not a lie detector test. I took a voice . . . where they check the voice . . ."

"Voice stress analysis?"

"Yeah, through Fawcett. Three times. Through the Connecticut state police actually."

Halt said, "That would be irrelevant because he could . . ."

And Warren interrupted, saying, "Oh right. I agree with you."

Interestingly, I spoke to Larry Fawcett on May 28, 1996, and asked him if he had subjected Warren to a voice stress analysis. Fawcett was very clear on that. "Never," he said. "Not with me."

We discussed it for a few moments, just so that I would be sure of my facts. Fawcett said, "I never voice-stress analyzed him."

Halt, later in their conversation, asked Warren a number of questions about the story. "Where did the story come from that, number one, Gordon Williams was there . . . Where did the little green men come from?"

Warren then interrupted and, parroting a line that was attributed to Mac Brazel during the Roswell UFO crash case in 1947, said, "They weren't green." But after chuckling, said, "There was something there that was alive."

Halt then said, "There are two nights there that are intertwined. Are you aware of that?"

"No."

At this point Halt was trying to end the confusion. Halt

said, "You have events from the first night in the second, or in the third night rather intertwined together. It's very puzzling."

Warren asked, cautiously, "What are the events that are intertwined?"

"The actual confrontation with a craft or whatever you want to call it."

"You don't feel there were several . . ."

Halt interrupted to say, "No."

"I have a witness I've talked to from the third night that says there were (unintelligible) lights . . ." Then Warren, keeping with his third night theory said, "Sounds like a lot of minds were jerked around with, then."

Then the third man in the conversation, Peter Robbins, said, "I have a question for you. Let's say there were real, unexplainable events that happened and they were taken advantage of . . . That if certain of the men, Larry, Adrian to name two, remember certain things that were a mixture of what happened and what was programmed for them to remember for other purposes. Larry remembers Colonel Halt being there . . ."

Warren interrupted to say, "Colonel Williams . . ."

Robbins agreed and continued, "Could that have been part, for some reason, to keep this . . ."

Robbins didn't finish the question. Warren said, "Okay, fair enough."

"When I took the tape on the following Saturday morning," said Halt, "it was the day after. I ran into Gordon Williams in the hallway of the office . . . I was going into the office to pick up some papers and he was coming in to do something similar . . . We stopped in the corner to talk and I told him about it. And I told him about the tape. He said, 'Do you have the tape?' And I said, 'Yeah. It's in the office.' He said, 'I want to take it down and play it for General . . .' He was totally surprised by the whole thing. He had a very keen interest. Took the tape down and played it and brought the tape back and I said, 'What happened?' He said, 'Nobody knew what to do.' He said, 'I played it at the staff meeting and [the general] asked, 'Is Halt credible?' . . . He brought the tape back and said, 'Call me the next time. I want to be there too.' "

Halt then talked about another event, several days or weeks later, when he received a call. He drove across the airfield with Williams close by. But Williams had a staff car and had to go the long way around. By the time Halt and Williams arrived at the scene, there was nothing to see.

Halt said, "It was only a light they thought they saw, and I'm not even sure they saw anything. They were looking for something."

Halt then said, "Gordon Williams did not know anything about it. I'm positive. We talked about it several times through the years . . ."

Then Halt said something that is very interesting. He was talking about how the story broke in 1983. He said, "I was fast enough to go to public affairs and pull my picture out of the file. His [Gordon Williams] appeared in the paper. I never thought they would take his picture. When they couldn't find mine, they took his."

Warren, a few minutes later, after discussing how "the women in England" had gotten everything wrong, said, "I am not married to anything I say. All I have done, or tried to do through the years . . ." He then said that he had told his mother, who was able to gauge whether he was lying or not. From Warren's point of view, his mother believed what he was telling about the events at Bentwaters.

Halt interrupted to ask, "Do you remember *two* separate distinct nights, or were you involved in one night?"

"One. But, what I remember on that night . . . I can remember people with me and that whole bit. Whether that is real or created or God knows now, but that's fine . . . The strange story with me where you can put a finger on it and say, God, something happened with this guy is in the paperwork . . . What my hopes are is that this is what my mind's eye says. There are a lot of possibilities here. But look at the paperwork here that I'm lucky enough to have. I can't touch other paperwork of mine."

But the discussion wasn't about paperwork generated by the events at Bentwaters, but documents that suggest that Warren's military career was less than sterling. The problems arise from areas that have nothing to do with Bentwaters, but Warren was suggesting that it does. He was missing documents, or the documents are coded, and he has a coded discharge from the Air Force. He wasn't sure what that meant, and neither did Halt, but it was irrelevant to trying to understand what happened in December 1980. Warren had, again, diverted the conversation from an area that would suggest he was not there into something that suggests high-ranking officials manipulated the situation and the people who were involved. Of course, Warren concluded, this is a result of what he claims to have seen at Bentwaters. There is no evidence that his conclusions are accurate.

There is no doubt, based on the documentation Warren

has shown to UFO researchers, that he was assigned to the base at Bentwaters in December 1980. Russ Estes allowed me to see a videotape that showed many of these same documents. But these were routine, such as orders assigning Warren to a security police flight at Bentwaters, the security police badge he wore while in the service, and the like. Again, it supports his statements that he was assigned to the base, but does nothing to support his story that there was a third night of UFO activity and that he saw little men who weren't green.

Warren then turned the conversation back to the events at Bentwaters. He asked Halt what he had seen that night. Halt said that he really didn't know what it was. But then said, "What we initially saw was what they put on the NBC thing [*Unsolved Mysteries*] because I worked with the guy from . . . Apogee . . . I sat down with the guy and described a lot of things to him. Then he did sketches and I said no it was this way or that way. His rendition of the craft or whatever is not very accurate. . . ."

Warren interjected, "They never are."

Halt continued by saying, "But whatever this first object was . . . actually moving in the trees around, maneuvering around and went back out into the field and broke into five objects."

"I saw that thing," said Warren. "You know, the damnedest thing here is that where the problem is, when you discount one thing, not you personally, but when you discount one thing, something else jumps in and you've got to look at it . . . I should have been easy to blow out of the water but there are too many problems . . . Soon after this I began to have eye problems, whether I saw a thing explode or didn't see a bright source of light . . ."

Halt interrupted and said, "You couldn't have been too close. You were not in front of us. There were no people in front of us. In other words, you were facing the sea from the access road, if you were there, that is where you had to be because nobody was permitted to go past that point. There were only five people past that point except when Burroughs came forward. You had to be well behind that, at least a hundred, two hundred yards . . ."

Warren jumped in, chuckled, and then after a hesitation said, "I've had marriages go. Every kind of the worst things from this . . . this circus. I don't know anymore."

He then began to talk about his eye problems again. He claimed the problems started within days. He said, "I went to the Bentwaters clinic. My eyes hurt. Burroughs, who I talked to . . . which is strange. He says whatever he says now but we met in California and talked at length about a lot of elements here. He says he has heart problems, eye problems due to this sort of thing . . . But this . . ."

Halt interrupted again and said, "I've talked to him on two occasions . . . He was one of the three cops . . . that approached something initially . . ."

Warren said, "I had nothing to do with that . . ."

"I came on duty that morning," continued Halt, "at about five o'clock I walked in and he was tidying up the blotters getting ready to close them out at six. He said, 'What do I put in there?' Burroughs and [I] forget who all were out chasing UFOs all night. I kind of laughed."

Halt explained that there had to be an entry in the blotter, but that they didn't have to identify it as a UFO. They had seen lights. Halt said to put they had seen lights and to put in the times when they had made their observations.

Halt then added a comment that was interesting. He said, "By the way, the blotters all disappeared."

Then Warren again returned to his eye problems. In the discussion of his eye problems, Warren said that the NSA had interviewed him. Apparently there was some kind of link between Warren's eye problems and the UFO event, or so he would have us believe.

Halt asked a relevant question: "Why would they approach you and not me?"

Warren suggested it was because he had gone public with the story. But even so, he was just an airman whose records suggest he wasn't involved. Why not let him shoot off his mouth, creating the perfect screen? Halt, on the other hand, as an Air Force colonel, who had made the audio tape, and who had written the letter detailing the events, was much more dangerous to the cover-up. If Halt corroborated the story, as he eventually did, then the case is just that much stronger. But, according to Halt, no one had talked to him about remaining quiet.

So what have we learned from this? There were two days of activities at Bentwaters. The first day seems to have involved some sort of craft that touched down, leaving depressions in the ground in a triangular-shaped pattern. Skeptics have suggested they were rabbit holes, but that seems unlikely.

The next night, there were lights seen and the officers and security police responded, moving into the woods.

Halt seems to have seen nothing solid, but did see lights. He and his party were the closest to the lights, in conflict with what Warren has claimed.

There was no third night. That was an invention so that Warren could become part of the story. He took parts from the second night and incorporated them into his tale. He claimed to have been close, to have seen the craft break into fragments, but Halt corrected him on that point.

There is one other argument which both Warren and Halt brought up that should be covered. When the story began to leak, a number of British UFO investigators started to pursue the case. Halt mentioned there had been a report that he had come to the door in his underwear, but he said that he had just returned from jogging. When the British UFO investigators arrived at his front door, he had picked up the red phone. The security police, and the local police, responded quickly to a call from a senior NATO officer. Halt just didn't want to be bothered.

Warren suggested that these same people had been talking to Halt's son while Halt was in the United States. They had been giving the youngster alcohol trying to get him to talk. If this is true, their actions are reprehensible.

So we've been able to sort through some of the problems at Bentwaters. We've seen how the situation has been altered and manipulated so that those who weren't there could claim they were. It seems that normal military response on a NATO base has been changed into some sort of conspiracy to hide the evidence.

But what we do learn is what is wrong with the UFO field. There are so many people in it who are claiming to be what they are not. Anyone who examines the Bent-waters case realizes that Warren is responsible for the confusion about it. He's not interested in correcting that confusion because to do so would eliminate his role. Instead, he changes his story as it becomes necessary so that he can continue to claim he was there.

As I listen to what Halt said during the discussion, I can see this clearly. Warren has suggested that the events Halt was a witness to, and chronicled in his tape and letter, happened while he, Warren, was not present. It is clear that those events took place on the second day. It was Warren who combined those events with what he claimed of the third day. A day that didn't happen.

The confusion that Larry Fawcett, Barry Greenwood, Timothy Green, and others wrote about comes from Warren. They believed that Warren was telling the truth because Warren had been at Bentwaters and could prove it. They believed Warren because he had spoken to friends who had been involved in the events of the two days. They could find some corroboration for what Warren said because he had enough details to convince them.

I spoke to John Burroughs about this a number of years ago. He told me that Warren hadn't been there. He knew who was there and who wasn't. He knew who had been in the field. According to Burroughs, Warren wasn't one of the security policemen who went out on either night.

If we eliminate the Warren story from Bentwaters, then there is no confusion. The dates line up and Halt's documentation provides us with what is still a puzzling case. Without Warren, we can understand it much better.

CHAPTER 11

December 29, 1980: The Cash-Landrum Encounter

The second important encounter of the 1980 Christmas season took place in southern Texas near Houston. It began after Betty Cash, then in her early fifties, traveling with her neighbor, Vicky Landrum, then in her late fifties, and Landrum's seven-year-old grandson, noticed that the sky ahead of them seemed to be bright. It was just after 9:00 P.M. when they saw a vertically oblong object hovering above the road in front of them.

Cash, driving her 1980 Cutlass Supreme, slowed down, pulling over so that she wouldn't have to drive under the object. Flames were flashing under it, down toward the road, creating a pool of blinding light. Later, speaking to one investigator, she suggested that the engine of her car had begun to run rough as she approached the object and that it finally quit. Unfortunately, this was a detail she added long after telling the tale to a number of people.

The object was about sixty feet in the air, diamond-shaped, with one of the points hanging down. It was only about a hundred feet from the stopped or stalled car, but so bright that none of the witnesses were able to clearly see the shape of it.

Cash got out of her car and walked toward the object, stopping after only a couple of feet. She noticed that the flames "whooshed" from the bottom, but didn't affect the roadway.

Landrum also got out, but didn't move forward, standing near the car behind the open door. After only two or three minutes, she got back into the vehicle because her grandson was screaming at her, demanding that she return.

The object was radiating an intense heat. Cash was surprised as she grabbed the door handle. The metal was too hot to touch. She took off her jacket and used it to protect her hand. When she got the door open, she climbed into the car. She'd been outside for five to seven minutes watching the hovering UFO.

As the object began to drift toward the west, heading in the direction of Houston Intercontinental Airport, both the women noticed dozens of helicopters in the area. Cash said she counted twenty-three, but Landrum stopped counting after only fifteen. Young Colby, the grandson, said that he could see the helicopters throughout the entire sighting. Most of them were large, twin-rotor aircraft known in the military as CH-47 Chinooks.

As the UFO moved away, Cash tried to start the car.

Landrum, who had been unaware that the engine had quit—and thought originally that it had been shut off by Cash—recalled that Cash did have to start it. As they drove along the road, and then turned toward Huffman, Texas, they saw the UFO and the helicopters three more times. After dropping off Landrum and her grandson, Cash arrived home just before ten. The object and helicopters had been in sight for something between ten to seventeen minutes, according to the witnesses.

The sighting, because of the duration, the shape of the object, and the fact that so many military helicopters were involved, would be interesting all by itself. But that wasn't the end of the case. Within hours, Betty Cash began to develop physiological symptoms, including a bright red "sunburn" on her skin, burning eyes, and vomiting. This, like the stalled car engine, is reminiscent of the Levelland, Texas, and the James Stokes sightings in November 1957.

By the next morning she was too weak to get out of bed. Her hair was coming out in clumps. She had a powerful and painful headache. Half-dollar sized blisters appeared on her skin which contained a clear fluid. Her neck and ears were swollen and her eyes were swollen shut so that she couldn't see. She also had diarrhea.

Both Vicky Landrum and Colby had similar symptoms, though nothing as severe as those experienced by Cash. Both were burned in a similar fashion, though not as badly. Researchers speculated that Cash, because she was outside of the car for the longest, was exposed to the radiation, or whatever it was, the longest. That would explain why her symptoms were so much more severe than those of the others.

Landrum, after four days, convinced Cash to go to the hospital. She was there for just over two weeks. Treatment included a salve and burn cream for her skin.

The doctor, B. B. Shenoy, called in specialists who couldn't explain the swellings, burns, or hair loss. All the tests performed failed to find a cause for her sickness. She was sent home with several medications designed to provide pain relief and comfort, but nothing to really cure her.

She was hospitalized again not long afterwards, this time for seven days. Her medical bills climbed and Shenoy was at a loss to explain the situation. Cash, however, feeling that the doctor should know what happened, told him about the UFO sighting. Shenoy, according to one researcher, seemed relieved to have a cause and entered the information in Cash's medical records.

It has been noted by various researchers that Betty Cash eventually developed breast cancer and had a mastectomy. It must be pointed out that the events of December 29, 1980, probably had nothing to do with the cancer. I mention it only because others seem to think the cancer was significant and might provide some sort of explanation for the report. It does not.

The other important feature of the Cash-Landrum case is the claim that so many military helicopters were apparently chasing the UFO. The problem is that the sighting took place during the Christmas holidays, and many military installations operate on a reduced schedule so that as many military personnel as possible can spend Christmas at home. It would be difficult to find enough pilots and aircraft to mount this sort of operation at that time of the year.

In fact, that was one aspect of the case that was deeply researched by believers and skeptics alike. Because of the medical problems experienced by the witnesses, Cash and Landrum believed that the U.S. government was responsible. Betty Cash didn't believe she had seen a flying saucer, but had witnessed some kind of classified government experiment that had gone wrong. She believed she had been injured by that crippled craft, whatever it was.

The investigation then, conducted by a number of people, including military officers, centered around all those helicopters. No one could figure out where so many Chinooks would have been stationed, especially given the time of the year.

There was one other important point. Betty Cash and Vicky Landrum were not the only ones to report a large number of helicopters operating in that area at that time. Dayton, Texas, police officer L. L. Walker and his wife, Marie, claimed to have seen the Chinooks in the Huffman area about four or five hours after Cash and Landrum saw them.

In a report to the J. Allen Hynek Center for UFO Studies, John F. Schuessler of Houston, Texas, included a transcript of an interview with Walker. At the interview were Lieutenant Colonel George Sarran, Vicky and Bertha Landrum, and Schuessler.

Walker said, "On December the 29th my wife and I were coming back home from her mother and dad's who live in Plum Grove. It's about 3 miles behind Splendora into the wood area. We was traveling New Caney Road, we just came through there, the cutoff, and hit Cedar Bayou and came across the river and cut down the school road at the Huffman new high school there and just got back on FM [farm-market road] 1960. We were approximately, we was inside the Liberty county city limits and just made a turn out there by the railroad tracks . . .

"And I made a remark. I said, 'Marie,' I said.

"She said, 'What's that noise?'

"I said, 'Well, I don't know.' But I said, 'It sounds like helicopters and it's getting louder.'

"She says, 'Well, I don't see any airplane.'

"And I said, 'It's not an airplane, it's a helicopter, Marie.'

"And she said, 'Whatever it is, it sure is low.'

"And I said, 'Yeah it is.' So I rolled my car window down and I started looking and I could see some flashing lights in the air approximately anywhere from four to five hundred feet in the air and I got to picking out more of them and as I was picking them out, I picked out three in a victor formation at about maybe a thousand. And a little bit off to the left of it was another sector of V with three choppers in it. And as I looked a little bit better I seen three more. The twin tops, front and aft, the shape and everything.

"I said, 'Well they must be on maneuvers again.' National Guard or something, out at Fort Polk [Louisiana] or the Coast Guard doing something and I looked a little bit closer and you could see some lower lights back off in the distance quite a ways back. I'd say about three-quarters of a mile—real good visibility that night and I just registered off and we went on home.

"And it wasn't about, oh, maybe three, four weeks, three, four days, maybe a little bit longer when I heard over the news of what happened . . . I even told the men around the office there. We [were] setting around talking one day and I said, 'What in the devil's all the helicopters around for?' I said, 'They have an airplane crash?'

"They said, 'No, not that I heard.' "

Private UFO investigator Schuessler noted that Colonel Sarran said that he was convinced that Walker was telling the truth. Sarran was convinced that Walker believed he had seen the helicopters. Schuessler also noted that no one had yet proven that helicopters had been in the area.

That is one of the interesting aspects of the case. Air Force officers denied that any helicopters had been in the area. It seems that all inquiries had been brushed off. Schuessler reported that Captain Jenny Lampley, because of congressional inquiry, was assigned to determine if Air Force helicopters had been involved. Two weeks later, another officer told Schuessler that the investigation had been completed and the results were negative. No Air Force helicopters were involved.

From that point on, the investigation rested in the hands of the Army and Lieutenant Colonel Sarran. He explained the problems and noted there were several bases in the area to which C-47 Chinooks were assigned. It seemed that it would be fairly easy to learn if any of them had been airborne on the night of December 29.

Sarran also explained that he had trouble accepting the Cash-Landrum concept of a government experiment escorted by military helicopters because of the date. He was not saying that UFOs didn't exist, only that because of the holidays, the flying operations at most facilities had been curtailed or shut down. Only skeleton staffs remained behind.

Sarran did try to learn the truth, contacting military bases in Texas, Oklahoma, and Louisiana. He checked regular Army, Reserve, and National Guard facilities. All denied that they had aircraft in the area at the time of the incident.

The FAA and its various air traffic control centers denied any knowledge of military maneuvers on the night of December 29. Sarran told Schuessler that such activities would have to be coordinated with the FAA because of the possibilities of an aircraft accident. No such notifications had been made.

Checks of the local units resulted in absolutely no hint that anyone was trying to hide anything. Pilots and enlisted crew who might have participated in such activities were questioned by both military officers and civilian researchers. No one gave even the slightest indication that flying operations had been conducted that night.

Sarran, among others, pointed out that an operation of the size indicated would have required massive support, including refueling capabilities. Refueling would have been a problem, but no one seemed to have noticed any jumps in the consumption of jet fuels in the area on the date in question. No trucks or fuel bladders were seen in the area. There just didn't seem to be any positive indication that Army Aviation was involved.

Cash and Landrum, because of their health problems, and because of the medical bills they had run up, wanted compensation from the government. A suit was filed against the Air Force because, according to some, "The Air Force has more money than the Army."

The problem there, however, is that no indications of governmental responsibility could be proven. The searches of military organizations that would have had access to sufficient numbers of helicopters could find no records to suggest that they had participated in any sort of exercise that would demand the numbers required.

A second problem also developed. Medical records of the three, Cash, Landrum, and Colby, were not presented as evidence. If, according to those records, there had been no signs of preexisting ill health or any medical problems, then a good case could be made that the events of December 29 caused the trouble. If, on the other hand, there was a record of various medical pathologies, then no such conclusion could be drawn.

New York attorney Peter Gersten filed suit on the behalf of Cash and Landrum, claiming twenty million dollars in damages. In August 1986, the case was dismissed on the grounds that the object seen by the women did not belong to the Army, Navy, Air Force, or NASA. Experts brought in denied any knowledge of such a craft, and clearly the helicopters, if they existed, were not the cause of the medical problems. That expert testimony was sufficient cause to dismiss the case.

That seems to be where the case stands today. Three witnesses claim they saw military helicopters chasing (or escorting) a craft that is not in any military inventory. The witnesses claimed they manifested a number of medical symptoms from exposure to the mystery craft, and medical records do show they were treated *after* the events. There is nothing to prove that the three were in perfect health prior to the events and that those events caused an erosion of their health. Betty Cash's cancer may have been a preexisting condition, though there is no record of it prior to the events. A comprehensive search by military officers and civilian researchers has failed to produce any evidence that the sighting took place.

Once again, we are left with nothing except our beliefs. Was the craft extraterrestrial? Was there any craft at all? Or was this some kind of elaborate hoax invented by the women (though neither has a history of creating practical jokes)? Without more data, we just can't answer any of the questions satisfactorily.

CHAPTER 12

November 29, 1989:
The Belgium Sightings

All the accounts of the Belgian wave of UFO reports begin by mentioning the first sightings of a triangular-shaped object on November 29, 1989. More than 120 people, including thirteen police officers, were among the witnesses near Eupen, Belgium. The object, with shining lights, was seen at close range. Although there were multiple witnesses, it was little more than a nocturnal lights event. It did, however, mark the beginning of a series of sightings that would produce some interesting and impressive evidence of UFOs.

Just two days later, Francesco Valenzano was driving through Ans in Liege Province, when his daughter shouted that he should look up. In the sky above them was a large, triangular-shaped object that drifted along slowly, just above the buildings of the town square. Finally it flew off toward another village.

There would be more sightings and the list of witnesses would continue to grow. Valenzano was an Air Force meteorological specialist. On December 11, a Belgian army lieutenant colonel, Andre Amond, while driving with his wife spotted a strangely lighted object moving slowly at low altitude. Amond stopped the car so that he could see the object better. It flashed a beam of light at him and began to approach. His wife began to shout, wanting to get out.

Amond said that the object then departed rapidly. He later told investigators that he had been impressed by the slowness with which the object moved originally, then its speed as it flashed away. The object made no noise as it maneuvered.

The day after Amond's sighting, and in response to the growing wave, the Eupen police and SOBENS (Belgian Society for the Study of Spatial Phenomena) held a press conference in Brussels. Also at the press conference were the Belgian Air Force officers who would be investigating the sightings, and Guy Coeme, the Belgium Defense Minister.

No solutions were offered. The purpose of the conference was to inform the media about the sightings and let them know what was to be done. It was the first time that anyone with the Belgium Ministry of Defense had spoken out on the topic of flying saucers.

Not long after the press conference, one of the daily newspapers in that area printed a story suggesting the UFOs were actually American F-117As. The article suggested that these were secret test flights and that the explanation had come from Washington. Although the F-117 bore a slight resemblance to the triangular UFO, it could not drift along slowly and the pattern of lights reported didn't match those on the aircraft.

Auguste Meessen, a professor of physics at the Catholic University at Louvain, investigated the explanation, learning that it hadn't come from Washington as the reporter had claimed, but from Finland. A writer for *Het Laatste Nieuws* said that he had just read an article about the F-117 and had wanted to inform his readers about the strange aircraft. To make the article interesting, he had suggested that the recent UFO sightings in Belgium might have been caused by the Stealth fighter. He had no inside knowledge, just a wild speculation, added to spice up his article. Other newspapers grabbed the explanation and ran with it rather than checking it first. After all, if it was in the newspaper, it must be right.

Lieutenant Colonel Wilfried De Brouwer, the chief of operations of the Belgian Air Force, told Meessen that they had sought help from the American embassy in an attempt to find solutions for the sightings. Had the F-117 been the culprit in the sightings, De Brouwer would have been told about the flights prior to them being made. The U.S. Air Force does not routinely invade the airspace of a friendly, foreign nation without alerting that nation to its presence.

What is interesting about the episode is the response Meessen received from the Eupen journalist who announced that Washington had explained the sightings. Told that an official denial was on the way, and asked why he had characterized the accounts as "hysterical," he said, "I am against all that." As Meessen pointed out,

so much for objectivity. The reporter doesn't believe in
UFOs, therefore there are no UFOs, and those reporting
them must be "hysterical."

But even the negative press in the local area didn't
discourage more sightings and more reports. On December 12, 1989, a witness, who wishes to remain unidentified, was awakened by a throbbing sound. He believed
that a circulation pump was about to fail, so he picked
up a flashlight and headed out toward the boiler. When
he shut down the pump, he could still hear the noise. It
had to be coming from outside.

As soon as he stepped out, his attention was drawn to
an oval-shaped object between two fir trees. In the bright
light of the moon, he could see the object clearly. There
were small lights around the perimeter that changed
color from blue to red and back to blue. The object was
metallic looking. At the front was a window or porthole
of some kind.

After a few minutes, the object rose slightly and the
sound coming from it changed. It began to drift toward
a meadow, shining searchlight-like beams under it. The
object then disappeared behind a house but a moment
later a well defined, bright light shot into the sky. The
witness was too frightened to investigate. Instead he returned to his own house.

Unlike so many others who saw the strange objects,
this man reported his sighting to the police. A search of
the fields conducted by the police and the Belgian army
turned up a giant circular area. The grass had been cut
as if by a lawn mower. There were also traces of some
sort of yellow material on the grass.

There were others who later claimed they heard the

noise from the craft, but didn't go out to investigate. A reporter living in the area said that he had been awakened by a bright light outside. He thought it was one of his own outdoor lights and rolled over to go back to sleep.

The witness also heard that photographs had been taken. He didn't know where the man lived and went to the local police for help. While there, he was shown a map that contained markings of several of the UFO sightings. The witness, studying the map, determined that the flight path of the object depicted showed that it would have flown over the area where he'd seen the UFO earlier.

He eventually found the man with the pictures. The witness drew his UFO for the man who said it looked like what he had photographed. The pictures, however, were poor. The man hadn't used a fast enough film so all that showed were spots of brightness.

Late on the evening of February 2, or in the early morning of February 3, 1990, a woman reported that her son, looking "haggard and acting oddly," told her of his UFO sighting. Outside to answer a call of nature, he had seen an object with three lights. It came toward him and, according to the boy, he thought, "They've come for me." That was the last he could remember.

The most spectacular of the sightings, and the ones that received the widest press coverage, occurred on the evening of March 30 and the early morning of March 31, 1990. It had been suggested that when there were reliable sightings of a triangular-shaped object, the Belgian Air Force would respond with American-made F-16 fighters. When several police officials and a host of other civilian witnesses reported seeing an object, the fighters were dispatched.

According to one account, though the fighter pilots made no visual contact with the UFO, the onboard radar did "lock on" to a target. It moved slowly, only about twenty-five miles an hour, but then would accelerate at fantastic speeds. It was reported to have dropped from an altitude of 7500 feet to 750 feet in about one second.

The fighters locked on to the target three times that night, but each time the UFO evaded them. Eventually both the UFO and the fighters left the area. SOBEP representatives are still unsure of what happened that night, but did express praise for the Belgian Air Force for its honesty in reporting the incident.

That wasn't, of course, the end of the sightings in Belgium. Although less than productive, from an evidence viewpoint, those sightings did call attention to the events. Other sightings were reported during the next several weeks.

A month later, for example, there was a close approach of an object near Stockay, Belgium. On May 4, 1990, a respected archaeologist walked outside to close his greenhouse door and heard the dogs in the neighborhood howling. As he returned to the house, he saw a huge object with a clearly defined outline in a field about five hundred feet from him.

He tried to alert his neighbors, but they were not home. Instead he told his wife and together they saw, at the front of the house, a cone-shaped object with a top that was mushroomlike in appearance.

After watching it for a number of minutes, his wife returned to the house. He went in with her, then decided to take another look. He walked along his field and saw that the object was only 100 to 150 feet away.

The object made no noise. The bottom was bright and opaque, the center was white, and the edges were yellowish. The craft seemed to be twenty-five to thirty feet in diameter at the base and was about fifteen to eighteen feet high.

The mushroom tip detached and began to climb. As it did, it turned a bright orange. After a few moments, the mushroom descended, reattached itself at the top, and the colors returned to their original shades.

Unable to find any other people to witness the event, the archaeologist returned to his house where his wife was waiting outside. They watched the UFO for a few more minutes, then went back inside.

Their son went to the spot of the encounter the next day. He found, and videotaped, four circular ground traces in a rectangular shape about twenty-five by thirty feet. The grass in each of the circular marks was twisted and depressed. A fine, yellowish powder was found on the blades of grass.

During that spring and summer, the French magazine *Science and Life* reported on the events in Belgium. The coverage, from a Belgian point of view, was less than flattering. The magazine took an anti-UFO view, refused to examine the evidence, and published myths about the sightings, suggesting the Belgians were less than adequate observers.

In January 1990, the French reporters rejected all the Belgian eyewitnesses based on an examination of a single photograph. Although the picture showed little more than a single glowing smudge, rather than analyze it, the magazine used it to suggest all the witnesses were fooled by some sort of undefined optical illusion.

In June, the same magazine dismissed the sightings by claiming they were the result of the Stealth Fighter. This despite the fact that the Belgian Air Force was satisfied that no American Stealth aircraft had been flown over Belgium, and denials by the head of the Belgian Air Force, not to mention the denials by the American Air Force.

In October, with the Stealth explanation ruined by un-cooperative Belgian and American officials, a new explanation was trotted out. Now, according to the magazine, it wasn't a Stealth aircraft, but some other experimental aircraft, flown by American pilots without notifying the Belgian Air Force that such flights would take place. Of course, there is absolutely no evidence that any American aircraft, Stealth, experimental, or otherwise, were involved in the Belgian sightings. The French were just not willing to let go of what, to them, was a good explanation for the sightings.

In fact, in October 1990 there were more and better sightings taking place. On Sunday, October 21, two residents of Bastogne were returning home late when two lights appeared, descending toward them. Echoing the words shouted by another Belgian witness, one of them screamed, "They're coming for us!"

They lost sight of the object for a few moments, but it reappeared, now behind a hedge bordering the right side of the road. They thought it might be a reflection on the car window, but when it was cranked down, the light was still there, now less than fifty feet from the car.

As they drove along, the object seemed to pace them,

staying with the car. They slowed and stopped, as did the object. When they accelerated, the light did the same. When they reached the end of the roadside hedge, they stopped. Now they could see a dark mass, more than forty-five feet in diameter. It climbed rapidly and silently into the sky. On the bottom was a ring of seven or eight lights.

Less than forty-eight hours later, more UFOs were seen. At 5:30 A.M. on October 23, a young woman identified only as Regine was awakened by her alarm clock. Through the window of her residence on the outskirts of Athus, near Luxembourg, she saw two bright lights hovering over a hill about a quarter of a mile away. Between the two bright lights was a smaller, dimmer blue light.

Ten minutes later, the lights rose into the sky and began drifting toward her silently. The lights passed over her house and she ran into the dining room where she could again see the object. She noticed that there was a small red light on the lower part of the craft.

The object kept moving in the direction of Athus. It then veered to the left, in the direction of Luxembourg, and disappeared. There were apparently no other witnesses to the event.

Later that same day, that is, October 23, four teenagers saw an object that came from behind a hill. It was about a quarter mile away and had a number of extremely bright lights on the lower part of it that were directed toward the ground. Centered among these lights was a smaller, dimmer light. They believed that the object was taking off because of the low altitude when they first spotted it.

This craft was shaped like a pyramid with the apex

pointing to the front. At the base were two more red lights. The object was in sight for about thirty seconds and disappeared behind another hill.

Another sighting was made of a craft quite close to the ground. On November 22, 1990, at the village of Fluerus, a young woman was lying in bed when an intense light penetrated the room. She got out of bed, wiped the frost from the glass, and saw that the bright light was coming from behind a neighbor's wall. Although the light wasn't more than a hundred feet away, it was just behind the wall and in an abandoned field. As the light dimmed, she noticed blue flashes from that area. When a train rumbled through, the last of the lights dimmed and vanished.

The sightings continued. On December 9, more than a year after the first of the reports, another couple traveling by car saw an object. At first it seemed to be a glowing triangle. Then, watching through one of the car's windows, they saw a huge, circular plate over the top of a group of trees. Around the edge were bright white lights. There were also four spoke-like lines that were a glowing brass color.

The UFO was about one hundred and fifty feet in the air. Although they wanted to stop the car, because of traffic they were unable to do so. They lost sight of it quickly.

The end of 1990 brought no respite. On January 6, 1991, two separate groups of witnesses saw a low-flying circular plate. The first group also reported they had seen a cupola on the top. There were many lights on the object.

Minutes later, another group reported they saw three

lights to the left of the road. At first they believed it to be the lights from a soccer field. They noticed, however, that the lights were on something hovering over a quarry.

The UFO was, according to one witness, about two hundred fifty feet long and forty to fifty feet high. The underside bulged outward and was dark gray. Fifteen portholes on the side were lighted. The rear was flat and seemed to have some fins.

The press lost interest in the sightings as they continued. The stories were all becoming the same. Witnesses were seeing brightly lighted, mostly triangular-shaped objects, floating silently above the ground. There were no real examples of physical evidence left behind, and the few photographs taken provided no proof of the visitation.

The sightings, however, continued, but apparently at a slower pace. SOBEP reported that the reports were not just lights in the night sky. These sightings were of objects quite close to the ground with the witnesses, in many cases, not far from the object. They were receiving good, detailed descriptions. The only difference was that the media were no longer interested in the reports.

Some of that must be laid at the feet of the French reporters who had decided, for their own reasons, that the reports were hoaxes or explainable as American military aircraft. Even in the face of facts demonstrating that such an explanation was unworkable, they insisted that it was true. It smacks of some sort of outside pressure.

Of course, it only *smacks* of that. The media, not only in Europe but also in this country, seem to believe that there is nothing to the stories of flying saucers. They believe that proper research would provide a good explanation. Flying saucers do not exist.

Rather than believe there is some sort of conspiracy to force the media to print stories showing UFOs are easily explainable, it seems more likely that it is a self-imposed belief. No reporter wants to look silly, especially in front of his or her colleagues. The solution, when assigned a UFO story, is to find the "silly" angle. This allows the reporter to complete the assignment without having to be exposed to ridicule.

But the blame doesn't rest wholly on the media. Those doing UFO research are also guilty of sloppy work. Many reporters have been impressed with the preliminaries of a story only to learn, through investigation, the case isn't as solid as originally portrayed.

This, however, does not excuse sloppy reporting by the media. To suggest, as one Belgium newspaper did, that Washington had "confirmed" the reports of Stealth aircraft in the vicinity, is reckless. Clearly there was no such confirmation. The reporter should have checked those facts, rather than accepting them as true because that is what he wanted to believe.

The one thing that came from the Belgian sightings was government cooperation. Rather than bury the details in a classified study that would be released in parts over the next decades, the Belgian Air Force was quite candid. They assisted researchers trying to find explanations for the series of sightings.

But Belgium wasn't the only location reporting the bright-lighted objects close to the ground at that time. On October 14, 1990, while the Belgian wave was in full swing, a witness in Switzerland saw a similar object. According to Auguste Meessen, writing in the *International UFO Reporter*, Mrs. Wengere and her husband were driving toward Zurich when she spotted two bright white lights.

At first she believed them to be the lights on electrical transmission towers on the mountains. There was still sunlight and she believed that the lights were not on the mountains but between her car and the mountains. She told her husband that she was looking at a UFO and asked that he stop their car.

Unfortunately the road conditions didn't allow him to stop. They continued their observations, suggesting that the lights were huge because they washed out the stars. An airplane appeared, but the pilots seemed unaware of the UFO and the object didn't react.

They drove into a village and lost sight of the lights. However, when they were back in the country, the lights reappeared, a little higher in the sky. Now a third light had appeared. At first it was motionless and then began drifting up, toward the other two lights.

Now the other two lights began to move, as if attached and circling a single point. The lone light orbited in the same fashion, around some central point, maintaining its distance from the other two lights.

They slowed so they could see the lights better, but there was now traffic behind them. They entered another built-up area and lost sight of the lights, this time for good.

In Canada, on August 11, 1993, a triangular-shaped object made an appearance. Several friends, out late to watch the Perseid meteor shower, spotted several of the meteors and a couple of satellites. They even saw an airplane, complete with navigation lights, warning beacons, and heard the faraway droning of the engine. All this is important because it demonstrates that the witnesses had already observed and identified many of the common, conventional objects used to explain UFO sightings.

Just after midnight they spotted something that crossed the sky from north to south in a matter of seconds. One of the witnesses, because of his poor eyesight, didn't get a good look at the object. But the others did.

One of them said it was dark gray-black and triangular or boomerang shaped. There were three dim red lights on it, one near each point of the triangle. The lights were not, according to one witness, points of light like a star, but circles of light. They didn't flicker or blink, but remained steady during the entire observation.

David Thacker, a member of the Alberta UFO Study Group (AUFOSG) investigated the case and wrote about it in the *International UFO Reporter*. According to him he could find no explanation for it. With the cooperation of Canadian authorities, he checked the radar records of the Lethbridge area. According to Thacker, Frank Hayden, a shift supervisor, reviewed the tapes and found nothing on them that would account for the UFO.

The sighting is important only because of the shape of the craft. Most people still report either nocturnal lights or disc-shaped objects. Triangular craft are not frequently reported, but such sightings are becoming more common. The sighting of a triangular-shaped object in Canada does not prove that such objects exist or that the Belgium sightings are somehow corroborated. It merely suggests that something is going on.

In fact, we can take it another step by pointing out that

similarly shaped objects continue to be seen in Europe. On January 6, 1995, a British Airways Boeing 737 had a near midair collision with a triangular-shaped object near Manchester in the United Kingdom. Both the captain, Roger Wills, and the first officer, Mark Stuart, reported seeing the craft. The only discrepancy in the report was that Stuart believed the object had been illuminated by the jet's landing lights.

The flight recorders from the incident have been released and are interesting. At about twelve minutes to seven, on the evening of January 6, the jet crew reported, "... we just had something go down the [right-hand side] just above us very fast."

The Manchester control facility responded, "Well, there's nothing seen on radar. Was it, er ... an ... ?"

"Well, it had lights, it went down the starboard side very quick."

"And above you?"

"Just slightly above us ..."

Because the near miss involved a commercial aircraft, the Joint Airmiss Working Group, part of the Civil Aviation Authority in Great Britain, conducted a year-long investigation. They were unable to identify what had come so close to the civilian jet. In fact, because there was no solid evidence that would explain the object, they were unable to assess either the cause or the risk to other aircraft. Had this been thirty years earlier and in the United States, the Air Force might have labeled the case as "unidentified." Or more likely, as insufficient data for a scientific analysis.

In March 1995 there was a series of sightings over St. Petersburg in Russia. While some of the sightings were of disk-shaped craft, at least one of them was of a triangular-shaped object with a number of lights on it.

The real point here, however, is that we had a wave of sightings in Belgium in the early 1990s. Hundreds saw the craft and reported it. Belgian Air Force fighters attempted one intercept. The evidence for the sightings is the same as it has always been: witness testimony. Can the judgments of these witnesses be trusted, or is there something that creates a mob psychology so that normally rational people believe they are seeing flying saucers in the night sky?

The real point is that through these events, we have seen the news media in Europe acting like the news media in this country. They ignored the evidence or proposed solutions that have no basis in fact. If they could identify the UFO as a "normal" occurrence, at least to their satisfaction, then the sightings didn't count. Their attitude seemed to be: "an explanation has been suggested and we'll believe in that."

According to SOBEP, the sightings have slowed and virtually disappeared in Belgium. There are a few still made, but not with the regularity of the early part of the decade. What is left is a core of interesting reports that suggest *something* invaded the airspace over Belgium, and other western countries, but there is no evidence that the craft were either real or extraterrestrial. All too often that is all that we have in the end.

Conclusions

We have examined a great deal of information in our search for the truth. We have seen how the Air Force and the government have concealed information, lied about the situation, and tried to cover their tracks with false statements. We have seen, through the documentation available to us and the witness testimony we have gathered, that UFOs have been considered real and not some illusion, delusion, hallucination, or outright fraud. There is something going on and the government has attempted to conceal it from us.

What we've seen is that, from the very beginning, we have not been told the truth. At the moment, it doesn't matter if the reasons are sound or if it was just another example of "Big Brotherism." It doesn't matter if the conclusions drawn are correct, even though the evidence doesn't support those very conclusions. What is important is that we don't know what the hell the truth is. That's what is shown by the examination of the cases and investigations presented here. We just don't know.

What is needed is a truly independent investigation of UFOs. One that is free of believers and debunkers. One that is made up of men and women who are dedicated to the truth and nothing else. That is something that has yet to be done.

It is interesting that the debunkers rarely refer to the Condon Committee these days. In 1966, as flying saucers were being seen all over the United States and public attention to the problem was growing, the Air Force decided that they needed help. They gave a contract to the University of Colorado to study the problem of flying saucers. This was supposed to be an independent investigation that would answer, to the satisfaction of everyone, the question of the reality of flying saucers. It is also important to remember that a number of universities turned down the contract before it was offered to the University of Colorado because they didn't like the strings attached to it.

The study seemed like a good idea at the time. If it was a truly independent investigation, carried out under the direction of a respected scientist who wouldn't be worried about his professional reputation being ruined by an association with UFOs, then answers might be found. If the scientists conducted a truly scientific investigation, then the final answer, or answers, might be found.

But as with the public studies before it, the Condon Committee was rigged to answer the questions in the way in which the Air Force wanted them answered. In fact, Dr. Michael Swords of the J. Allen Hynek Center for UFO Studies found proof that the Condon Committee was a setup from the very beginning. According to a letter discovered by Dr. Swords and written by Air Force Lieutenant Colonel Robert Hippler, there was no intention of performing an objective and scientific investigation of flying saucers. Hippler wrote to Condon and his staff that no one knew of any extraterrestrial visitation and, therefore, there "has been no visitation." That spells out the opinions of the Air Force in 1966 and suggests exactly what Condon and his committee were assigned to "discover."

Hippler also pointed to the cost of continued investigation and asked Condon "if the taxpayer should support this" for the next several years. Hippler warned Condon that another such "independent" investigation couldn't be mounted for several years if Condon determined there was something to the flying saucers. It should be noted that other similar studies had always suggested that the investigation be continued. Hippler, apparently, didn't want to fall into that trap.

Condon understood exactly what Hippler was trying to tell him. Just three days after reading the Hippler letter, Condon was in Corning, New York, to lecture to scientists, including members of the Corning Section of the American Chemical Society and the Corning Glass Works Chapter of Sigma Xi. He told them, "It is my inclination right now to recommend that the government get out of this business [UFO investigation]. My attitude right now is that there is nothing in it. But I am not supposed to reach a conclusion for another year."

So much for scientific objectivity.

Skeptics also point to the investigation conducted by Dr. H. P. Robertson in January 1953. Although sponsored by the CIA, that point is probably irrelevant. What is important is that Robertson, who created the panel and selected the members, picked men who were openly hostile to the concept of UFOs, extraterrestrial space flight, and flying saucers. Then, as we detailed earlier in this book, Robertson apparently wrote a final report on a Friday evening—a report which appeared to have actually been written beforehand.

So the two public studies made by "independent" scientists and sponsored by federal tax dollars were apparently nothing more than propaganda designed to convince the public that there was nothing to reports of flying saucers. Saucer enthusiasts, of course, attacked the reports when they were made, but the propaganda machinery could deal with that easily. Reporters, reading only the conclusions of the studies and not the available supporting documentation, determined that the Air Force had been right all along. There were no flying saucers. There were just poorly trained observers who misinterpreted natural phenomena, who were plagued by illusions, delusions, and hallucinations, and who were guilty of creating practical jokes, hoaxes, and faked pictures of flying saucers.

But we have seen, by studying complete case files and investigations, that neither study was particularly scientific nor objective. They reached the conclusion they were supposed to reach, and that was the end of it: the public was foolish for believing in something as silly as flying saucers.

The Air Force has provided us with another example of this. In September 1994, they released a report on their investigation into the events outside of Roswell, New Mexico, in July 1947. An Air Force colonel, Richard Weaver, spent time, money, and effort in an attempt, according to the Air Force, to review the Roswell incident. Weaver's report, published in 1994, suggested that the event could be explained by a balloon from the 1947 top secret Project Mogul.

As with both the Robertson panel and the Condon Committee before it, Weaver's report leaves out important information and draws conclusions that aren't warranted by the evidence that he cites. The report implies that Mogul was highly classified, and they that those stationed at the Roswell Army Air Field in July 1947 wouldn't have been aware of it and therefore could have been fooled by the unusual debris. Weaver forgets to point out that some of the officers at Roswell were, in fact, briefed on Project Mogul because their assistance in recovering the equipment was wanted by those associated with Mogul.

But more importantly, while the project *was* highly classified, the balloons and equipment *were not*. The balloons were standard neoprene weather balloons and the arrays included rawin targets that had been standard equipment for years. Nothing about the balloons and equipment was classified, and they should have been easily identifiable to the officers and men at the Roswell Army Air Field, even if they knew nothing about Project Mogul and the information it was designed to retrieve.

The other side of the flying saucer controversy coin is no better. Those who truly believe in the reality of the

flying saucers are often willing to endorse the most out-
rageous cases because they *must* be true. There are hundreds of examples of this from the contactees of the 1950s
to the witnesses of today.

Larry Warren demonstrates this better than most. UFO
researchers believe his tale even though it does not fit in
with the rest of the Bentwaters case. They believe him,
even when those who were truly involved in the sightings over two nights, have suggested that Warren was
not there, or have challenged his testimony about the
case. The UFO believers accept him as a legitimate witness, even though he has said, repeatedly, that his whole
story might be imagination.

Might be? Or is?

Instead of rejecting Warren and his information, they
try to fit it into the Bentwaters UFO framework by suggesting mind control experiments, governmental lies,
and an international cover-up to account for any date
confusion. But if Warren is eliminated from the story,
then the dates all track and there is no more problem.
Larry Warren created the confusion because, without it,
he was just another airman stationed at Bentwaters when
the UFO sightings were made. Like them, he would have
no role to play and no television crews or UFO investigators would speak to him.

Another fine example are the Majestic-Twelve documents received by researchers about a decade ago. These
documents allege that the U.S. government recovered a
flying saucer outside of Roswell and that a super-secret
oversight committee made up of twelve scientists, government leaders, and high-ranking military officers was
created by President Truman to exploit the find. The

MJ-12 documents, according to proponents, prove everything we have seen here in a single short example.

Research into the MJ-12 documents by both opponents and proponents has for the most part revealed many flaws, such as an incorrect dating format, ranks of military officers that are wrong, combination of two levels of classification on the title page, lack of a top secret control number, and an improper executive order format. There are few in the UFO community who accept the documents as authentic today. The problem is that there are a few who believe the documents are "disinformation." That is, they believe the documents were created by "insiders" to fool the UFO community. They believe that the insiders were attempting to discredit all UFO researchers by providing them with information that close scrutiny would reveal to be tainted.

So even when we *know* there are problems with the evidence, we create rationalizations to explain away those problems. And when more problems are discovered, more rationalizations are created until there are so many rationalizations that the case begins to collapse under its own weight.

The point here is to suggest something that can be done to eliminate the problems. We don't need another government-sponsored investigation that is supposed to be objective and scientific. We don't need another research paper, document, or briefing filled with the same things that have filled all the rest. What we need is a single, solid investigation, in which the conclusions are not drawn *before* the evidence is examined and the research had been completed.

We have examined a number of cases, documents, and

investigations. We have seen that those cases we examined were not as the government and the military would have us believe. We have also seen, however, that those same cases are not as the UFO researchers and investigators would have us believe. The truth, as always, is somewhere in between the two.

I should also point out that we UFO researchers labor under an additional handicap. We have no official status. If the witnesses refuse to speak with us, for whatever reason, we can't suggest that we go "downtown" to talk about it. If they close the door in our faces, our only recourse is to climb into the car and go home. We can hope to learn things from other sources, but sometimes they are not available to us. Investigation, from a private point of view, without official status, is a very difficult task.

During the years-long investigation of the Roswell case, I spoke a number of times to Major (later, Colonel) Edwin Easley, the man who had been provost marshal at the Roswell Army Air Field when the UFO crash took place. During the very first conversation, Easley told me a number of times that he had been sworn to secrecy. He didn't want to violate his oath and said that he couldn't talk about it.

But Easley also wanted to help, providing clues about the event. He helped me understand the situation on the base at Roswell, who was doing what, and gave limited but very helpful clues when and where he could. Official status of some sort might have helped crack through the decades-old veil of secrecy if it had been available. Instead I was forced to rely on the kindness of Edwin Easley.

I say *might* have helped because I have seen the result of Colonel Weaver's interview with Captain (later, Lieutenant Colonel) Sheridan Cavitt, the officer in charge of counterintelligence at Roswell in July 1947. I have seen the transcript of that interview and realize that it follows the party, meaning Air Force, line. I have seen the letter from the secretary of the Air Force to Cavitt telling him that he can share everything he knows about the Roswell case with Colonel Weaver because the colonel holds the highest of clearances.

Weaver, naturally, showed the letter to Cavitt, then conducted the interview. What we don't know is what was said before the tape began to roll, if Weaver and Cavitt discussed the nature of his testimony before the tape was started, or if Weaver provided Cavitt with the "answer" to the Roswell debris before anyone there said much of anything on tape.

Cavitt's story, as told to Weaver, does confirm parts of the tale told by others, such as Major Jesse A. Marcel, Sr., the air intelligence officer assigned to the base, and Lewis Rickett, Cavitt's NCO in the counterintelligence office at Roswell. Cavitt said that he had picked up a balloon, and had been accompanied to the site by Marcel. But Cavitt had told me, years earlier, first that he hadn't been at Roswell at the time, and then that he had been assigned to the base, but not involved in anything like the recovery described by Marcel and Rickett. And, he told me that he had never participated in the recovery of a balloon, weather, Mogul, or otherwise. He was quite specific about that.

Had Cavitt said, in those earlier interviews, "Yeah, I was there and I picked up a balloon," the situation would have been radically altered. In fact, there was so little importance attached to the balloons that the Alamogordo, New Mexico, city newspaper reported on them just two days *after* the events in Roswell were reported nationally. Of course, the newspaper didn't mention Project Mogul, but did publish pictures of the balloons and arrays that were being launched. Professor Charles Moore, of New York University and a member of the Mogul team, told me that the ladder featured in one of the pictures was one that he had bought to help launch the balloon flights.

In other words, Cavitt was under no directive to lie about the recovery of the balloons, if that is what had happened in 1947. While the purpose of Mogul was classified, the recovery of the equipment was not. When I spoke to Cavitt in 1990, at his home, it would have been very simple for him to say that he had, in fact, helped recover balloons. Instead he told me that he had never done that.

Official status for private investigations might have gotten us answers earlier. Official status, if Cavitt had told Weaver the same thing he told mc, would have brought everything he said into question immediately. But because I, like the other private investigators, have a "financial" interest in UFOs in general or the Roswell case in particular, our investigations are dismissed as flawed. We're just a "bunch of UFO nuts" who want to believe and who are making a buck at it.

Of course, the argument can be turned around on the Air Force. It can be said that the Air Force has a financial stake in proving UFOs don't exist. After all, their mission is to keep American skies clear of foreign invaders, whether those invaders were launched from terrestrial bases or outer space. If flying saucers are real, then it is clear the Air Force has failed at their mission.

There is a second point to be made. If there was no crash of a flying saucer at Roswell, why does the Air Force care what we think? We are just a bunch of UFO nuts. Yet they have gone to considerable taxpayer expense to convince us that there was no UFO crash at Roswell. Why is that?

The point is we have uncovered repeated incidents in which government officials and military officers have not told the truth about flying saucers. We have found the paper trail that suggests something extremely unusual has been happening and that our government has been less than candid about it. We have demonstrated that the public investigations by the Air Force, the Robertson panel, and the Condon Committee were more interested in convincing us that UFOs were not real than they were in learning just what was going on.

And, we have learned that they did take the problem seriously for years, contrary to their claims otherwise. They manipulated the press so that they never had to answer the tough questions. When Blue Book became too public, they switched the investigation to another unit, but never said a word. When UFO researchers said there was a secret investigation, which the Air Force always denied, it turns out *they were right*. We've examined the documents proving secret investigations did exist.

Once we have uncovered the problem, it is up to us to provide the solution. And the solution is simple. A solid, independent investigation that doesn't have its conclusions drawn before the scientists even hear or see the first bit of evidence. A solid, independent investigation that will look at all the evidence carefully, objectively, and scientifically. An independent investigation that will not be swayed by scientific or public opinion, but one that will review all the evidence.

People have talked about how it is impossible to solve the UFO problem. The answer is that it isn't impossible, it just requires a solid, objective study of the evidence. Carl Sagan liked to say, "Where is the evidence? Where is the physical evidence?"

The answer is: The evidence is all around for those who want to see it. The only real question is if UFOs are extraterrestrial. The evidence presented here suggests that it might be true. It suggests that the situation isn't as we have been led to believe. Now is the time to try to learn the truth rather than pretend that we know it.

Appendix A:

1946: The Ghost Rockets

In their report of December 10, 1948, Air Force and naval officers suggested that some of those reporting flying saucers might be doing it for publicity. There were, and are, people who will do about anything to see their names in the newspaper or see themselves on television. Examples of this can easily be found everywhere. Not too many years ago, someone reported finding a syringe in a can of Pepsi. Within days there were dozens of such cases, with those who found the syringes claiming they were going to sue for damages.

It made no difference that Pepsi denied that anything could be found inside their cans. According to them, and as per videotape of the production line, nothing could accidentally be sealed in the cans. Before the cans are filled, the production line turns them upside down so that anything in them would fall out. Still the stories persisted.

Within weeks it was over. Surveillance cameras in mini-marts and convenience stores showed some of the "victims" actually inserting the syringes into the cans after they had opened them. When confronted with the evidence, they denied they had done anything at all. When the episode ended, there wasn't a single case where anyone had found anything inside a Pepsi can except Pepsi.

What this shows is that the authors of the December 10 report were right. There were, and are, people who would do almost anything to see their names in the newspaper or see themselves on television. But that doesn't mean that everyone reporting UFOs fits into that category.

The authors did point to the episode of the Scandinavian ghost rockets in 1946 and suggest that publicity had brought some witnesses to the attention of the authorities. They had no evidence that such was the case, but it is a valid point. The ghost rockets could be considered the first of the modern UFO wave of sightings, and it might be illustrative to compare them to the flying saucer reports that developed in the United States in the following years.

The first of the ghost rockets to be reported *after* World War II appeared in the skies of Helsinki on February 26, 1946. A radio station reported that "numerous meteors have recently fallen" in northern Finland. It was interesting, but the reaction of many was to believe that the objects seen were, in fact, meteors.

On June 9, the question about the identity of the objects

surfaced again in Helsinki where a glowing body, trailing smoke behind it, was seen heading to the southwest at a low altitude.

On June 10, witnesses reported something resembling the German V-2 rockets overhead. It was in sight for about ten minutes, and about two minutes after it disappeared, an explosion was heard.

And then, over the next several weeks, there would be other reports of ghost rockets. In many of them, it was reported that the object or rocket had crashed. On July 9, 1946, for example, near Lake Barken, Sweden, a witness watched an object with alternating blue and green lights come from the northeast and plunge into the lake about a hundred and ten yards away.

On July 10, 1946, at Bjorkon, Sweden, a number of people watched as a "projectile trailing luminous smoke" slammed into a beach leaving a yard wide, shallow crater containing a slag-like material, some of it reduced to powder. A newspaper reporter found a cylinder about twenty or thirty meters in diameter. Military authorities investigated, produced ambiguous results, and finally accused the witnesses of imagining things.

Just over a week later, on July 18, 1946, at Lake Mjosa, Sweden, two eight-foot-long missiles with wings set about three feet from the front plunged into the lake, creating "notable turbulence." While in flight, the wings seemed to flap, as if made of cloth, and the objects whistled.

The next day, at Lake Kolmjarv, Sweden, witnesses watched a gray, rocket-shaped object with wings crash into the lake, sparking a three-week hunt for it by military authorities. Nothing was found. Nearly forty years later, a Swedish UFO researcher, Clas Svahn, interviewed some of the civilian witnesses and military investigators. An Air Force officer speculated that the object might have been made of a light-weight material that could disintegrate easily. A civilian witness claimed she heard a "thunderclap" that might have been the object exploding. There were several additional witnesses to this, and a governmental investigation team was dispatched. All the information about this case would not be available until the Swedish government released the details of their investigation into the ghost rockets some time later.

The *Chicago Tribune*, on July 27, reported that there had been more than 500 sightings of the ghost rockets in just twenty-six days. It was about that time that the Swedish government began to censor the reports. The press could continue to report specific incidents as long as the locations were deleted. It is also important to note that the names of the witnesses were also left out of the accounts. That, of course, prevented anyone from doing any followup investigation and learning things that the military, and the government, might not want them to learn.

About the beginning of August, the Swedish Defense Staff announced that "radio-controlled rockets" were entering Sweden from the south and exiting in an easterly direction. In a statement that would be echoed in the United States the following year, Swedish officials suggested that the number of reports was probably exaggerated because of the publicity, but when those were eliminated there was still a solid core of reports.

As noted, there were a number of reports of the ghost rockets crashing and debris was retrieved on several occasions. The fragments that were examined showed the presence of common materials. Nothing was produced to suggest that the ghost rockets had been manufactured anywhere other than on Earth.

It shouldn't come as much of a surprise that the Swedish authorities were concerned about the ghost rockets. World War II had been over for less than a year. During the final months of the war, the Nazis had launched hundreds of V-2 rockets against the Allies. It seems reasonable to assume that the Swedish were worried that someone, possibly a pocket of Nazi fanatics, or the Soviets using captured German scientists, was responsible for the invasion of Swedish territory.

The situation in Sweden didn't change in August. On the twelfth a cigar-shaped object, about five feet long and trailing smoke, passed over a small town and then "landed" on a small, uninhabited island. The thick undergrowth "discouraged" the searchers who worked their way to the site. They found nothing.

At Malmö, Sweden, on August 16, one of the "ghost" rockets exploded, breaking windows and dropping fragments.

About a month later, in mid-October 1946, over southern Sweden two people on a lake heard a noise that drew their attention to an object that appeared over the trees. They described it as looking like a small dart with wings and a ball-shaped tip. It exploded as it crashed into the water.

But probably the most important event of August was the arrival of Lieutenant General James H. Doolittle, the man who had planned and led the first bombing raid on Tokyo just months after the beginning of World War II. Doolittle had been briefed by U.S. intelligence about the events. It had been announced that Doolittle was in Sweden on business for Shell Oil Company, but documents released in later years have revealed the truth. American military officers were highly interested in the ghost rockets and Doolittle had been dispatched to learn what he could.

August also brought reports from other areas in Europe. On August 20, witnesses in Dijon, France, reported large, elongated objects that whistled overhead at great speed.

During the last week in August, Norway joined the ranks of the countries reporting the ghost rockets. The London *Daily Telegraph* reported, "Two of the projectiles have been seen over Oslo during the past week, and two are reliably reported to have landed in Lake Mjoesen, north of the city. Unfortunately the lake is too deep for the authorities to be able to hold out any hope of dredging the pieces ... The Norwegian General Staff issued a statement to the press asking it not to make any mention of the appearance of the rockets over Norwegian territory but to pass on all reports to the Intelligence Department of the High Command."

At the end of the August, there was a report from Denmark. Witnesses said that "a rocket bomb" fell from the sky with a "thundering explosion." The witnesses said the object was a speeding bullet-shaped body soaring through the sky before it fell.

In September more of Europe became involved. In Greece, "Acting Foreign Minister Stephanos Stephano-polos supported a statement in London by Premier Constantin Tsaldaris that flying rockets had been seen over Greece."

On September 17, north Africa entered the arena. From Morocco came the report that, "A flying projectile with a 'tail of flame' was seen last night over the town of Fez; it was reported at Casablanca today."

Over the next few days reports would be made in Germany, Portugal, Belgium, and Holland. The reports would detail points of light, elongated rockets and even disc-shaped craft. The sightings included everything that would become a staple of the UFO waves that were to follow, including an investigation by governmental officials and attempts to suppress the information being reported by the newspapers.

On October 10, 1946, the Swedish Defense Staff released its findings. They concluded that the majority of the sightings were of conventional objects seen in unusual circumstances (doesn't that sound familiar?). The staff also reported, "In some cases clear, unambiguous observations have been made which cannot be explained as natural phenomena, Swedish aircraft, or imagination on the part of the observer. Echo, radar, and other equipment registered readings, but gave no clue as to the nature of the objects." The few samples of physical evidence that had been recovered by the military were identified as routine and provided no clues to the identity of the ghost rockets.

Jerry Clark and Lucius Farish, two men who have completed a great deal of research into the ghost rockets, reported in *Saga's UFO Report* in 1974 that one of the first ghost rocket sightings would have eliminated the belief that they were of Soviet design if it had been reported in 1946. The story was first published in the Swedish magazine *Allers*.

According to the story, Gosta Carlsson, a resident of Angelholm, a town sixty miles from Malmö in southern Sweden, told reporters:

"It was an evening in May 1946. I had been out walking and was resting for a while close by the shore. By the time I started to walk back it was almost dark, so I used a forehead lamp.

"When I saw a light among the trees I thought at first that someone had made a fire. The light was coming from an open space in the forest a short distance away. When I reached the place, however, I saw that in the farthest end of the open ground there was a disc-shaped object with a cupola. The cupola seemed to be a cabin with oval windows. Above it there was a mast, almost like the periscope of a submarine. Beneath the disc there was a big oblong fin which stretched from the center to the edge of the underside. There were also two metal landing legs. A small ladder reached to the ground from a door beside the fin.

"The object was approximately 53 feet in diameter and 13 feet from top to bottom at the middle. I know this because I measured the marks on the following day. There were a lot of holes around the edge of the disc, like those of a turbine, and jet-beams darted from the holes which burned the grass when the object departed. The light came from the mast. It was about 17 feet in height, and three antennae were suspended from its top. Lower down something like a lamp shade was hanging. It was shining with a strange purple light which covered not only the whole object but also the ground a couple of feet beyond it. The light was flowing and pulsating from the 'lamp shade' like water from a fountain. Where the light hit the ground I could see a sparkling effect.

"On the ground, beyond the area of the light, a man in white, closely fitting overalls was standing. He seemed to be some sort of guard. He raised his hand toward me: it was a gesture that could not be misunderstood, so I stopped. I was less than 30 feet from him. He was approximately as tall as I am, maybe a few inches shorter, but he was thinner than me. There were others like him, but the strange thing was that nobody said a word. It seems as if they had just finished repairing a window, because they put their tools away and looked at me. Everything was silent. The only thing I heard was the sound from the guard when he walked on the grass. There were three men working at the window, and two more were standing alongside. There were three women as well, and one more came out of the object later. On the far side there was another guard. In all I saw 11 persons.

"They all wore short black boots and gloves, a black belt around the waist, and a transparent helmet. The women had ashen-colored hair, but I could not see the hair of the men as they wore black caps. There were all brown-colored, as if sunburned.

"I went a few steps closer, but then the guard raised his hand again. After that I stood still. The guard had a black box on his chest which was suspended by a chain around his neck. It looked like an old black camera. He turned toward me and I thought he was going to take a picture of me, but nothing happened, except that I thought I heard a click from my forehead lamp. The lamp did not work after that, but that may have been purely coincidental. When I returned home I found that the battery had run out, although it was a new one.

"It seemed as if the 'cheese-dish cover' of light stood like a wall between us. I think it was created to isolate them from our world and atmosphere. One of the women came out of the cabin with an object in her hand. She went to the edge of the wall of light and threw the object beyond the area of light. At the same time I heard her laugh.

"Afterwards it is difficult to explain what one does, and why he does it. I thought the disc-like object could be some sort of military device. The whole scene seemed so strange. I never take alcohol, and I knew it was not an hallucination, but nevertheless I decided to go back to the seashore, and from there return to the opening to see if the object was still present. I was aware of a smell like that from ozone following an electrical discharge."

A few comments about this case must be made. First and foremost, though the witness said the events took place in May 1946, he didn't report it until 1971. It could be said that his story is an invention influenced by the reports of flying saucers that have been made for twenty-five years before he came forward.

According to Clark and Farish, Swedish UFO researcher Sven-Olaf Frederickson reported that Carlsson had retrieved the object the being had seemed to throw away. Here, once again, is a report of an object that was supposed to have been made on another planet. The 1971 investigation by Frederickson revealed nothing extraordinary in the object. And, according to Carlsson, it had changed shape over the years.

And finally, looking at the tale from an anthropological point of view, it seems strange that a being from another planet would use human gestures to stop Carlsson. Even among different cultures around the world, gestures have different meanings. The confusion over gestures is sometimes funny and sometimes tragic. To assume that a race from another world would develop gestures that would be understood by Carlsson seems unlikely.

If, however, the report is an accurate representation of what Carlsson saw in 1946, it was certainly predictive of the UFO sightings that would begin about a year later. And, if the report is accurate, it certainly eliminates the possibility that the ghost rockets, or whatever, were something of Soviet manufacture or German design.

And, if we are to believe what has been written before, the Swedish government actively suppressed the tales of the ghost rockets. If people were reporting them for the publicity they would receive, then the government was doing what it could to stop the wave. It must be noted that the suppression of the reports did not stop people from making observations of the objects.

This is, of course, the same claim that American officers would make about similar waves of sightings in this country. But it seems that few of those reporting sightings had visions of their names in the newspapers. While the reports might have been of astronomical phenomena, unusual weather events, or conventional aircraft seen under less than perfect conditions, few of those making the reports sought any sort of publicity. In fact, in many cases, the people in this country only made their reports when promised their names *wouldn't* appear in the newspapers.

With the Swedish and Scandinavian ghost rockets, we can trace the reports back, beyond 1946 and the Second World War, and into the 1930s. The first time that a ghost rocket report surfaced in a Swedish newspaper was in 1939. Over the next few years there would be other reports, but some of those seem to be traceable to the German experiments on the V-1s and V-2s.

But the phenomenon seems to have originated in November and December 1933, near the border with Norway and just below the Arctic Circle. These sightings were not of rockets, but of lights that seemed to fly or float along the valleys near the border. The only known aircraft in the area could be accounted for, but there was the possibility that some sort of smuggling was taking place.

As the number of reports grew, and in some respect because of newspaper reports, the various Scandinavian governments tried to find explanations. The Norwegians, Swedes, and Finns all shared their information and co-operated with one another to either force down or capture one of these "mysterious airplanes."

Studies made by the various governments came to the same conclusions that modern authorities do when confronted with UFO sightings. Many are from reliable observers, but many, if not most, are from people unfamiliar with the sky around them. In a Swedish study of 487 cases reported during the winter of 1933–1934, they wrote off nearly a quarter of them as "unbelievable." But more importantly, there was a solid core of reliable reports that couldn't be explained in a conventional sense.

Just over a decade later, the Swedish Defense Staff would be investigating nearly a thousand ghost rocket reports. What separates the ghost rockets from other UFO waves is that nearly 100 impacts of the craft were reported, and thirty pieces of debris were submitted to the military for analysis.

One of the most important, and the most interesting, was the July 19 event mentioned earlier. It was just before noon when a farmer, Kurt Lindback, and others heard a rumbling that drew his attention to the sky. He spotted something that he thought, at first, was an airplane. It was about seven feet long and had two stubby wings.

The light gray object fell into the lake about a mile from where he was standing. There was a large splash, followed by a second one, suggesting some sort of explosion.

Another witness, standing on the shore, told of the horrible noise. He said that it was as if a bomb had detonated nearby. Of course, there was no one dropping bombs on Sweden a year after the war had ended.

The Swedish military did investigate at length. The military cordoned the area and erected a raft over the area where the object fell. From the raft, they could see that something had detonated underwater. The lake bed was disturbed, and the plant life had been thrown up and out to land onto the nearby shore.

Two engineers arrived shortly after the military. They searched for signs of radioactivity but found none. The military search was finally suspended when nothing physical was located.

Although the sightings and investigations have been well documented not only by Swedish authorities but by other Scandinavian officials, no solution to the ghost rocket epidemic has been found. The introduction of radar and other monitoring equipment only proved that something physical was being seen. And, although many in Sweden thought in 1946 that the ghost rockets were from the Soviet Union, no credible evidence has ever been found to support that. Instead, the Swedish officials are left with no solution. All they know is that something that resembled a modern cruise missile was being fired at and seen over much of Europe, but there was no one in 1946 who had the technology to do that.

This then is what the Air Force and Naval officers were referring to in their December 10, 1948 report. Doolittle might have contributed some of the information to them. But, in 1948, the Scandinavian ghost rockets meant little or nothing to United States Air Force officers. They were having their own trouble trying to identify the flying discs that had been reported over all of the United States since 1947.

Appendix B:

The Documentation Against Roswell

S ince the Roswell case first broke in the UFO community with Len Stringfield's 1978 MUFON Symposium speech, the skeptics have suggested that it
never happened. They have ignored a large body of eyewitness testimony, suggesting the witnesses were mistaken, caught up in the hysteria of the moment, or were
spreading lies for personal gain.

The case the skeptics make now encompasses three
documents, or reports, that were originally classified,
some as high as Top Secret. These documents, suggest
the skeptics, mean that no such crash took place, because
they make no mention of the Roswell crash debris. These
documents kill the idea completely, at least in their
minds.

The Roswell story began late on the evening of July 4

when something slammed into the ground just north of the small New Mexican town of Roswell. The next day, according to a number of eyewitnesses including Major (later, Colonel) Edwin Easley, Frank Kaufmann, Sergeant Thomas Gonzales, Dr. W. Curry Holden, and Lieutenant Colonel Albert Lovejoy Duran, the remains of an alien craft that had crashed were recovered. The object, triangle-shaped with a batlike rear wing, was taken by the Army, first into the base at Roswell, and later transported to Wright Field outside of Dayton, Ohio.

Several of the witnesses, including those mentioned earlier, apparently saw the bodies of the alien flight crew. The bodies were also moved from the impact site to the base and then on to Wright Field. By late July 1947, the evidence of the craft and bodies had been covered up.

About that same time, Mac Brazel, a rancher living near Corona, New Mexico, seventy-five to eighty miles northwest of Roswell, reported to the Chaves County sheriff that something had fallen on his ranch. Major Jesse A. Marcel, the air intelligence officer of the 509th Bomb Group, based at Roswell, responded to the sheriff's telephone call. With another officer, identified by Marcel as Sheridan Cavitt, the base counterintelligence officer, Marcel traveled to the Brazel ranch. There he recovered strange metallic debris that, according to him, wouldn't burn, was extremely light-weight, and unbreakable. Marcel was convinced that he handled something "that came to Earth but wasn't of Earth." In other words, it was an extraterrestrial craft.

These are the facts of the case boiled down to almost nothing. I spent more than six years investigating this report, spoke to all the witnesses who are mentioned earlier as having seen the bodies, and to four dozen people who claim to have handled the strange metallic debris. The point here is to provide a synopsis of the case so that the rest of the material can be understood.

To me, Roswell reflects the crash of an alien craft and the recovery of it by Army personnel. Both military and civilian officials, all very high in the government, were aware of the crash and the recovery. Now, if it happened as I believe, there would be a paper trail that could be located. Something should give us a hint about the Roswell case.

First, there are some newspaper articles. Originally, the reports suggested that the officers of the Roswell Army Air Field had recovered one of the mysterious flying saucers that had been reported for about two weeks. There is no speculation in the first story about the nature of the flying saucers, only that one had been recovered by the Army with the help of a local rancher.

Less than twenty-four hours later, the debris was identified by Brigadier General Roger Ramey, commanding officer of the Eighth Air Force, parent organization of the 509th, as a rather common weather balloon and radar target. Photographs of that debris appeared in newspapers around the country. It looked as if the flying saucer was nothing more than a weather balloon, as General Ramey said.

Jesse Marcel, Sr., who appeared in two of the photographs, told various people, including television reporter Johnny Mann, that the pictures were not of the material he had found on the Brazel ranch. He suggested the pictures were staged for the media.

Colonel (later, Brigadier General) Thomas J. DuBose

confirmed that the material in Ramey's office was not the stuff that had been found outside of Roswell. According to DuBose, the material had been switched with that of a weather balloon. DuBose told investigators, on videotape, that the weather balloon story was a cover to be provided to reporters.

But newspaper reports are not the same thing as military documents that were originally classified. The debate over Roswell should not include the newspaper articles because, no matter how objective the reporters, they are, in fact, reporting on what others said. No one is holding their feet to the fire. If they get a few facts wrong, they will be corrected in small boxes buried inside the newspaper days later. Besides, sometimes the rush to get there first overshadows the accuracy of their stories.

But official documents passed among the top military leaders are different. We can expect them to be an accurate representation of the situation. The men charged with the defense of the United States can't make intelligent decisions about that defense if there are inaccuracies in the information upon which they base their decisions. A review of that documentation should give us clues about the nature of the situation and flying saucers in 1947.

First, we must remember that all this took place during July 1947. During that period there were dozens of flying saucer sightings. It was a time of great intensity, just as it had been during the summer of 1952 and the late fall of 1957. But unlike those periods, there was no official investigation and no mechanism in place for proper research. The officers in the then Army Air Forces were as much in the dark as anyone else. A review of the statements made by top military and government officials during late June and early July 1947 shows that they didn't know what was happening either. Just like the rest of us, they were guessing.

In fact, in one newspaper article, an Air Army Forces officer, Tom Brown, was quoted as saying that they didn't know what was causing the sightings. This is a rather startling admission from an officer charged with the defense of the United States.

It was during July that Brigadier General George Schulgen, the assistant chief of staff for intelligence, prepared a document for the commanding general of the Air Materiel Command, Lieutenant General Nathan F. Twining. It is important to understand the nature of the document. It was not a letter requesting information, or asking for an opinion about the flying discs, but a report that contained sixteen specific cases involving military and civilian pilots and other specific flying saucer sightings. Schulgen's document, then, contained a great deal of evidence that Schulgen wanted analyzed by the intelligence officers at AMC.

Twining, or rather the intelligence officials assigned to AMC, did exactly what Schulgen wanted. They analyzed the reports and wrote their conclusions in a three-page letter signed by Twining.

Again, it must be pointed out that the response was drafted after an analysis of the materials and reports that Schulgen himself had forwarded. In other words, there is no evidence that those at AMC added anything to the reports. All they did was analyze the material sent by Schulgen. That point will become important later.

UFO believers have often quoted from the beginning of the letter signed by Twining who wrote, "2. It is the opinion that: a. The phenomenon reported is something real and not visionary or fictitious. b. There are objects probably approximating the shape of a disc, of such appreciable size as to appear to be as large as manmade aircraft . . ."

Twining and his staff were saying that the situation was real and that investigation into it was important. They didn't believe that flying saucers were hoaxes or illusions. The question was what they were and if they posed a threat to the security of the United States.

Skeptics, especially those who believe that the Roswell case is, at best, a misidentification of a common weather balloon and at worst a hoax, also quote from the Twining letter. Twining, on page three wrote, "Due consideration must be given the following: (2) The lack of physical evidence in the shape of crash recovered exhibits which would undeniably prove the existence of these objects."

Twining, as the head of the AMC, would have known if an object had crashed outside of Roswell. The laboratory facilities for the study of the debris were at Wright Field. There is no way that such studies could have been undertaken at AMC without Twining knowing about it.

That would seem to suggest that the Roswell crash didn't happen. How else to explain the statement about the lack of recovered exhibits? Does this mean there was no crash outside of Roswell, or is there another explanation?

It seems reasonable to believe that the statement is an outgrowth of the package sent to AMC by Schulgen. It seems that the men at AMC reviewed the material sent and responded to it without adding anything. It is also possible that the response, signed by Twining, was written by someone else at AMC for Twining's signature. In other words, because there was no mention in Schulgen's material about Roswell, AMC made no mention of it.

What this means is that although Twining knew about the events in Roswell, it was not necessary to compromise that knowledge to accomplish the mission. Twining and his people needed a project to study the flying discs, and that was the recommendation they made based on the material sent by Schulgen. There was no need to mention the Roswell material.

It should also be pointed out that Schulgen's material and Twining's response were classified only as Secret. The Roswell case would be Top Secret. Military regulations require that the highest level of classification in a document be the overall classification. That would mean that even if most of a report was unclassified, but a single paragraph contained top secret information, then the whole document must be classified Top Secret. Either that, or the top secret paragraph must be removed.

If we look at this objectively, we can see that there was no need to mention Roswell in order to accomplish the goal of a priority investigation. All the data used for the analysis was submitted from Schulgen, which contained nothing about Roswell. The analysis pointed out that crash-recovered debris would prove the case and none was submitted.

But the Twining letter doesn't mean that Twining didn't know about Roswell, or that he lied to Schulgen and Schulgen's superiors in Washington. The data about Roswell would have been communicated to them at the time it happened, through other channels, and at a classification appropriate for it.

The Twining letter creates a dilemma, but it is, in and of itself, inconclusive. We can argue about the motives and the interpretations of it all we want, but with the parties involved in its creation dead, we can only argue about the interpretations. We can find no final answers.

There is another document, dated December 10, 1948, that was classified as Top Secret and detailed earlier. It is Air Intelligence Report No. 100-203-79, entitled "Analysis of Flying Object Incidents in the U.S." and apparently was a joint effort between the Directorate of Intelligence of the Air Force and the Office of Naval Intelligence. It is so sensitive that it contains a warning that states, "This document contains information affecting the national defense of the United States within the meaning of the Espionage Act, 50 U.S.C., 31 and 32, as amended. Its transmission or the revelation of its contents in any manner to an unauthorized person is prohibited by law. Reproduction of the intelligence in this publication, under the provisions of Army Regulation 380-5, is authorized for United States military agencies provided the source is indicated."

The document, then, was highly classified. It was a report created to brief high-ranking officers on the flying object situation. It would seem that the officers creating the document would have access to all the classified information needed to accurately assess the situation. In fact, Philip Klass, arch skeptic and UFO debunker, has made just that argument. The officers writing the report would not lie about the state of the situation to their superiors. They would tell their superiors everything they knew. And, if Roswell was the crash of an alien spacecraft, it should be mentioned in this report.

Or should it?

The problem, according to the document was "TO EXAMINE patterns of tactics of 'Flying Saucers' (hereinafter referred to as flying objects) and to develop conclusions as to the possibility of existence."

Under facts and discussions, the report said, "THE POSSIBILITY that reported observations of flying objects over the U.S. were influenced by previous sightings of unidentified phenomena in Europe, particularly over Scandinavia in 1946, and that the observers reporting such incidents may have been interested in obtaining personal publicity have been considered as possible explanations. However, these possibilities seem to be improbable when certain selected reports such as the one from U.S. Weather Bureau at Richmond are examined. During the observations of weather balloons at the Richmond Bureau, one well trained observer has sighted strange metallic disks on three occasions and another observer has sighted a similar object on one occasion. The last observation of unidentified objects was in April, 1947. On all four occasions the weather balloon and the unidentified objects were in view through a theodolite. These observations at the Richmond Bureau occurred several months before publicity on the flying saucers appeared in U.S. newspapers."

The report included an interesting paragraph about the origins of the objects. To understand the situation, that paragraph is important. It said, "THE ORIGIN of the devices is not ascertainable. There are two reasonable possibilities: (1) The objects are domestic devices, and if so, their identification or origin can be established by a survey of the launchings of airborne devices . . . (2) Objects are foreign, and if so, it would seem most logical to consider that they are from a Soviet source . . ."

The conclusions, at the bottom of page two, and marked Top Secret, were, "SINCE the Air Force is responsible for control of the air in the defense of the U.S., it is imperative that all other agencies cooperate in confirming or denying the possibility that these objects are of domestic origin. Otherwise, if it is firmly indicated that there is no domestic explanation, the objects are a threat and warrant more active efforts of identification and interception."

And finally, the report said, "IT MUST be accepted that some type of flying objects have been observed, although their identification and origin are not discernible. In the interest of national defense it would be unwise to overlook the possibility that some of these objects are of foreign origin."

What we observe in this document, however, is not the all-knowing access to every classified report that Klass has suggested. Instead, we find the authors speculating that the flying objects might be a domestic project and their suggestion that any such project be revealed to the Air Force because of its responsibility for air defense. In other words, the authors of the top secret report did *not* have complete access to everything. They admitted that there were areas they were not allowed to examine. That leaves the door open for Roswell.

Again, the information at Roswell was considered, according to many of the officers I spoke to, including Edwin Easley, so highly classified that the president of the

United States suggested Easley not talk about it. President Truman was telling a major (later a full colonel) that the events at Roswell were highly classified and highly sensitive.

The fact that these events are left out of the Air Intelligence Report, then, is not significant. The authors admitted that they did not have all privileged information. The report does not prove that Roswell didn't happen, or that these officers were lying to their superiors if it did. They didn't know about Roswell, didn't have access to that highly restricted information, and therefore couldn't include it because they didn't know about it.

Neither of these documents sounds the death knell for the Roswell case. Explanations that make sense can be offered. They allow for the Roswell crash and the lack of mention of it in those documents. Another has surfaced, however, that is more disturbing.

William LaParl, a researcher living in Maine, uncovered what is, if nothing else, quite disturbing. Using the Freedom of Information Act, he asked to see the minutes of the Air Force Scientific Advisory Board conference that took place at the Pentagon on March 17 and 18, 1948.

LaParl noted that he had first received a letter telling him that there were "no records responsive" to his request. He was told that many of the minutes of the meetings had been destroyed in 1960 by a colonel who was trying to clean out his safe. Later another Air Force agency found a copy of the minutes and it was declassified in response to LaParl's request.

According to the information found by LaParl, Dr. Theodore Von Karman presided over the meeting. General Hoyt S. Vandenberg sat in, representing General

Carl Spaatz, who was busy somewhere else. Devlin Bronk was also unable to attend.

What is important is that the meeting was attended by Colonel Robert McCoy who was chief of the Intelligence Department at the Air Materiel Command. McCoy and another colonel gave a detailed briefing on the Utilization of Technical Intelligence. Brief descriptions were given on a number of projects, such as Paper Clip and Sign.

About Sign, McCoy said, "We have a new project—Project Sign—which may surprise you as a development from the so-called mass hysteria of the past summer when we had all the unidentified flying objects or discs. This can't be laughed off. We have over 300 reports which haven't been publicized in the papers from very competent personnel, in many instances—men as capable as Dr. K. D. Wood, and practically all Air Force, Airline people with broad experience. We are running down every report. *I can't even tell you how much we would give to have one of those crash in an area so that we could recover whatever they are* (emphasis added)."

LaParl points out that as far as he could tell, all participants had top secret clearances so there shouldn't have been a problem with discussing top secret material at the meeting. It doesn't seem reasonable that McCoy would have made the statement to confuse people in the far future. It was not a "throw away" line.

But the point here is that McCoy, because of who he was, could be expected to know about the Roswell crash, if one had taken place. He was assigned to AMC, and my investigations show that many of the people there were aware of the crash. Brigadier General Arthur Exon (a lieutenant colonel in 1947) told me that he had heard about the stuff coming into Wright Field. Although not assigned to an intelligence function, he heard the rumors and had spoken to the men involved in the analysis of the debris. Although Exon didn't see any of the debris, or the bodies himself, he was aware of the situation, just as McCoy should have been. McCoy, after all, was assigned to the intelligence functions at Wright Field.

There are only two arguments that can be made intelligently at this point. Either McCoy didn't know of the crash, or it never happened. This is an either/or situation and there is no real middle ground.

If the crash never happened, then McCoy's statement, in the context of how he said it, makes sense. He was telling the assembled committee that flying saucers were a real problem, but they didn't know what kind of problem. A recoverable crash would reveal the nature to them.

If the crash happened, it is difficult to believe that McCoy wouldn't know about it because of who he was and where he was. In my investigations of the Roswell case, I have spoken to a number of people who were assigned to Wright Field as military personnel or civilians. I have also interviewed people whose husbands were assigned to the base. They all knew that something had happened, but were not directly involved.

Helen Wachter, for example, was a nursing student whose fellow student's husband was an MP at Wright Field. While visiting her friend, who had just given birth, the husband arrived in a state of excitement. He told his wife about the alien bodies that had been brought into the base. Wachter thought, at first, he was referring to people from another country, but it soon became clear he was talking about beings from another planet.

Of course, if McCoy, for some reason, had been cut out of the loop, he might have assumed that the stories were little more than rumor. He might have asked questions of those above him and been told there was nothing to it. He would, therefore, tell others that nothing like that had happened, which would explain his statement at the committee meeting.

As one of the primary investigators of the Roswell case, I find McCoy's statement to be quite disturbing. Having served in the military as an intelligence officer, I realize that there are many things that are classified for various reasons that I have not been given. Although I held a top secret clearance, it didn't mean that I was authorized access to everything classified as top secret. There were many things I knew, because of the job, that even the commander didn't know. That is not to say that I wouldn't have told him if he had asked, but until the situation changed, I was not required to brief him. I merely had to have the information available in case he needed it.

We could argue this point for years. Did McCoy know and lie about it? Was he kept in the dark because he wasn't part of the small, inner circle who had access to the data? Did he tell the truth about there being no crash? How can we ever work our way through this problem? And, is there anything out there, other than the testimony of eyewitnesses, to suggest that something extraterrestrial crashed outside of Roswell?

First, on the other side of the argument is an FBI document dated July 10, 1947. The FBI was being asked by the Army Air Forces, specifically Brigadier General Schulgen, to assist in the investigation. According to the letter, "He [Schulgen] advised that to complete the picture he desired the assistance of the Federal Bureau of Investigation in locating and questioning the individuals who first sighted the so-called flying disks in order to ascertain whether or not their statements were prompted by personal desire for publicity or political reason."

Of course, this means nothing to us today. That the FBI was asked to assist in the investigation, especially in checking out the backgrounds of witnesses, is not surprising. What is important, however, is that the FBI seemed to agree. Clyde Tolson, on July 15, endorsed the letter, writing, "I think we should do this."

Under that was the endorsement of J. Edgar Hoover. He wrote, "I would do it but before agreeing to it we must insist upon full access to discs recovered. For instance in the La [though this has been interpreted as saying SW, gov or Sov] case the Army grabbed it and would not let us have it for cursory examination."

This would seem to suggest that something had crashed and that the Army had recovered it. Unfortunately, the reference is vague and open to interpretation. Hoover's sloppy handwriting leaves us guessing about the "La" case. It doesn't seem to fit Roswell, but how many other flying saucer crashes had been reported?

The answer is quite a few.

Skeptics have suggested that Hoover was referring to an incident that took place in Shreveport, Louisiana, on July 7, 1947. There is no doubt that this case is a hoax, and not a very clever one. If that was what Hoover meant in his endorsement on the letter, then the question has been answered, and we are no closer to understanding the situation in July 1947.

But, and this is a big *but*, the FBI was not cut out of the Shreveport case. In fact, the FBI was an important part of the investigation. The FBI reported through the commanding general at Barksdale Field, Louisiana, to the commanding general of the Army Air Forces (General Carl Spaatz) in Washington, D.C. The report said, in part, "FBI resident agent, Shreveport, was informed and contacted FBI office, New Orleans, by phone, made initial report and later informed that office that discovery was hoax and rendered complete report of investigation. Summary of information on case will be forwarded."

Because the FBI was involved heavily, because the case was an obvious hoax, and because pictures of the "flying disk" were included in the newspapers, it doesn't seem likely that this is the case Hoover mentioned, simply because the Army didn't grab it and not let anyone else see it.

To this point no one has figured out what the "La" stands for. The other cases, one from Bozeman, Montana, one from Wisconsin and one from Houston, Texas, have all been shown to be hoaxes. The only case that seems to fit is Roswell, but then what does "La" mean?

So we do have one official document that mentions a recovered disk. It is as vague in the references as those attributed to Twining and McCoy. It doesn't prove there was a crash at Roswell, but it does provide a bit of paper for those who demand it.

There is also a letter written by Dr. Robert I. Sarbacher who claimed that he had been asked to participate in the study of a craft that had been recovered.

Actually, the documents surrounding this concern more than just a letter by Sarbacher. It began in 1950 when Wilbert B. Smith, a Canadian, wrote a top secret memorandum about "Geo-Magnetics" for the Canadian Department of Transport. In the text, he mentioned, "We believe that we are on the track of something which may well prove to be the introduction of a new technology. The existence of a different technology is borne out by the investigations which are being carried out at the present time in relation to flying saucers."

Smith's memorandum continues, "I made discreet inquiries through the Canadian Embassy staff in Washington who were able to obtain the following information: a. The matter is the most highly classified subject in the United States Government, rating even higher than the H-bomb. b. Flying saucers exist. c. Their modus operandi is unknown but concentrated effort is being made by a small group headed by Doctor Vannevar Bush. d. The entire matter is considered by the United States authorities to be of tremendous significance."

While this does not suggest there was a crash at Roswell, or anywhere else, it does show a high level interest in flying saucers. If, however, we look at the statements made publicly, and we try to learn what was happening at those high levels, we are told that no one thought much of flying saucers. They were nothing more than hoaxes, misidentifications, and illusions. Something just isn't quite right here.

But there is other information to take us to the crashed flying saucers. Arthur Bray, who uncovered the memorandum and shared it with UFO researcher Len Stringfield, also found an interview conducted by William B.

Smith with Dr. Robert I. Sarbacher in September 1950. Smith said, "I have read Scully's book [*Behind the Flying Saucers*] and I would like to know how much of it is true."

Sarbacher said, "The facts reported in the book are substantially correct."

"Then flying saucers exist?"

"Yes, they exist."

What we have then, is an American scientist telling a Canadian scientist that flying saucers are real and that they crash. Sarbacher, who hadn't been privy to the details because of circumstances, believed that Scully's stories were correct, but it is easy to believe that a flying saucer crash in New Mexico at Roswell might have been the incident that inspired the reports. Details were wrong, but the overall report was accurate.

Of course, we are left with the question of Sarbacher's knowledge. How did he learn about the crash? And, more importantly, is the information accurate?

William Steinman, a California UFO researcher who was chasing the Scully story, after learning of what Bray was claiming, and reading what Stringfield had written, decided to contact Sarbacher. According to him, he wrote Sarbacher and then called him. According to Sarbacher, the notes found by Bray of the Smith interview were accurate.

Steinman received a long letter from Sarbacher. Sarbacher wrote, on letterhead from the Washington Institute of Technology, "Relating to my own experience regarding flying saucers, I had no association with any of the people involved in the recovery and have no knowledge regarding the dates of the recoveries."

Sarbacher was confirming from his position in government service that there had been recoveries, but when asked to participate in the research surrounding it, was unable to do so because of personal and business reasons. But the point was that he knew what had happened because of the information provided to him when he was asked to assist.

Later in the letter, he wrote, "About the only thing I remember at this time is that certain materials reported to have come from the flying saucer crashes were extremely light and very tough."

Sarbacher confirmed what he said to a number of others, including Jerry Clark of CUFOS and Barry Greenwood, Larry Fawcett and Larry Byrant of Citizens Against UFO Secrecy. Clark wrote about the case in August 1985, confirming that Dr. John von Neumann and Dr. Vannevar Bush were told that flying saucers were extraterrestrial. In the article Clark quoted from his own interview with Sarbacher, confirming many of the things that Steinman had reported to the UFO community.

What all this does is suggest that there was an "insider circle" who knew about crashed saucers and who discussed it. This information, though vague, suggests that the crash at Roswell took place. The Hoover note puts a time frame on it and Sarbacher confirmed the location as New Mexico.

There are some other documents available. During my research into the Roswell case, one of the witnesses provided me with a copy of a log and a few pages of a final report that went on to Washington, D.C. These two documents suggest a crash outside of Roswell with the recovery of the craft by members of the military.

The problem here is that the documents are in private hands so that others can't use Freedom of Information Act to acquire copies of them. Although I do have photocopies and have seen the originals, there is no way to verify their accuracy.

One of the documents was created on paper that clearly came from the right time frame and was official letterhead from the Roswell Army Air Field. It provided a look at the craft and the bodies of the alien flight crew.

The craft is like nothing that was in the inventory in 1947. It is a triangular-shaped object. From the front it has the look of the SR-71 Blackbird, although the rear fins are tilted sharply inward. From the top or bottom it looks like nothing created on this planet.

The description of the bodies provides little in the way of detail. There is a drawing of the heads, showing eyes that are only slightly larger than human eyes. They do have a high forehead, small eyes, and a very small mouth.

The other document in my possession is a log beginning on July 1 and continuing to July 6, 1947. There is little in the way of detail in it, only suggesting that something extremely unusual happened early in the morning, and suggesting that a target had been tracked on radar. Then the note, "Object down—2317 [11:17 P.M.]—Radar target gone."

The next entry notes, "Found wreckage 0200 proceed to station and execute ... All units survey perimeter from entr [sic] point of impact."

What we have then, are several documents that seem to suggest that something crashed outside of Roswell and that it was not from our planet. Eyewitness testimony, published in great detail in *The Truth about the UFO Crash at Roswell,* corroborates this point of view.

Documents recovered by a variety of researchers suggest both that the crash at Roswell happened and that it didn't happen. Those who truly believe can point to documents and say that the paper trail, though skimpy, does exist. If the incident was as highly classified as it has been suggested, then those outside the governmental agencies with responsibility for it would have an extremely difficult time recovering any documentation supporting their view. Compartmentalization and need to know rears its ugly head. That a few documents do exist is extremely good fortune.

On the hand, those who truly don't believe can point to a few documents and insist that the case is closed. Colonel McCoy should have known about the crash and clearly didn't. General Twining wrote about a lack of crash recovered exhibits. He, too, should have known.

When all the debate ends, we are left with no clear-cut answer here. All we can do is decide, for ourselves, which set of circumstances and documents are the most persuasive.

1996: The Freedom of Information Act

There are those who ask why I haven't used the Freedom of Information Act to retrieve the documents, reports, and secrets that I have searched for. Just send in the request and all that I want should be forwarded to me.

Of course, nothing is ever as easy as it seems. The Freedom of Information Act, which was passed to provide American citizens with the information that the government has collected and stored over decades, is useful. News agencies, reporters, historians, and private citizens have used the act to obtain everything from their personal records of military service, or dossiers created about them by the FBI, to the documents that proved the government had used unwitting citizens in scientific experimentation. The Freedom of Information Act has provided the clues that have unraveled some of the most puzzling mysteries. It has been, and will be, a useful tool in many instances.

It is not, however, the magic key that opens all the doors to the secret vaults. There are exceptions to the rules, and there are petty bureaucrats who refuse to cooperate out of meanness. And there are those who believe that releasing some information might be harmful to the nation. All of these roadblocks keep us from learning much of what we want to learn.

That is one thing that must be clear. Information, whether from intelligence, scientific, military, or government agencies, which is deemed important to the national security, is exempt from the Freedom of Information Act. Requests come back suggesting that the information is sensitive, or is properly classified and not releasable. At that point, the person filing the request can appeal. But that appeal often involves hiring lawyers and courtroom appearances.

So let's take a look at what the act does. In my investigations into UFOs in general, and the Roswell case in particular, I have filed dozens of requests. I have filed requests with the Army, Air Force, Navy, CIA, DIA, FBI, and a variety of other government agencies. I have gone after records held in the Air Force Archives, presidential libraries, and various repositories. I have tried to find documents that are no longer classified, but which might help answer some questions that I have about UFOS and Roswell.

For example, I was interested in Navy balloon projects that might have been confused with flying saucers in 1947. There were hints about various launches at various locations, but nothing in the public record which was very useful. Using the public library, I learned what Naval organization had conducted what research and where that organization was located today. I wrote them a letter, but after two months it was clear that I would receive no response. So, I filed a Freedom of Information request.

In that request, I cited the United States Code (U.S.C.) sections which were relevant to my research. The first sentence of my letters says, "I am writing to request agency records pursuant to the Freedom of Information Act, 5 U.S.C. 522." This requires the agency to respond in ten working days or about two weeks when weekends and holidays are figured in.

That does not mean you'll receive the information in ten working days. It usually means you'll receive a letter saying that your request has been received and that it will be processed as quickly as it can be. Remember, many agencies do not have full-time employees who fill only Freedom of Information requests.

In the case of the Navy balloon projects, once I filed a Freedom of Information request, I got the information quickly. It wasn't as helpful as I had hoped, but it did provide clues which led me to the answers that I sought.

In another instance, I had called the White Sands Missile Range to ask about a specific technical bulletin. They asked me *not* to send a Freedom of Information request. I complied, and received no response. When I filed the Freedom of Information request, I received a prompt response.

I wrote them then, and after citing the U.S.C., said, "I am trying to locate all records and documents that relate to Project Mogul which was operated by New York University and Watson Laboratories. Technical Report No. 93.02 prepared by James R. Smith, covered some of the data. Launches took place in June and July 1947. Although originally classified, it has long since been declassified."

Their response? "In accordance with Army Regulation 25-55, paragraph 1-503 (2) and 5-201 c requesters must reasonably describe the information requested. You have not sufficiently identified the information you want searched. You need to describe the record of information with sufficient particularity to enable this agency to locate it by conducting a reasonable search."

Let's see. How about a search of Technical Report 93.02 prepared by James R. Smith? As side clues what about New York University and the Watson Laboratories? And, how about the dates of June and July 1947?

It really didn't matter, because I was able to find the information from another source. But, how could I supply more specific information when I had already given them the name of the report and the author of it? I had even provided them with the classified name of the project. And, I had given them the reference number of the document. I confess I don't know what more they would have wanted.

In other cases the information has been received with pages and pages of material deleted. For example, one State Department document contained the header, a routing slip showing the initials of those who had read the whole document, and the secret classification. Everything else for five pages had been deleted.

And that brings us to the important points of Freedom

of Information. Although the various agencies must respond, it doesn't mean they are required to forward the information. In some cases, they won't even admit if the information exists. These answers carry the sentence, "We can neither confirm nor deny . . ."

Of course, if such information didn't exist, they could tell us that, so the sentence, in its own strange way, is confirmation that the information does exist. It is just one of the games played at the highest levels which are designed, I suppose, to keep us guessing.

In each of the responses that does not contain helpful information, or in which the responding agency suggests that the information may or may not exist, or when it is claimed to be properly classified, there is a suggestion that an appeal can be made. The first round of appeals is just a letter back explaining why the information should be released. If it is denied a second time, then legal action is sometimes necessary. The costs of attorneys are often prohibitive.

In the 1980s, the Citizens Against UFO Secrecy did file suit and did go to court to receive documents held by various intelligence agencies. Those agencies responded with a short document explaining why the information shouldn't be released into the private sector. The judge reviewed the reasons himself (in camera in legal terms), agreed with the government, and denied access to the documents. He wouldn't even release the argument for keeping the documents classified. Instead, he released the legal arguments in which seventy-five percent of the information was blacked out.

So, the Freedom of Information Act, while a valuable tool, is not the be-all and end-all of research. It provides

us with some ammunition and allows us to read documents that we once would not have had the privilege to
read. It has let us find clues that help us understand the
situation as it existed in the past. It allows us to glimpse
into the world of secrecy. And it provides us with clues
about where to look for the information we want.

But, it doesn't give us everything we need. It only lets
us go so far and then it stops. So, when you wonder why
I haven't filed a Freedom of Information request about
some aspect of the UFO field, the answer is, if I haven't
done it, someone else has. And the answer we received
was less than enlightening.

Bibliography

Air Defense Command Briefing, January 1953, Project Blue Book Files.

ALBERTS, Don E. and PUTNAM, Allan E. *A History of Kirtland Air Force Base 1928–1982*. Albuquerque, NM: 1606th Air Base Wing, 1985.

"Analysis of Flying Object Incidents in the U.S." Air Intelligence Report No. 100–203–79 (December 10, 1948).

ANDERSON, Michele. "BIOSPEX: Biological Space Experiments." NASA Technical Memorandum 58217, Washington, DC: NASA, 1979.

ANDERSON, Ted. Alleged diary for July 1947.

ASIMOV, Isaac. *Is Anyone There?* New York: Ace Books, 1967.

ATIC UFO Briefing, April 1952, Project Blue Book Files.

BAKER, Raymond D. *Historical Highlights of Andrews AFB 1942–1989*. Andrews AFB, MD: 1776th Air Base Wing, 1990.

BARKER, Gray. "America's Captured Flying Saucers—The Cover-up of the Century." *UFO Report* (May 1977).

————. "Archives Reveal More Crashed Saucers." *Gray Barker's Newsletter 14* (March 1982).

————. "Von Poppen Update." *Gray Barker's Newsletter* (December 1982): 8.

BARNETT, Ruth. Personal Diary, 1947.

BAXTER, John. and ATKINS, Thomas. *The Fire Came By*. Garden City, NY: Doubleday, 1976.

BECKLEY, Timothy Green. *MJ-12 and the Riddle of Hangar 18*. New Brunswick, NJ: Inner Light, 1989.

BERLITZ, Charles and MOORE, William L. *The Roswell Incident*. New York: Berkley, 1988.

"Big Fire in the Sky: A Burning Meteor." *New York Herald Tribune* (December 10, 1965).

BINDER, Otto. *What We Really Know About Flying Saucers*. Greenwich, CT: Fawcett Gold Medal, 1967

————. *Flying Saucers Are Watching Us*. New York: Tower, 1968.

BLOECHER, Ted. *Report on the UFO Wave of 1947*. Washington, DC: self-published, 1967.

BLUM, Howard. *Out There: The Government's Secret Quest for Extra-terrestials*. New York: Simon and Schuster, 1991.

BLUM, Ralph, with BLUM, Judy. *Beyond Earth: Man's Contact with UFOs*. New York: Bantam Books, 1974.

BOWEN, Charles (ed). *The Humanoids*. Chicago: Henry Regnery, 1969.

BREW, John Otis and DANSON, Edward B. "The 1947 Reconnaissance and the Proposed Upper Gila Expedition of the Peabody Museum of Harvard University." *El Palacio* (July 1948): 211–222.

Briefing Document: Operation Majestic 12, November 18, 1952.

"Brilliant Red Explosion Flares in Las Vegas Sky." *Las Vegas Sun* (April 19, 1962): 1.

BRITTON, Jack, and WASHINGTON, George, Jr. *Military Shoulder Patches of the United States Armed Forces*. Tulsa: MCN Press, 1985.

BROWN, Eunice H. *White Sands History*. White Sands, NM: Public Affairs Office, 1959.

BUCKLE, Eileen. "Aurora Spaceman—R.I.P.?" *Flying Saucer Review* (July/August 1973): 7–9.

BUSKIRK, Winfred. *The Western Apache: Living in the Land Before 1950*. Norman, OK: University of Oklahoma, 1986.

CAHN, J. P. "Flying Saucer Swindlers." *True* (August 1956).

———. "The Flying Saucers and the Mysterious Little Men." *True* (September 1952).

CAMERON, Grant and CRAIN, T. Scott, Jr. *UFOs, MJ-12 and the Government*. Seguin, TX: MUFON, 1991.

CANADEO, Anne. *UFO's The Fact or Fiction Files*. New York: Walker, 1990.

CANNON, Martin. "The Amazing Story of John Lear." *UFO Universe* (March 1990): 8.

CAREY, Thomas J. "The Search for the Archaeologists." *International UFO Reporter* (November/December 1991): 4–9, 21.

CATOE, Lynn E. *UFOs and Related Subjects: An Annotated Bibliography*. Washington, DC: Government Printing Office, 1969.

CHARITON, Wallace O. *The Great Texas Airship Mystery*. Plano, TX: Wordware, 1991.

CHAVARRIA, Hector. "El Caso Puebla." *OVNI*: 10–14.

CITIZENS AGAINST UFO SECRECY. "MJ-12: Myth or Reality?" *Just Cause* (December 1985).

———. "Confirmation of MJ-12?" *Just Cause* (June 1987).

———. "The MJ-12 Fiasco." *Just Cause* (September 1987).

———. "More On MJ-12." *Just Cause* (March 1989).

———. "MJ-12 Update." *Just Cause* (June 1989).

———. "Conversation with Dr. Sarbacher." *Just Cause* (September 1985).

CLARK, Jerome. "The Great Unidentified Airship Scare." *Official UFO* (November 1976).

———. "The Great Crashed Saucer Debate." *UFO Report* (October 1980): 16–19, 74, 76.

———. "Crashed Saucers—Another View." *Saga's UFO Annual 1981* (1981).

———. *UFO's in the 1980s.* Detroit: Apogee, 1990.

———. "Crash Landings." *Omni* (December 1990): 92–91.

———. "UFO Reporters. (MJ-12)." *Fate* (December 1990).

———. "Airships: Part I." *International UFO Reporter* (January/February 1991): 4–23.

———. "Airships: Part II." *International UFO Reporter* (March/April 1991): 20–23.

CODDINGTON, Robert H. "An Analysis of the Rendlesham

Forest Incident Tape." *International UFO Reporter* (November/December 1985): 9–13.

COHEN, Daniel. *Encyclopedia of the Strange.* New York: Avon, 1987.

———. *The Great Airship Mystery: A UFO of the 1890s.* New York: Dodd, Mead, 1981.

———. *UFOs—The Third Wave.* New York: Evans, 1988.

Committee on Science and Astronautics. Report, 1961.

COOPER, Milton William. *Behold a Pale Horse.* Sedona, AZ: Light Technology, 1991

COOPER, Vicki. "Crashed Saucer Stories." *UFO* 6, no. 1 (1991): 15.

———. "The Roswell Case Revived: Was It An Alien Saucer." *UFO* (January/February 1991): 25–29.

CRARY, Dr. Albert. Personal Diary, June–July 1947.

CREIGHTON, Gordon. "Close Encounters of an Unthinkable and Inadmissible Kind." *Flying Saucer Review.* (July/August 1979).

———. "Further Evidence of 'Retrievals.' " *Flying Saucer Review* (January 1980).

———. "Continuing Evidence of Retrievals of the Third Kind." *Flying Saucer Review* (January/February 1982).

———. "Top U.S. Scientist Admits Crashed UFOs." *Flying Saucer Review* (October 1985).

DAVIDSON, Leon (ed). *Flying Saucers: An Analysis of Air Force Project Blue Book Special Report No. 14.* Clarksburg, VA: Saucerian Press, 1971.

DAVIES, John K. *Cosmic Impact.* New York: St. Martin's, 1986.

DAVIS, Isabel and BLOECHER, Ted. *Close Encounter at Kelly and Others of 1955.* Chicago: CUFOS, 1978

DAVIS, Richard. "Results of a Search for Records Concerning the 1947 Crash Near Roswell, New Mexico." Washington, DC: GAO, 1995

"The Day a UFO Crashed Inside Russia." *UFO Universe* (March 1990): 48–49.

DENNETT, Preston. "Project Redlight: Are We Flying the Saucers Too?" *UFO Universe* (May 1990): 39.

DOBBS, D. L. "Crashed Saucers—The Mystery Continues." *UFO Report* (September 1979).

"DoD News Releases and Fact Sheets." 1952–1968.

EARLEY, George W. "Crashed Saucers and Pickled Aliens." *Fate* Part I (March 1981): 42–48, Part II (April 1981): 84–89.

EBERHART, George. *The Roswell Report: A Historical Perspective.* Chicago: CUFOS, 1991.

ECKER, Don. "MJ-12 'Suspected Forgery,' Air Force Says." *UFO 8*, no. 3 (1993): 5.

EDITORS OF LOOK. "Flying Saucers." *Look* (1966).

EDWARDS, Frank. *Flying Saucers—Here and Now!* New York: Bantam, 1968.

———. *Flying Saucers—Serious Business.* New York: Bantam, 1966.

———. *Strange World.* New York: Bantam, 1964.

Eighth Air Force Staff Directory, Texas: June 1947.

ENDRES, Terry and PACKARD, Pat. "The Pflock Report in Perspective." *UFO Update Newsletter*, vol. 1, no. 5 (Fall 1994): 1–6.

ESTES, Russ (producer). "Quality of the Messenger." *Crystal Sky Productions*, 1993.

"Experts Say a Meteor Caused Flash of Fire." *Deseret News* (April 19, 1962): 1.

Fact Sheet, "Office of Naval Research 1952 Greenland Cosmic Ray Scientific Expedition," October 16, 1952.

FAWCETT, Lawrence and GREENWOOD, Barry J. *Clear Intent: The Government Cover-up of the UFO Experience.* Englewood Cliffs, NJ: Prentice-Hall, 1984.

Final Report, "Project Twinkle," Project Blue Book Files, Nov. 1951.

FINNEY, Ben R. and JONES, Eric M. *Interstellar Migration and the Human Experience.* Berkeley, CA: University of California Press, 1985.

"Fireball Explodes in Utah." *Nevada State Journal* (April 19, 1962): 1.

First Status Report, Project STORK (Preliminary to Special Report No. 14), April 1952.

Flint (Michigan) City Directories 1945–1950.

"Flying Saucers Again." *Newsweek* (April 17, 1950): 29.

"Flying Saucers Are Real." *Flying Saucer Review* (January/February 1956): 2–5.

FORD, Brian. *German Secret Weapons: Blueprint for Mars.* New York: Ballantine, 1969.

FOSTER, Tad. Unpublished articles for Condon Committee Casebook. 1969

FOWLER, Raymond E. *Casebook of a UFO Investigator*. Englewood Cliffs, NJ: Prentice-Hall, 1981

———. "What about Crashed UFOs?" *Official UFO* (April 1976): 55–57.

———. *The Watchers*. New York: Bantam Books, 1990

FULLER, John G. *The Interrupted Journey*. New York: Dial, 1966.

———. *Incident at Exeter*. New York: G. P. Putnam's Sons, 1966.

———. *Aliens in the Sky*. New York: Berkley Books, 1969

Genesee County (Michigan) Telephone Directories 1945–1950.

GILLMOR, Daniel S. (ed). *Scientific Study of Unidentified Flying Objects*. New York: Bantam Books, 1969.

GOLDSMITH, Donald. *Nemesis*. New York: Berkley Books, 1985.

———. *The Quest for Extraterrestrial Life*. Mill Valley, CA: University Science Books, 1980.

GOOD, Timothy. *Above Top Secret*. New York: Morrow, 1988.

———. *The UFO Report*. New York: Avon Books, 1989.

———. *Alien Contact*. New York: Morrow, 1993.

GORDON, Stan. "After 25 Years, New Facts on the Kecksburg, Pa. UFO Retrieval Are Revealed." *PASU Data Exchange #15* (December 1990): 1.

———. "Kecksburg Crash Update." *MUFON UFO Journal* (September 1989).

———. "Kecksburg Crash Update." *MUFON UFO Journal* (October 1989): 3–5, 9.

———. "The Military UFO Retrieval at Kecksburg, Pennsylvania." *Pursuit*, vol. 20, no. 4 (1987): 174–179.

GORDON, Stan and COOPER, Vicki. "The Kecksburg Incident." *UFO*, vol. 6 no. 1 (1991): 16–19.

"Great Lakes Fireball." *Sky & Telescope* (February 1966): 78, 79, 80.

GRIBBIN, John. "Cosmic Disaster Shock." *New Scientist* (March 6, 1980): 750–52.

"Guidance for Dealing with Space Objects Which Have Returned to Earth. Department of State Airgram, July 26, 1973.

GUTIERREZ, Peter. "Close Encounters of the Belgium Kind." *The Bulletin* (January 11, 1996): 26–29

HALL, Richard. "Crashed Discs—Maybe." *International UFO Reporter*, vol. 10, no. 4 (July/August 1985).

———. *Uninvited Guests*. Santa Fe, NM: Aurora Press, 1988.

———. "MJ-12: Still Holding Its Own Through Thickets of Debate." *UFO* (January/February 1991): 30–32.

——— (ed). *The UFO Evidence*. Washington, DC: NICAP, 1964.

HANRAHAN, James Stephen. *History of Research in Space Biology and Biodynamics at the Air Force Missile Development Center 1946–1958*. Alamogordo, NM: Office of Information Services, 1959.

———. *Contributions of Balloon Operations to Research and Development at the Air Force Missile Development Center 1947–1958*. Alamogordo, NM: Office of Information Services, 1959.

HAUGLAND, Vern. "AF Denies Recovering Portions of 'Saucers.' " *Albuquerque New Mexican* (March 23, 1954).

HAZARD, Catherine. "Did the Air Force Hush Up a Flying Saucer Crash?" *Woman's World* (February 27, 1990): 10.

HEGT, William H. Noordhoek. "News of Spitzbergen UFO Revealed." *APRG Reporter* (February 1957): 6.

HENRY, James P. and MOSELY, John D. "Results of the Project Mercury Ballistic and Orbital Chimpanzee Flights, NASA SP-39." NASA: 1963.

HIPPLER, Lt. Col. Robert H. Letter to Edward U. Condon, January 16, 1967.

"History of the Eighth Air Force, Fort Worth, Texas." (Microfilm) Air Force Archives, Maxwell Air Force Base, AL.

"History of the 509th Bomb Group, Roswell, New Mexico." (Microfilm) Air Force Archives, Maxwell Air Force Base, AL.

"History of the 4602d AISS." (Microfilm) Air Force Archives, Maxwell Air Force Base, AL.

HOGG, Ivan U. and KING, J. B. *German and Allied Secret Weapons of World War II*. London: Chartwell, 1974.

HUNEEUS, J. Antonio. "Soviet Scientist Bares Evidence of 2 Objects at Tunguska Blast." *New York City Tribune* (November 30, 1989): 11.

———. "Great Soviet UFO Flap of 1989 Centers on Dalnegorsk Crash." *New York City Tribune* (June 14, 1990).

————. "Spacecraft Shot out of South African Sky—Alien Survives." *UFO Universe* (July 1990): 38–45, 64–66.

————. "Roswell UFO Crash Update." *UFO Universe* (Winter 1991): 8–13, 52, 57.

————. "A Full Report on the 1978 UFO Crash in Bolivia." *UFO Universe* (Winter 1993).

HURT, Wesley R. and MCKNIGHT, Daniel. "Archaeology of the San Augustine Plains: A Preliminary Report." *American Antiquity* (January 1949): 172–194.

HYNEK, J. Allen. *The UFO Experience: A Scientific Inquiry*. Chicago: Henry Regnery, 1975

HYNEK, J. Allen and VALLEE, Jacques. *The Edge of Reality*. Chicago: Henry Regnery, 1972.

"Internation Reports: Tale of Captured UFO." *UFO*, vol. 8, no. 3 (1993): 10–11.

"It Whizzed Through the Air; Livonia Boys Find Fireball Clues." *Livonian Observer & City Post* (December 16, 1965).

JACOBS, David M. *The UFO Controversy in America*. New York: Signet, 1975.

JOHNSON, J. Bond. " 'Disk-overy' Near Roswell Identified As Weather Balloon by FWAAF Officer." *Fort Worth Star-Telegram* (July 9, 1947).

JONES, William E. and MINSHALL, Rebecca D. "Aztec, New Mexico—A Crash Story Reexamined." *International UFO Reporter*, vol. 16, no. 5 (September/October 1991): 11.

JUNG, Carl G. *Flying Saucers: A Modern Myth of Things Seen in the Sky*. New York: Harcourt, Brace, 1959.

KEEL, John. "Now It's No Secret: The Japanese 'Fugo Balloon.' " *UFO* (January/February 1991): 33–35.

————. *UFOs: Operation Trojan Horse*. New York: G. P. Putnam's Sons, 1970.

————. *Strange Creatures from Space and Time*. New York: Fawcett, 1970.

KENNEDY, George P. "Mercury Primates." *American Institute of Aeronautics and Astronautics*, 1989.

KEYHOE, Donald E. *Aliens from Space*. New York: Signet, 1974.

KLASS, Philip J. *UFOs Explained*. New York: Random House, 1974.

————. "Crash of the Crashed Saucer Claim." *Skeptical Enquirer*, vol. 10, no. 3 (Spring 1986).

————. *The Public Deceived*. Buffalo, NY: Prometheus Books, 1983.

————. "Roswell UFO: Coverups and Credulity." *Skeptical Enquirer*, vol. 16, no. 1 (Fall 1991).

KNAACK, Marcelle. *Encyclopedia of U.S. Air Force Aircraft and Missile Systems*. Washington, DC: Office of Air Force History, 1988.

LAPAZ, Lincoln and ROSENFELD, Albert. "Japan's Balloon Invasion of America." *Collier's* (January 17, 1953): 9.

LESTER, Dave. "Kecksburg's UFO Mystery Unsolved." *Greenburg Tribune-Review* (December 8, 1985): A10.

Library of Congress Legislative Reference Service. "Facts about UFOs." (May 1966).

LOFTUS, R. *Eye-Witness Testimony*. Cambridge, MA: Harvard University Press, 1979.

LORE, Gordon, and DENEAULT, Harold H. *Mysteries of the Skies: UFOs in Perspective*. Englewood Cliffs, NJ: Prentice-Hall, 1968.

LORENZEN, Coral and Jim. *Flying Saucers: The Startling Evidence of the Invasion from Outer Space*. New York: Signet, 1966.

————. *Flying Saucer Occupants*. New York: Signet, 1967.

————. *Encounters with UFO Occupants*. New York: Berkley Medallion Books, 1976.

————. *Abducted!* New York: Berkley Medallion Books, 1977.

LOW, Dr. Robert J. Letter to Lt. Col. Robert Hippler, January 27, 1967.

MACCABEE, Bruce. "Hiding the Hardware." *International UFO Reporter* (September/October 1991): 4.

————. "What the Admiral Knew." *International UFO Reporter* (November/December 1986).

————. "The Arnold Phenomenon: Part I, II, and III." *International UFO Reporter* (January/February 1995–May/June 1995).

MACK, John E. *Abduction*. New York: Charles Scribner's Sons, 1994.

MATTHEWS, Mark. "Armageddon at Tunguska!" *Official UFO* (May 1979).

MCCALL, G. J. H. *Meteorites and Their Origins*. New York: Wiley & Sons, 1973.

MCCLELLAN, Mike. "The Flying Saucer Crash of 1948 Is a Hoax." *Offical UFO* (October 1975): 36–37, 60, 62–64.

"McClellan Sub-Committee Hearings," March 1958.

"McCormack Sub-Committee Briefing," August 1958.

MCDONALD, Bill. "Comparing Descriptions, An Illustrated Roswell." *UFO* vol. 8, no. 3 (1993): 31–36.

MCDONOUGH, Thomas R. *The Search for Extraterrestrial Intelligence.* New York: Wiley & Sons, 1987.

MEESSEN, Auguste. "The Belgium Sightings." *International UFO Reporter* (May/June 1991): 4–11, 22, 24.

MENZEL, Donald H. and BOYD, Lyle G. *The World of Flying Saucers.* Garden City, NY: Doubleday, 1963.

MENZEL, Donald H. and TAVES, Ernest H. *The UFO Enigma.* Garden City, NY: Doubleday, 1977.

"Meteor Lands in Utah, Lights Western Sky." *Los Angeles Times* (April 19, 1962).

MICHEL, Aime. *The Truth about Flying Saucers.* New York: Pyramid, 1967.

MOORE, Charles B. "The New York University Balloon Flights During Early June, 1947." Self-published: 1995

MOORE, William L. and SHANDERA, Jaime H. *The MJ-12 Documents: An Analytical Report.* Burbank, CA: Fair Witness Project, 1991.

MUELLER, Robert. *Air Force Bases: Volume 1, Active Air Force Bases within the United States of America on 17 September 1982.* Washington, DC: Office of Air Force History, 1989.

MURPHY, John. "Object in the Woods." *WHJB Radio*, radio broadcast (December 1965).

National Security Agency. Presidential Documents. Washington, DC: Executive Order 12356, 1982.

NEILSON, James. " Secret U.S./UFO Structure." *UFO*, vol. 4, no. 1 (1989): 4–6.

"New Explanation for 1908 Siberian Blast." *Cedar Rapids Gazette* (January 25, 1993).

NICAP. *The UFO Evidence.* Washington, DC: NICAP, 1964.

NICKELL, Joe. "The Hangar 18 Tales." *Common Ground* (June 1984).

NICKELL, Joe, and FISCHER, John F. "The Crashed-Saucer Forgeries." *International UFO Reporter*, vol. 15, no. 2 (March/April 1990): 4–12.

————. "Further Deception: Moore and Shandera." Unpublished paper, 1993.

"No Reputable Dope On Disks." *Midland Reporter Telegram* (July 1, 1947).

NORTHROP, Stuart A. *Minerals of New Mexico*. Albuquerque, NM: University of New Mexico, 1959.

OBERG, James. "UFO Update: UFO Buffs May Be Unwitting Pawns in an Elaborate Government Charade." *Omni*, vol. 15, no. 11 (September 1993): 75.

O'BRIEN, Mike. "New Witness to San Agustin Crash." *MUFON Journal*, no. 275 (March 1991): 3–9.

OLIVE, Dick. "Most UFO's Explainable, Says Scientist." *Elmira Star-Gazette* (January 26, 1967): 19.

PACKARD, Pat and ENDRES, Terry. "Riding the Roswell-go-round." *A.S.K. UFO Report*, vol. 2, no. 1: 1–8

PALMER, Raymond and ARNOLD, Kenneth. *The Coming of the Saucers*. Amherst, WI: Privately printed, 1952.

PAPAGIANNIS, Michael D. (ed). *The Search for Extraterrestrial Life: Recent Developments*. Boston: 1985.

PEEBLES, Curtis. *The Moby Dick Project*. Washington, DC: Smithsonian Institution Press, 1991.

PEGUES, Etta. *Aurora, Texas: The Town that Might Have Been*. Newark, TX: Self-published, 1975.

PFLOCK, Karl. *Roswell in Perspective*. Mt. Ranier, MD: FUFOR, 1994.

————. "In Defense of Roswell Reality." *HUFON Report* (February 1995): 5–7.

————. "Roswell, A Cautionary Tale: Facts and Fantasies, Lessons and Legacies." In Walter H. Andrus, Jr. (ed), *MUFON 1995 International UFO Symposium Proceedings*. Seguin, TX: MUFON, 1990: 154–68.

————. "Roswell, The Air Force, and Us." *International UFO Reporter* (November/December 1994): 3–5, 24.

PLEKHANOV, G. F., KOVALEVSKIY, A. F., ZHURAVLEV, V. K., VASIL'YEV, N. V. "The Effect of the Tungussk Meteorite Explosion on the Geomagnetic Field." *U.S. Joint Publications Research Service*, December 21, 1961.

Press Conference—General Samford, Project Blue Book Files, 1952.

"Press Release—Monkeynaut Baker is Memorialized." Huntsville, AL: Space and Rocket Center, December 4, 1984.

"Project Blue Book" (microfilm). National Archives, Washington, D.C.

"Project Moon Dust" (microfiche). Department of State, Washington, D.C.

PRYTZ, John M. "UFO Crashes." *Flying Saucers* (October 1969): 24–25.

RAAF Base Phone Book, Roswell, NM, August 1947.

RAAF Yearbook, Roswell, NM, 1947.

RANDLE, Kevin D. "Mysterious Clues Left Behind by UFOs." *Saga's UFO Annual* (Summer 1972).

———. "The Pentagon's Secret Air War Against UFOs." *Saga* (March 1976).

———. "The Flight of the Great Airship." *True's Flying Saucers and UFOs Quarterly* (Spring 1977).

———. *The October Scenario*. Iowa City, IA: Middle Coast Publishing, 1988.

———. *The UFO Casebook*. New York: Warner, 1989.

———. *A History of UFO Crashes*. New York: Avon, 1995.

RANDLE, Kevin D. and CORNETT, Robert Charles. "Project Blue Book Cover-up: Pentagon Suppressed UFO Data." *UFO Report*, vol. 2, no. 5 (Fall 1975).

RANDLE, Kevin D. and SCHMITT, Donald R. *UFO Crash at Roswell*. New York: Avon, 1991.

RANDLES, Jenny. *From Out of the Blue*. New York: Global Communciations, 1991.

———. *The UFO Conspiracy*. New York: Javelin, 1987.

———. "Bentwaters: The Secret File." *UFO Universe* (Spring 1992): 24–31, 64.

"Report of Air Force Research Regarding the 'Roswell Incident.'" Washington, DC: Government Printing Office, July 1994.

"Rocket and Missile Firings." White Sands Proving Grounds, January–July 1947.

RODEGHIER, Mark. "Roswell, 1989." *International UFO Reporter* (September/October 1989): 4.

RODEGHIER, Mark and CHESNEY, Mark. "The Air Force Report on Roswell: An Absence of Evidence." *International UFO Reporter* (September/October 1994).

ROSIGNOLI, Guido. *The Illustrated Encyclopedia of Military Insignia of the 20th Century*. Secaucus, NJ: Chartwell, 1986.

RUPPELT, Edward J. *The Report on Unidentified Flying Objects*. New York: Ace, 1956.

RUSSELL, Eric. "Phantom Balloons Over North America." *Modern Aviation* (February 1953).

SAGAN, Carl and PAGE, Thornton (eds). *UFO's: A Scientific Debate*. Ithaca, NY: Cornell University Press, 1972.

SANDERSON, Ivan T. "Meteorite-like Object Made a Turn in Cleveland, O. Area." *Omaha World-Herald* (December 15, 1965).

————. "Something Landed in Pennsylvania." *Fate* (March 1966).

————. *Uninvited Visitors*. New York: Cowles, 1967.

————. *Invisible Residents*. New York: World Publishing, 1970.

SAUNDERS, David and HARKINS, R. Roger. *UFOs? Yes!* New York: New American Library, 1968

SCHAFFNER, Ron. "Roswell: A Federal Case?" *UFO Brigantia* (Summer 1989).

SCHMITT, Donald R. "New Revelations from Roswell." In Walter H. Andrus, Jr. (ed.), *MUFON 1990 International UFO Symposium Proceedings*. Seguin, TX: MUFON, 1990: 154–68.

SCHMITT, Donald R. and RANDLE, Kevin D. "Second Thoughts on the Barney Barnett Story." *International UFO Reporter* (May/June 1992): 4–5, 22.

SCULLY, Frank. "Scully's Scrapbook." *Variety* (October 12, 1949): 61.

————. *Behind the Flying Saucers*. New York: Henry Holt, 1950.

SHANDERA, Jaime. "New Revelation about the Roswell Wreckage: A General Speaks Up." *MUFON Journal* (January 1991): 4–8.

SHEAFFER, Robert. *The UFO Verdict*. Buffalo, NY: Prometheus, 1981.

SIMMONS, H. M. "Once Upon A Time In the West." *Magonia* (August 1985).

SLATE, B. Ann "The Case of the Crippled Flying Saucer." *Saga* (April 1972): 22–25, 64, 66–68, 71, 72.

SMITH, Scott. "Q & A: Len Stringfield." *UFO*, vol. 6, no. 1, (1991): 20–24.

Special Report No. 14 (Project Blue Book), 1955.

SPENCER, John. *The UFO Encyclopedia*. New York: Avon, 1993.

SPENCER, John and EVANS, Hilary. *Phenomenon*. New York: Avon, 1988.

Status Reports, "Grudge—Blue Book, Nos. 1–12."

STEIGER, Brad. *Strangers from the Skies*. New York: Award, 1966.

———. *Project Blue Book*. New York: Ballantine, 1976.

STEIGER, Brad and STEIGER, Sherry Hanson. *The Rainbow Conspiracy*. New York: Pinnacle, 1994.

STEINMAN, William S. and STEVENS, Wendelle C. *UFO Crash at Aztec*. Boulder, CO: Self-published, 1986.

STEVENSON, William. *Intrepid's Last Case*. New York: Villard, 1988.

STONE, Clifford E. *UFO's: Let the Evidence Speak for Itself*. Self-published, 1991.

———. "The U.S. Air Force's Real, Official Investigation of UFO's." Self-published, 1993.

STORY, Ronald D. *The Encyclopedia of UFOs*. Garden City, NY: Doubleday, 1980.

STRINGFIELD, Leonard H. *Situation Red: The UFO Siege!* Garden City, NY: Doubleday, 1977.

———. *UFO Crash/Retrieval Syndrome: Status Report II*. Seguin, TX: MUFON, 1980.

———. *UFO Crash/Retrieval: Amassing the Evidence: Status Report III*. Cincinnati, OH: Self-published, 1982.

———. *UFO Crash/Retrievals: The Inner Sanctum: Status Report VI*. Cincinnati, OH: Self-published, 1991.

———. "Roswell & the X-15: UFO Basics." *MUFON UFO Journal*, no. 259 (November 1989): 3–7.

STURROCK, P.A. "UFOs—A Scientific Debate." *Science* 180 (1973): 593.

SULLIVAN, Walter. *We Are Not Alone*. New York: Signet, 1966.

SUMNER, Donald A. "Skyhook Churchill 1966." *Naval Reserve Reviews* (January 1967): 29.

SWORDS, Michael D. (ed). *Journal of UFO Studies, New Series, Vol. 4*. Chicago: CUFOS, 1993.

Tech Bulletin. "Army Ordnance Department Guided Missile Program." January 1948.

Technical Report. "Unidentified Aerial Objects, Project SIGN." February 1949.

Technical Report. "Unidentified Flying Objects, Project GRUDGE." August 1949.

TEMPLETON, David. "The Uninvited." *Pittsburgh Press* (May 19, 1991): 10–15.

THOMPSON, Tina D. (ed). *TRW Space Log*. Redondo Beach, CA: TRW, 1991.

TODD, Robert G. "MJ-12 Rebuttal." *MUFON Journal* (January 1990): 17.

TODD, Robert G., RODEGHIER, Mark, GREENWOOD, Barry, and MACCABEE, Bruce. "A Forum on MJ-12." *International UFO Reporter* (May/June 1990): 15.

U.S. Congress, House Committee on Armed Forces. *Unidentified Flying Objects*. Hearings, 89th Congress, 2nd Session, April 5, 1966. Washington DC: U.S. Government Printing Office, 1968.

U.S. Congress Committee on Science and Astronautics. *Symposium on Unidentified Flying Objects*. Hearings, July 29, 1968. Washington, DC: U.S. Government Printing Office, 1968.

VALLEE, Jacques. *Anatomy of a Phenomenon*. New York: Ace, 1966.

———. *Challenge to Science*. New York: Ace, 1966.

———. *Dimensions*. New York: Ballantine, 1989

———. *Revelations*. New York: Ballantine, 1991.

VIDAL, Patrick and ROSENCWAJG, Michel. "The Belgium Wave." *International UFO Reporter* (July/August 1991): 4–8, 23

"Visitors From Venus." *Time* (January 9, 1950): 49.

War Department. *Meteorological Balloons* (Army Technical Manual). Washington, DC: Government Printing Office, 1944.

WEBBER, Bert. *Retaliation: Japanese Attacks and Allied Countermeasures on the Pacific Coast in World War II*. Corvallis, OR: Oregon State University Press, 1975.

WHEELER, David R. *The Lubbock Lights*. New York: Award Books, 1977.

WHITING, Fred. *The Roswell Events*. Mt. Ranier, MD: FUFOR, 1993.

WILCOX, Inez, personal writings, 1947–1952.

WILKINS, Harold T. *Flying Saucers on the Attack*. New York: Citadel, 1954.

———. *Flying Saucers Uncensored*. New York: Pyramid, 1967.

WISE, David and ROSS, Thomas B. *The Invisible Government*. New York: Random House, 1964.

YOUNG, Robert. "Old-Solved Mysteries: What Really Happened at Kecksburg, PA, on December 9, 1965." *Skeptical Inquirer*, vol. 15. no. 3 (1991).

ZEIDMAN, Jennie. "I Remember Blue Book." *International UFO Reporter* (March/April 1991): 7.

Index

S

V

Valentich, Frederick,
    disappearance of, 172–77,
    177–78
  explanations for, 175–77
Valenzano, Francesco,
    sighting, 215–16
Vandenberg, Hoyt S., 11, 267
Von Karman, Theodore, 267

W

Wachter, Helen, Roswell
    incident and, 269–70
Walker, L.L. and Marie,
    interview with, 209–11
War of the Worlds (movie), 35
Warren, Larry, 179, 236
  Bentwaters sightings
    account, 191–204
Washington Nationals, 46–58,
    70–71, 79–80
  second sightings, 51–55
Way, Harold C., 48
Weaver, Richard
  Cavitt interview, 238–39

Roswell incident report,
    235
Wheeler, Jim, sighting, 138–
    39
White Sands sightings, 97–
    104, 142–43
Willemoes (Danish destroyer),
    62
Williams, Frank, sighting, 139
Williams, Gordon, 197–98
Wills, Roger, 229
Wilson, R.R., 166
Woodward, A., 175
The World of Flying Saucers
    (Menzel and Boyd), 106
Wright-Patterson Air Force
    Base, report, 146–47
Wynn, Edward H., 62

Y

YB-49 aircraft, 18

Z

Zacko, Joe, 57